MW00637660

THE VALUES
OF THE
KINGDOM OF GOD

A PRACTICAL GUIDE TO KINGDOM LIVING

How God's Righteousness Leads to His Kingdom Values.

John Hatton

The Values of the Kingdom of God

And I pray this: that your love will keep on growing in knowledge and every kind of discernment, so that you can approve the things that are superior and can be pure and blameless in the day of Christ, filled with the fruit of righteousness that comes through Jesus Christ to the glory and praise of God.
Philippians 1:9-11 – HCSB

First published in May, 2019
ISBN 978-0-9994500-1-7

www.kingdomsecret.org

Cover, illustrations and book design by John Hatton.
Cover background adapted from NASA public domain photo.

Bible versions used, abbreviations and copyright permissions

Note: Scripture references with words which appear in bold, italic or bold italic were highlighted by the author to help readers quickly identify the main terms being considered. Since this is a modern technique and obviously not part of the Biblical manuscript, there is no need to mention this fact next to each case, as is the custom of most publishers.

To Monique and Melissa

My wife Monica and I often remind each other that our daughters are the greatest and best contribution we have given to the world.

I am honored to be Monique and Melissa's father and to dedicate this book to them.

Kingdom Paradigm

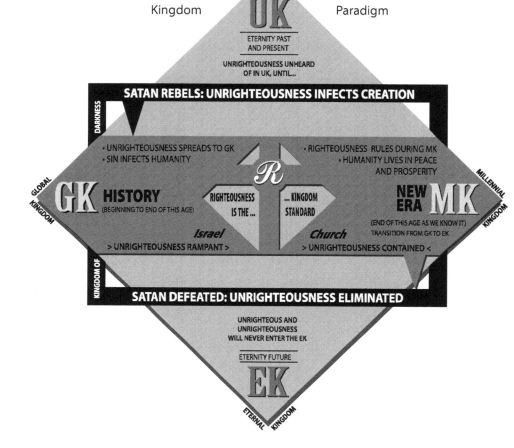

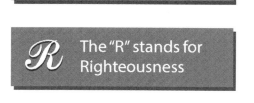

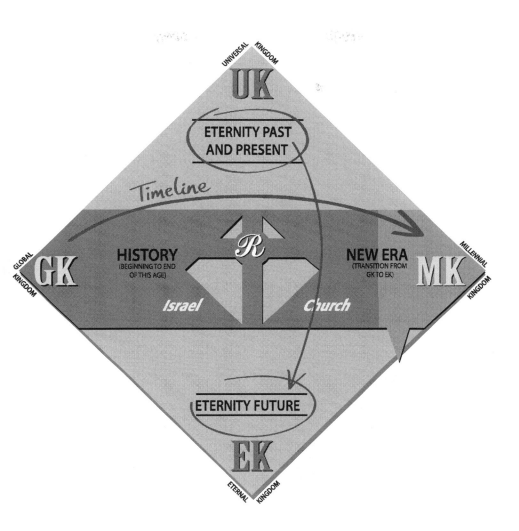

- **UK** to **EK** = **U**niversal **K**ingdom (eternity past to present) to **E**ternal **K**ingdom (present to eternity future).

- **GK** to **MK** = **G**lobal **K**ingdom to **M**illennial **K**ingdom timeline ("the beginning" to "the end of the age" and Millennium).

- **R** = **R**ighteousness as the core value of the Kingdom, gained for believers by **Jesus**, Who is the gateway to the Kingdom.

What others are saying about
The Values of the Kingdom of God

I have known author John Hatton for most of his life. I have followed his spiritual growth and am impressed with his practical writings on the Kingdom of God. The Bible is a map for our lives as we all prepare for eternity. Many Christians are confused about the subject of the Kingdom of God. Hatton writes a clear explanation of this subject. I recommend his book on Kingdom Values as trustworthy and truthful.

— **Jerry Stanley Key, Ph.D.**
Former Professor at *Seminário Teológico Batista do Sul do Brasil* in Rio de Janeiro, Brazil, and at Southwestern Baptist Theological Seminary in Fort Worth, Texas. International Mission Board (IMB) Missionary to Brazil (1959-1997).

John Hatton's latest book, "The Values of the Kingdom of God" is a masterpiece! After reading his introduction to the series, "The Secret of the Kingdom of God," which I found the best overview on the subject, I wondered how he would follow-up on it with enough content for another book. He sure has! "The Values of the Kingdom of God" is not only a "practical guide to kingdom living" as the subtitle says, but it is the most comprehensive treatment of the values of the kingdom that I have ever seen. In fact, I never imagined that there were so many values – John's book identifies 70 of them. Each one is clearly defined and described, with principles that derive from it, practical implications, and even an assessment at the end of each section. But the most valuable insights I took away from John's book were about "Righteousness." I thought I knew a lot about righteousness, but now I know so much more about what John describes as the "core value of the Kingdom of God." John clearly shows how all the other values flow from that core value.

As with his previous book, John's writing is very clear, concise, understandable, and non-academic. John does an excellent job of supporting all his points with scripture and citing major authorities on the various topics he covers in his book. John also includes diagrams and charts that help to summarize and visualize his powerful content. However, readers should be aware that reading about 70 Kingdom Values is not something that should be done in a single sitting, or even in a few. This book is a wealth of knowledge that should be read and pondered over a period of time – even a lifetime. Readers will come away with much greater self-awareness about how we fall short of the righteousness of God in so many areas. But our failures in these areas should be the source of a better appreciation of God's grace toward us and motivate us to strive to meet God's standards in an ever greater way – without condemnation. This is an amazing handbook full of wisdom to enable and empower Christians to live in the Kingdom of God – present and future.

— **Dr. Dean R. Spitzer**
Award-winning author, management consultant, and Bible teacher

John has provided a great service to followers of Jesus with this book. Some books are a quick scan, but you'll want to consider this a study course that is highly memorable. The listing of 70 Kingdom Values is worth the price of the book alone! I personally have appreciated the definitions, organizational approach (with awesome graphic depiction), analogies using Scripture, and personal touches throughout.

— **Mark Snowden**, Director of Missional Leadership (DOM), Cincinnati Area Baptist Association, Cincinnati, Ohio. Owner of Snowden Ministries International, http://truthsticks.us.

I think this book will have a tremendous impact on all who embrace it and invest themselves in exploring the depth and breadth of its content. My hat is off to you, my friend. Thank you for sharing this with me.

— **Dr. David Garrison**, Executive Director of the Global Gates mission agency. Author of ***Church Planting Movements*** and ***A Wind in the House of Islam: How God is Drawing Muslims to Faith in Jesus Christ Around the World***.

The author of this fine book has made a significant contribution to evangelicals by exploring kingdom themes and their application to God's children and His world, both for the here-and-now and for the hereafter. Reading this book will raise fervor within your heart to pray (and actually understand the prayer) "Let your kingdom come and your will be done on earth as it is in heaven."

— **David Bledsoe, D.Min, Th.D**, International Mission Board missionary to Brazil in the area of training, and the Brazil-side Coordinator of the Master of Theological Studies (MTS) program for the Southeastern Baptist Theological Seminary (SEBTS). Author of articles and books in the area of missions.

Contents

The Values of the Kingdom of God
A Practical Guide to Kingdom Living

How God's Righteousness leads to His Kingdom Values

Preface

Ambassadors of the King

Every Christian is a representative of the King. We bear His name, we represent His Kingdom, and as "Christ's ambassadors" we invite – even implore – others to "be reconciled to God" (2 Corinthians 5:20 - NIV).

I had the privilege of being raised in the home of William Alvin Hatton and Lydia Catherine Jordan Hatton (Katie), the pioneer missionaries who began the Royal Ambassador organization in Brazil (find "Royal Ambassadors" on wmu.com). In the past this was to Baptist Churches in the United States what Awana is to several Christian churches today. Although the RA's have virtually disappeared in this country, they are still very active in Brazil. But there they are called "Ambassadors of the King".

I could hardly wait until I was nine years old to "officially" qualify as a candidate in order to belong to the RA chapter in our local church. Over the years I memorized many Bible verses, learned about missionaries and their work around the globe, went to several camps, handed out gospel tracts in public squares, and knew how to recite "The Commitment of the Ambassadors of the King" by heart. I have translated this pledge below:

I pledge to strive for a worthy life of an ambassador of the King, to keep my lips from lying, from impurity and from taking the Lord's name in vain. To keep my body clean and ready for service. To study the lives of great ambassadors of the King in God's Word and in missionary books. Give all I can to support missions and, through my work, help to establish God's Kingdom on earth.

I promise to be loyal to Jesus Christ, live for Him and serve Him always. I will lead a pure life, always tell the truth, correct my mistakes, and follow Christ the King. If not for this, for what then was I born?

Every Christian is one of Christ's ambassadors to the world. As such, we must strive to live in a way that honors our King and attracts people to Him. We honor our Lord by living righteously and attract people to Him by living out Kingdom Values.

Of course, Kingdom Values are much more than a means to witness or authenticate our walk with the Master to outsiders. They are a reflection of His character and the practical expression of His will (see "The Mirroring Principle" in ***The King of the Kingdom of God***, volume four in this series).

The Secret of the Kingdom, the first book in this series of four, lays down the theoretical foundation on which this study on the Kingdom is constructed. ***The Values of the Kingdom*** is the natural result of inheriting and living in the Kingdom. It answers the question "what then should we do?" (Luke 3:10, 12, 14). When John the Baptist was asked this question by the crowds, tax collectors and soldiers, his answers were practical and to the point. It is my hope that you will find this book to be a relevant guide as you relate to others, and applicable to your daily walk with the King.

Acknowledgments

I am grateful

To my parents

Dad had a passion: organize preteens and early teens to teach them Kingdom Values through sports, camping activities and Bible memorization. As the youngest of Mom and Dad's four kids, I grew up going to camps and participating in our church's Royal Ambassadors chapter. The "Ambassadors of the King" laid the groundwork for my growing interest in the Kingdom of God. I am so thankful the Lord gave me parents who were both fine examples of how to live out Kingdom Values.

To "Uncle" Jerry Key

For a large portion of my spiritual formation and church involvement. Dr. Jerry Key was not only my pastor for many years in Rio de Janeiro, but my Homiletics teacher at the Baptist Seminary as well. Being my mission "uncle" and next door neighbor, he was never shy about giving me good advice, for which I am truly grateful.

To World Vision

In my twenties I began to work for World Vision Brazil, where the Director, Manfred Grellert, and social workers spoke often about the need to stick to a "Kingdom agenda," abide by "Kingdom Values" and seek Kingdom justice for the poor and needy.

To the International Mission Board

In my thirties, my wife Monica and I joined the International Mission Board and served with that organization for 23 years. Throughout those years our leaders and colleagues often included Kingdom references in their meetings, training and sermons.

To family and friends

My wife, Monica, sister Lidia Dell, and daughters Monique and Melissa have all encouraged me through prayer, advice, ideas and by helping to promote the first volume of this series. Friends have given me feedback which has been very positive and encouraging.

Introduction

Righteousness in action

As earth dwellers and Kingdom citizens we live in a constant tension between the here and now and the hereafter. The Bible advises us to keep our eyes on the wonderful life we have to look forward to in the future, eternal state. Paul says, "So we don't look at the troubles we can see now; rather, we fix our gaze on things that cannot be seen. For the things we see now will soon be gone, but the things we cannot see will last forever" (2 Corinthians 4:18 - NLT). Even though we know that in this life we will have problems, we can be encouraged when we focus on the fact that Jesus conquered this world and has readied a place for us in the next one (John 16:33; 14:2).

However, we are not there yet. And, as Thomas Dreier reminds us, "Our beliefs in a rich future life are of little importance unless we coin them into a rich present life."[1] Our hope in the future should mold our lives in the present. And that is where Kingdom Values come in. They are "the good, pleasing, and perfect will of God" (Romans 12:2 - HCSB), lived out in our daily lives. They are righteousness in action!

Although *The Secret of the Kingdom of God*, the first in this series, also addresses God's Global Kingdom (His rule over planet earth) and how it affects our lives, it is primarily about the overarching and future aspects of the Kingdom. *The Values of the Kingdom of God*, on the other hand, is concerned with the way we can and should live our lives in God's Global Kingdom – during our earthly pilgrimage.

On the following pages you will find charts covering the 70 Kingdom Values which appear in this book. Notice that there is a summarized description of each and an "opposite" characteristic in the right column. These are not always strictly opposites, but express what one can expect to find, absent the corresponding Kingdom Value. These can be negative character traits, behavior, feelings or attitudes.

The content of this book begins with a discussion of the term "righteousness," since this is the standard of the Kingdom, the starting point and basis for all Kingdom Values. Following, are eight chapters on the 70 Kingdom Values identified in this study, organized under different categories from the beatitudes to "overall and generic" values.

At the end of each Kingdom Value there is a Kingdom Value Scale which you can use to evaluate your strengths and weaknesses in your daily walk, as it relates to the value being discussed.

We live in a society that glorifies the flesh and ridicules Christian morals. This has contributed to carelessness and confusion in the lives of many Christians. Teaching and preaching Kingdom Values can be an excellent way of creating awareness, combating wrong ideas, and providing Christians with the tools they need to better understand what God expects from them.

If your goal in life is to please God (2 Corinthians 5:9), you will lead a life of righteousness which expresses itself via Kingdom Values. Whether your primary aim is to deepen your own personal Christian relationship with God or to help others do so, here are some ways this book can be read and taught:

1. Readers can identify the values they most want to read about and skip around form topic to topic accordingly.

2. Kingdom Value descriptions can be read one at a time as daily devotionals.

3. Youth leaders can determine or inquire which values are the most challenging for their students and organize weekly Bible studies around them.

4. Preachers may find the discussions a good way to begin their own study and sermon preparation.

5. Ministers can organize their yearly sermon plan around these values, selecting one for each week. Since there are 70 Kingdom Values listed and 52 weeks in the year, there will still be 18 which may be covered during midweek Bible studies or prayer meetings.

However you chose to read this book, I believe you will be blessed, if nothing else, because of the many Bible verses which are quoted in the context of each Kingdom Value. God's Word keeps our minds supplied with God's patterns and ideals, counterbalancing the influence that is pushed our way via social media, streaming videos, and movies. God's Word comforts our spirit, trains our emotions, directs our steps and keeps us on the right path. May God use His Word and this study to bless you on the journey!

KINGDOM	VALUE	DESCRIPTION	OPPOSITE
1 Beatitude	Humility	• Poor in spirit possess Kingdom; • Humble will be exalted	Pride
2 Beatitude	Repentance	• Those who mourn are comforted; • Key to entering Kingdom	Unrepentant
3 Beatitude	Meekness	• Power under control; • Jesus: meekest Man ever	Bullying
4 Beatitude	Burning desire for Righteousness	• Righteous' thirst is quenched; • Desiring what God desires	Complacency
5 Beatitude	Mercy	• Merciful receive mercy • What goes around comes around	Harshness
6 Beatitude	Purity	• Will be ready to be with Him; • Will see God	Impurity
7 Beatitude	Reconciliation	• Pacifiers act like their Father; • They bless and are blessed	Unforgivingness, Conflict
8 Beatitude	Being Persecuted	• Blessed like prophets and Jesus; • Proof of uncompromising faith	Living in a Comfort Zone
9 Fruit of the Spirit	Love	• Unconditional commitment and desire for another's well-being	Hate
10 Fruit of the Spirit	Joy	• By-product of righteous living; • Inner satisfaction and gladness	Sadness, emptyness
11 Fruit of the Spirit	Peace	• State of well-being, inner balance; • Result of reconciliation with God	Turmoil
12 Fruit of the Spirit	Patience	• Willing to wait for God's timing; • Enduring – with good attitude	Impatience
13 Fruit of the Spirit	Kindness	• Showing good will; a sweet spirit; • Being nice and civil	Rudeness
14 Fruit of the Spirit	Goodness	• Doing good and blessing others; • Maintaining good values, virtue	Badness
15 Fruit of the Spirit	Faithfulness	• Being loyal to God; • God is faithful to the faithful	Unfaithfulness
16 Fruit of the Spirit	Gentleness	• Courteous, mild-mannered; • Calm respect for others	Abusiveness
17 Fruit of the Spirit	Self-control	• Freedom to do what's right; • Putting evil desires in check	Out of control

KINGDOM	VALUE	DESCRIPTION	OPPOSITE
18 Purpose of the Church	Worship	• Paying homage to the King; • Praising, loving, submitting	Denigrate
19 Purpose of the Church	Fellowship	• Enjoying God and each other; • Promoting community	Individualism
20 Purpose of the Church	Discipleship	• Following and mirroring Christ; • Practicing Christian disciplines	Not following
21 Purpose of the Church	Proclamation	• Proclaiming the Good News about the Kingdom	Failing to proclaim
22 Purpose of the Church	Service	• The Kingdom's M.O. • Contributing to church, society	Egocentrism
23 Mutuality: "one another"	Forgiving	• Forgetting faults, canceling debts; • Offering a second chance	Grudges; getting even
24 Mutuality: "one another"	Honoring	• Showing respect and regonition; • Thinking highly of others	Dishonoring
25 Mutuality: "one another"	Harmony	• Agreeing to agree; • Unity and like-mindedness	Disunity
26 Mutuality: "one another"	Hospitality	• Opening heart and home; • Receiving and entertaining guests	Social phobia
27 Mutuality: "one another"	Preferring other believers	• Putting faith community first; • Showing favor to other believers	Preferring non-believers
28 Mutuality: "one another"	Submiting	• Validating the gifts of others; • Respecting the authority of others	Competing
29 Mutuality: "one another"	Brotherly affection	• Showing and acting in love; • Appreciating and enjoying others	Antagonism
30 Mutuality: "one another"	Serving one another	• Focusing on the needs of others; • Helping, caring, providing	Self-serving
31 Mutuality: "one another"	Tenderhearted	• Showing lovingkindness: caring, sympathetic, warm	Rough and callous
32 Mutuality: "one another"	Encouraging	• Infusing courage in others; • Lifting up, lending strength	Discouraging
33 Mutuality: "one another"	Celebrating (rejoice together)	• Rejoicing together over victories; • Sharing a praise; thanksgiving	Isolating self
34 Mutuality: "one another"	Speaking Scripturally	• Incorporating Bible into speech; • Quoting and applying Scripture	Trash talk

KINGDOM	VALUE	DESCRIPTION	OPPOSITE
35 In Relation to God	Glorifying God	• Praising, promoting, pleasing God • Giving Him all the credit	Crediting, praising self,
36 In Relation to God	Honoring God's Name	• Keeping His Name holy and separate from the profane	Dishonoring; taking in vain
37 In Relation to God	Obedience	• Doing what God says to do; • Aligning our lives with His will	Rebellion
38 In Relation to God	Rest	• Depending on God's provision • Leaving results to Him	Anxiety
39 In Relation to God	Faith	• A key to the Kingdom; • Confidently trusting God	Doubt, unbelief
40 In Relation to God	Hope	• Waiting expectantly for the fulfilment of God's promises	Despair
41 In Relation to God	Grace	• Receiving God's unmerited favor; • Depending on it for salvation	Wrath
42 In Relation to God	Thanksgiving	• Nurturing a thankful attitude; • Expressing gratitude to God	Murmuring
43 In Relation to God	Prayer	• Speaking and listening to God; • Kingdom cooperation with God	Prayerlessness
44 In Relation to God	Rejoicing in the Lord	• Finding joy and fulfilment in God; • Celebrating life in King Jesus	Pessimism
45 Life Mission	Fruitfulness	• Producing much fruit; • Being productive in the Kingdom	Fruitlessness
46 Life Mission	Compassion	• Practicing the golden rule; • Being moved by people's needs	Insensitivity
47 Life Mission	Stewardship	• Acknowledging God's ownership • Taking care of God's possessions	False sense of ownership
48 Life Mission	Work	• Contributing to society; • Supporting family and church	Laziness, idleness
49 Life Mission	Witnessing	• Offering the keys to the Kingdom; • Being salt and light	Failing to share the faith
50 Life Mission	Missions	• Evangelizing, discipling nations; • Transcultural Gospel sharing	Lack of vision
51 Life Mission	Benevolence (charity, giving)	• Contributing materially and financially to poor and needy	Greediness

KINGDOM	VALUE	DESCRIPTION	OPPOSITE
52 Character: inner self	Spirit Controlled	• Yielding to the Spirit's will • Walking under His direction	Controlled by the flesh
53 Character: inner self	Holiness	• Separate from all that is unholy; • Dedicated for God's use	Worldliness
54 Character: inner self	Self-denial	• Taking up cross, dying to self; • "Yes" to God, "no" to evil desires	Indulgence
55 Character: inner self	Integrity	• Saying what we do; • Doing what we say	Being Doubleminded
56 Character: inner self	Contentment	• Satisfied with who we are; • Just fine with what we have	Greed
57 Character: inner self	Enduring Suffering	• Holding up in pain, persecution; • Faithful through loss and sorrow	Failing the suffering test
58 Character: inner self	Perseverance	• Keep on keeping on in the faith; • Focusing on the future prize	Giving up
59 Character: inner self	Honesty	• Dealing openly and sincerely; • Fair and correct dealings	Dishonesty, cheating
60 Character: inner self	Truth	• Adopting God's worldview; • Who He is, what He says	Falsehood
61 Character: inner self	Wisdom	• Living according to God's values; • Applying God's truth to life	Foolishness
62 Character: inner self	Overcoming	• Remaining faithful to the end; • Victory over trials and temptations	Falling short
63 Character: inner self	Freedom	• Free from sin, idolatry, death; • Free to live righteously	Bondage
64 Character: inner self	Courage	• Strength to face fears and foes; • Power to stand for righteousness	Timidity and cowardice
65 Overall and generic	Justice	• Social justice in society; • Being fair at home, work, church	Injustice, being unfair
66 Overall and generic	Authority and Power	• The right to decide, order, rule; • The means to perform, enforce	Weakness
67 Overall and generic	Life	• God is pro-life; we should be too; • Life is God's precious gift	Death
68 Overall and generic	Family structure	• Cornerstone of civilization; • Biblical model for all generations	Alternative or no structure

| 69 | Overall and generic | **Morality** | • Conforming to God's morals;
• Sexually, socially, personally pure | Immorality |
| 70 | Overall and generic | **Exposing evil** | • Dennouncing unrighteous, evil "values" and practices. | Connivance |

Download color-coded charts from www.kingdomsecret.org.

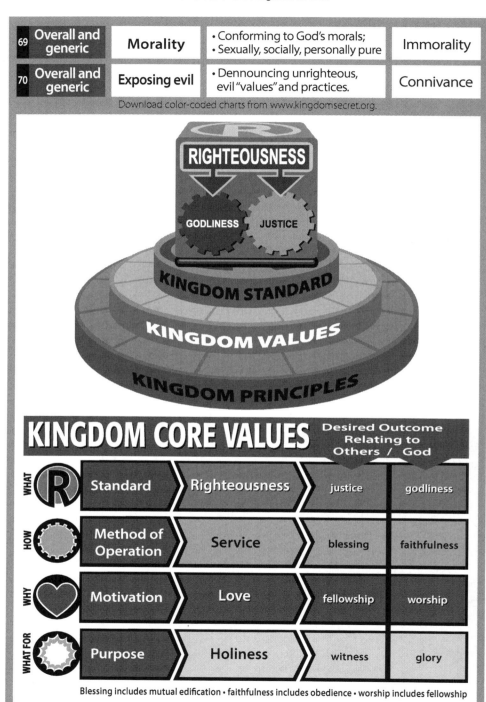

Blessing includes mutual edification • faithfulness includes obedience • worship includes fellowship

Chapter

1

Righteousness: the Standard of the Kingdom

The LORD reigns, let the earth be glad;
let the distant shores rejoice.
Clouds and thick darkness surround him;
righteousness and justice are the foundation of his throne.
Psalm 97:1-2

He Who rules makes the rules

It should come as no surprise that the Ruler of the universe gets to make the rules of the universe. If God says something is important, it is. If He says something is good, it is. If He says something is evil, it is. Take God out of the equation and it's anybody's guess, preference or opinion. Confusion, frustration and depression ensue.

Yet, for citizens of the Kingdom, God's authority stands unchallenged. I am so glad God is in charge! Because God is always right and God is always good. Everything He does is for His glory and our ultimate good. Have you ever wondered just how bleak our future would be if the forces of evil were one day able to overthrow God and take over the universe? We know Satan is a terrible tyrant who has no interest in anyone but himself. Thank God – literally – we do not have to worry about that. Our benevolent, loving King will be in charge for ever! And that's a very good thing.

In the first eight verses of Psalm 119, the psalmist speaks of God's law, statutes, ways, precepts, commands, righteous laws, and decrees. These terms express what is important to God, communicated to us as rules to be followed. Those who do follow them are called "blessed." God rewards those who live according to His ways and obey His orders. Some of those rewards are built in, much like natural laws: if you eat well, exercise frequently and get enough sleep you reap the benefits of better health.

And yet it is important to remember we live in a fallen world where bad things happen even to those who do things God's way. God's rewards and blessings do not make us immune to suffering and pain. In fact, it is many times through these – not in spite of them – that God teaches us more about Himself. King Jesus warned us that "here on earth you will have many trials and sorrows. But take heart, because I have overcome the world" (John 16:33b - NLT). This is the balance we need: to know we will have to deal with suffering but to be courageous and even cheerful because Jesus is in control and guarantees the ultimate positive outcome.

From the Ten Commandments to the teachings of Jesus, God has made clear what He demands and desires from us. Unfortunately, we all seem to suffer from "selective amnesia," needing to be reminded quite often of God's requirements. True, the Law was not given so that by obeying it we could obtain salvation. We are justified by faith. But the Law remains as God's standard of conduct and He expects those saved by grace to diligently observe His commands. Jesus said it plainly: "If you love Me, you will keep My commands" (John 14:15 - HCSB).

Kingdom Standard, Values, and Principles

If we really want to be pleasing or acceptable to God we will not "copy the behavior and customs of this world" but will adhere to God's code of conduct (Romans 12:2a - NLT). And in so doing we "will be able to test and approve what God's will is—his good, pleasing and perfect will" (Romans 12:2b - NIV). God's commandments tell us how He wants us to relate to Him and to others. In a nutshell, "those who say that they live in [Jesus] must live the same way he lived" (1 John 2:6 - GW).

As we reflect on this matter, it may help if we organize God's commands under the following categories:

1. Kingdom Standard (this and the next chapter)

A standard is "a required or agreed level of quality or attainment; an idea or thing used as a measure, norm, or model in comparative evaluations; principles of conduct informed by notions of honor and decency used or accepted as normal or average."[1]

The standard of the Kingdom, which sums up all that God requires (Matthew 3:15) and all that God desires (Psalm 33:5), and against which everything is measured, is righteousness. In a sense, righteousness is God's code of conduct.

John MacArthur teaches: "here is the standard, and the key to it all is one word: 'righteousness.' Jesus is saying, 'If you are a child of the King, the characteristic of your life will be righteousness.'"[2] Righteous conduct flows out of a holy character. Dr. Brian Stephens teaches "we were not called to be assimilated by the world, but to be different and set apart from it."

Godliness is the personal – and justice the social – face of righteousness. Later on in this chapter we will look at the concept of righteousness and how it is found everywhere in the Bible. We will reflect on its implications for the Kingdom and its application to our lives. Righteousness is the over-arching standard of the Kingdom and Kingdom Values and Principles help us better understand how to flesh out righteousness in everyday living.

2. Kingdom Values (chapters 3 through 10)

Value has to do with worth. It is "the regard that something is held to deserve; the importance or preciousness of something; the usefulness of something considered in respect of a particular purpose," and relates to "a person's principles or standards of behavior; one's judgment of what is important in life."[3]

This leads us to ask: what is of value and precious to our King? How does our King want us to conduct our lives? What specific areas are mentioned and examples are given in His Word? There are so many we will need to limit ourselves to some of the more obvious and common ones (I stopped at 70). We can divide Kingdom Values into personal (having to do with our character and behavior), relational (dealing with mutuality or the "one another" commands), social (life mission and how we conduct our work, service and ministry in the world), and spiritual values (in relation to God).

3. Kingdom Principles (interspersed throughout)

What happens when we live out Kingdom Values? What happens if we don't?

Principles are "fundamental norms, rules, or values that represent what is desirable and positive for a person, group, organization, or community, and help it in determining the rightfulness or wrongfulness of its actions."[4]

But I would like to extend the definition to include the notion that "a principle is a law or rule that ... is an inevitable consequence of something, such as the laws observed in nature..."[5] In other words, I am using "principles" here to mean those actions we take which have important positive or negative consequences, the cause-and-effect laws of the Kingdom of God. I decided against bunching all the principles I came across together in one place. Instead, they are associated with certain Kingdom Values, or appear after the consideration of specific verses related to the Kingdom.

A call to righteous living by a Righteous King

"God writes straight on crooked lines." So goes a popular saying in Brazil. How true that is! Though "there is none righteous, not even one" (Romans 3:10), God still uses imperfect people who have surrendered to His will to carry out His plans in the world. And the saying is right on target since the Hebrew word **yashar**, sometimes translated into English as "upright," *means* "straight."

The Bible says God is righteous (Psalms 11:7; 116:5; 119:137; 145:17; Ezra 9:15; Daniel 9:7; 14). Psalms 7:11 says He is a Righteous Judge. His very laws and ordinances are righteous (Psalms 19:9; 119:75; 160). Jesus, the Messiah, is called "The Righteous Servant" (Isaiah 53:11), "The Righteous Branch" (Jeremiah 23:5) and "The Righteous One" (Isaiah 24:16; Acts 3:14; 7:52; 22:14; and 1 John 2:1).

"Righteousness" is all over the Bible
From now on be on the alert every time you read your Bible and make a mental note every time you come across the word "righteousness." You will be surprised to find it everywhere. It will pop up in the middle of some of your most treasured passages. It is the path to which God led David in the most quoted chapter of the Psalms (Psalm 23:3); the hunger and thirst of the blessed in the beatitudes (Matthew 5:6); the breastplate of the armor of God that every Christian is to wear (Ephesians 6:14); and the credit Abraham received because of his faith in God (Genesis 15:6 – a verse quoted in Romans 4:3, Galatians 3:6 and James 2:23). Over and over again, righteousness is the term used to sum up what God is looking for in humanity and that which really pleases Him. King David wrote that "the Lord is righteous; He loves righteousness; the upright will behold His face" (Psalm 11:7 - NASB).

While righteousness is a recurring theme in most books of the Bible, there are at least three books which have righteousness as their central focus. All three are part of the poetic and wisdom literature of the Hebrew scriptures. They are Job, Psalms, and Proverbs. Close examination of the first book will reveal "the purpose of the book of Job is to explore the justice of God's treatment of the righteous,"[6] not so much the problem of suffering, in and of itself.

As for the book of Psalms, the first chapter "draws a brief but sharp distinction between the conduct of the righteous person and that of the wicked person. It also addresses their respective destinies. We find that this accurately introduces one of the major themes of Psalms: concern for the ultimate vindication of the righteous and the ultimate punishment of the wicked."[7]

Proverbs itself states its main purposes as "learning what wisdom and discipline are" with the goal of "receiving wise instruction in righteousness, justice, and integrity" (Proverbs 1:2-3 - HCSB; reiterated in chapter 2:6-10). "Ultimately the way of wisdom is keeping to the path of righteousness."[8] For the Christian, it is comforting to know that Jesus "became for us wisdom from God, and righteousness and sanctification and redemption" (1 Corinthians 1:30 - NET Bible).

When you get right down to it, "all Scripture is inspired by God and is profitable... for training in righteousness." (2 Timothy 3:16-17 - HCSB). Righteousness is central to the message of the Bible because it is also central to the Kingdom of God. It is the standard of the Kingdom because it is a direct expression of one of God's main attributes – holiness. Therefore, righteousness has been, is and always will be the standard of every aspect of God's Kingdom. We are told, "But of the Son He says, "YOUR THRONE, O GOD, IS FOREVER AND EVER, AND THE RIGHTEOUS SCEPTER IS THE SCEPTER OF HIS KINGDOM" (Hebrews 1:8 - NASB).

Jesus was "designated by God a high priest after the order of Melchizedek" (Hebrews 5:10 - ESV). Melchizedek was "king of Salem" (Genesis 14:18). Salem was short for what would become Jerusalem and means "peace" or "peaceful." Therefore, He is "king of peace" (Hebrews 7:2b). And Melchizedek literally means "king of righteousness" (from the Hebrew *malki* for "king" and *tsedeq* for "righteousness") (Hebrews 7:2a). God's Kingdom has righteousness as its scepter and the King of Righteousness as its eternal Ruler.

What is righteousness?
The Word of God tells us the Kingdom of God is a matter of righteousness (Ro-

mans 14:17a). We may deduce that if we want to understand the Kingdom, we must understand righteousness.

The word "righteousness" in the English Bible comes from two words in Hebrew (**sedaqah** and **sedeq**) and two words in Greek (**dikaiosune** and **euthutes**). The Hebrew **sedeq** (or **tsedeq**) means "accurate, fairly, just, justice, righteous, righteousness, what is right."[9] The word transliterated **sedaqah** (or t**sedaqah**) is from the same root but includes the notions of "honesty, merits, righteous acts, and rights."[10]

God's standards are right, fair, just and honest. There *is* a right way to live. There *is* a correct way to relate to others. There *is* a proper way to relate to God. Righteousness is, therefore, doing the right thing in the right way. Or better, doing God's will, God's way.

Being politically correct, culturally sensitive and tolerant of other people's value system are all part of the current trend. But over and above trends, fads, human value systems and even human laws is God's code of conduct. God's laws, decrees, and precepts are not up for debate – whether or not we find them to be natural, sensible, logical or convenient. "Let those who are wise understand these things. Let those with discernment listen carefully. The paths of the LORD are true and right, and righteous people live by walking in them. But in those paths sinners stumble and fall" (Hosea 14:9 - NLT).

More than merely abiding by a code of conduct

Holiness has to do with character (who we *are*) and righteousness has to do with actions and behavior (what we *do*). "The Hebrew mind did not understand righteousness to be an attribute of the divine, that is a characteristic of God's nature. Rather, God's righteousness is what God *does* in fulfillment of the terms of the covenant that God established with the chosen people, Israel."[11] While the Kingdom standard of righteousness (along with Kingdom Values and Principles) constitutes a "code of conduct" for the citizens of God's Kingdom, we must understand that "in biblical usage righteousness is rooted in covenants and relationships. For biblical authors, righteousness is the fulfillment of the terms of a covenant between God and humanity or between humans in the full range of human relationships" so that "as Israel kept the covenant law, the nation was righteous."[12]

This applies to Christians as well, for all who have entered the Kingdom after the time of Christ do so under the New Covenant, which He established. Under the New Covenant, validated by our Lord's own blood, those who repent and believe may enter a special relationship with the Father, through which God provides the forgiveness of sins, the indwelling of the Holy Spirit, and eternal life. Through the New Covenant, "He made the One who did not know sin to be sin for us, so that we might become the righteousness of God in Him" (2 Corinthians 5:21 - HCSB). The believer agrees to submit to the Lordship of God, becoming both son and servant, being used of God to produce much fruit, to be a blessing in the world and to serve others. This relationship is so special that the apostle John exclaimed: "Look at how great a love the Father has given us that we should be called God's children. And we are!" (1 John 3:1a - HCSB).

Righteousness is not a cold, mechanical, and disinterested conformity to God's laws. That's how the Pharisees saw it, and for this they were severely rebuked by our Lord. As concerned as they were for "the law," they overlooked the greatest commandment ever delivered by Moses to the Israelites: "Love the LORD your God with all your heart and with all your soul and with all your might." What God desired was that "these words that I command you today shall be on your heart" (Deuteronomy 6:5-6 - ESV).

Righteousness is our eager response to a loving God with Whom we have entered a special relationship. We desire to live according to God's standards because we love Him and wish to please Him. And when we do, we end up discovering that, "Whoever pursues righteousness and love finds life, prosperity and honor" (Proverbs 21:21 - NIV). When we are in covenant with God, we honor Him and He honors us! (For more on the covenants of the Bible, see chapter 5 of **The Secret of the Kingdom** under "The Global Kingdom").

Seeking righteousness is priority number one

We are commanded by Jesus to seek the Kingdom of God and God's righteousness before all else (Matthew 6:33). Jesus had been speaking about the cares of life, about the need to eat, drink, and clothe our bodies (Matthew 6:25). He tells us not to worry about these things, not because we don't need them, but because God already knows we need them. Jesus did not say "seek *only* the Kingdom." He said, "seek *first* the Kingdom." He had just stated we could take our physical and material needs to the Father. He taught His disciples to pray "give us today our daily bread" (Matthew 6:11).

Jesus was coming from a covenant perspective. The idea is "you trust and obey, making the Kingdom and righteousness your focus, and the King, Who is your Father, will take care of your needs." It could be stated as **the "you concentrate on God's interests and He will take care of yours" Kingdom Principle**.

Inversely, we could conclude that if we concentrate on the cares of life and do not intentionally keep the Kingdom and righteousness as our priority, we will end up being fruitless, our fellowship with the Father will be negatively affected, and we should not be surprised if we have a harder time than usual taking good care of our day-to-day necessities. Not because God would love us any less (He *is* our Father and cares deeply about us and desires to bless us). But because our lives would be out of balance and our priorities would be in disarray.

After returning from the 70-year Babylonian captivity, the people of Jerusalem kept putting off rebuilding the Temple. Yet they felt the time was right to rebuild and remodel their own homes. God challenges them to carefully weigh what they were doing. This was the reason, He tells them, "You have planted much, but harvested little. You eat, but never have enough. You drink, but never have your fill. You put on clothes, but are not warm. You earn wages, only to put them in a purse with holes in it" (Haggai 1:6 - NIV). This was also why, "You expected much, but then it amounted to little. When you brought the harvest to your house, I ruined it." God did this "because My house still lies in ruins, while each of you is busy with his own house" (Haggai 1:9 - HCSB).

God tells them it was their fault "the skies have withheld the dew and the land its

18

crops" and the reason He had ordered a "drought" on crops, people, animals and "on all that your hands produce" (Haggai 1:11 - HCSB).

Those who only focus on the cares of life are like seeds sown among thorns, Jesus said. They "hear the kingdom news but are overwhelmed with worries about all the things they have to do and all the things they want to get. The stress strangles what they heard, and nothing comes of it" (Mark 4:18-19 - The Message). But those who concentrate on the Kingdom and righteousness of God are like "those who hear the Word, embrace it, and produce a harvest beyond their wildest dreams" (Mark 4:20 - The Message).

Jesus' whole life, mission, and time on earth was fully dedicated to God's Kingdom and righteousness. He told His disciples that "My food (nourishment) is to do the will (pleasure) of Him Who sent Me and to accomplish and completely finish His work" (John 4:34 - AMP). We are to follow in the footsteps of Jesus, "the Righteous One" (Acts 22:14), and He taught that "it is proper for us to... fulfill all righteousness" (Matthew 3:15).

God is "just and justifier"

If there is an attribute of God that stands out, it is that He is holy. Both the Old and the New Testaments proclaim: "Holy, holy, holy is the Lord Almighty" (Isaiah 6:3 and Revelations 4:8). This is the God Who created us in His likeness so that we could enjoy serving, worshiping and having fellowship with Him. The God Who "chose us in [Jesus] before the creation of the world to be holy and blameless in his sight" (Ephesians 1:4 - NIV). A holy God Whose original purpose was to have holy sons and daughters.

But when humanity fell, we lost our innocence and became guilty, corrupted and sinful. God still loves and wants us back as we were meant to be. In order to accomplish this goal, God does something astonishing: He declares those who repent and place their faith in Him to be "not guilty" and credits His righteousness to them (Colossians 1:22; 2:13, 14; Romans 3:22; 4:3, 6; Galatians 2:16). By so doing, He imparts His own holiness to those who trust in Him.

We see in the Bible two sides of righteousness: one is shown in God's actions; the other is received as a gift which leads to "right standing" with God, by being "justified" or declared not guilty. This means God is both "**just** and the **justifier**" of the one who has faith in Jesus" (Romans 3:26b - NASB). This is the Good News of the Kingdom which had been foretold by the Old Testament prophets. In speaking of the Messiah Who was to come, Isaiah foretold that "the Righteous One, My Servant, will justify the many, as He will bear their iniquities" (Isaiah 53:11 - NASB).

The Apostle Paul said his aspiration was to "be found in [Jesus], not having a righteousness of my own from the law, but one that is through faith in Christ —the righteousness from God based on faith" (Philippians 3:9 - HCSB; see also Galatians 2:16 and Titus 3:5). As soon as a new believer has been justified, the Holy Spirit of God begins the work of sanctification in order to make him or her more and more like Himself. It is crucial to be holy because God desires to have fellowship with us. And that is not possible as long as we remain in sin (holiness does not mix with unholiness). One of us has to change – and it isn't God! God holds the standard. He tells us to "be holy, because I am holy" (1 Peter 1:16; Leviticus 11:44,45; 19:2; 20:7).

Even in the Old Testament, righteousness was associated with salvation. Using marriage symbols similar to those of Revelation 19, Isaiah writes: "I am overwhelmed with joy in the LORD my God! For he has dressed me with the clothing of salvation and draped me in a robe of righteousness. I am like a bridegroom in his wedding suit or a bride with her jewels" (Isaiah 61:10 - NLT). The Psalmist cries out: "Open the gates of righteousness for me; I will enter through them and give thanks to the Lord. This is the gate of the Lord; the righteous will enter through it. I will give thanks to You because You have answered me and have become my salvation" (Psalms 118:19-21 - HCSB).

While we are saved by grace by no work of our own, after we have been saved we are to engage in doing "good works, which God prepared in advance as our way of life" (see the sequence in Ephesians 2:8-10 - BSB). We are not saved *by* but *for* good works. Good works relate to fulfilling the mission God assigned to us and result in fruit which bring glory to the Father (John 15:5, 8). Performing righteous actions and bearing much fruit are expected of all who have been made righteous (Revelation 19:8 - NIV).

Righteous acts
What are some of the righteous acts the righteous should perform? Here is a sampling.

The righteous:
• Do what is right (1 John 2:29; 3:7);
• Do things God's way, like Abel (1 John 3:12);
• Walk with God, as Noah (Genesis 6:9);
• Walk in God's ways (Hosea 14:9);
• Give generously and without sparing (Psalms 37:21; Proverbs 21:26);
• Refrain from the bad kind of anger (James 1:20);

20

- Care about justice for the poor (Proverbs 29:7);
- Say what is wise and speak what is just (Psalms 37:30; Proverbs 10:31);
- Make plans that are just (Proverbs 12:5);
- Hate what is false (Proverbs 13:5);
- Lead blameless lives (Proverbs 20:7);
- Are overjoyed when justice is done (Proverbs 21:15);
- Get up after falling (Proverbs 24:16);
- Are bold as a lion (Proverbs 28:1);
- Detest the dishonest (Proverbs 29:27);
- Take good care of their animals (Proverbs 12:10).

What does living righteously look like?
In Psalm 15 King David shares some of what the Lord had taught him about righteous living. He asks who could come close to and fellowship with God (literally, dwell in His sanctuary and live on His holy hill). The answer is "he whose walk is blameless and who does what is righteous." What follows in that psalm is a description of what it means to be righteous.

He who is righteous:
- Speaks the truth from his heart;
- Has no slander on his tongue;
- Does his neighbor no wrong;
- Casts no slur on his fellowman;
- Despises a vile man;
- Honors those who fear the LORD;
- Keeps his oath even when it hurts;
- Lends his money without usury;
- Does not accept a bribe against the innocent.

Leaders are especially expected to be righteous
Proverbs tells us that:
- "Kings detest wrongdoing, for a throne is established through righteousness" (16:12 - NIV).
- "When the righteous thrive, the people rejoice; when the wicked rule, the people groan" (29:2 - NIV).
- It is by wisdom that kings reign and rulers make just laws (8:15).
- "Arrogant lips are unsuited to a fool – how much worse lying lips to a ruler!" (17:7 - NIV)
- "Remove the wicked from the king's presence, and his throne will be established through righteousness" (25:5 - NIV).

Practical righteousness, from Zechariah 7:9, 10 and 8:16-19
People who live righteously:
- Administer true justice;
- Show mercy and compassion to one another;
- Do not oppress the widow or the fatherless, the alien or the poor;
- Do not think evil of each other;
- Speak the truth to each other;
- Render true and sound judgment in their courts;
- Do not plot evil against their neighbor;
- Do not love to swear falsely;
- Love truth and peace.

A reminder from Micah 6:8 (HCSB)
"Mankind, He has told you what is good and what it is the LORD requires of you:"
- To act justly (an aspect of righteousness);
- to love faithfulness (some versions have "mercy");
- To walk humbly with your God.

John the Baptist's message
John the Baptist was "preaching a baptism of repentance for the forgiveness of sins," telling the people to "produce fruit consistent with repentance" (Luke 3:3, 8 - HCSB). He told them not to think they were in a good place simply because they were Abraham's descendants. He warned them judgment was near, "So every tree not producing good fruit will be cut down and thrown into a fire" (Luke 3:9 - ISV).

So the crowd asks John what they were supposed to do. Remember the message was they needed to repent and produce results in line with their repentance. Instead of giving them a theoretical lesson on the subject, he gave them practical examples of what they needed to do. "The man who has two shirts must share with the man who has none, and the man who has food must do the same." To the Tax collectors, he said: "You must not demand more than you are entitled to." And to the soldiers, he said, "Don't bully people, don't bring false charges, and be content with your pay" (Luke 3:10-14 - PHILLIPS).

Paul on righteousness in action (Ephesians 4:1-6:9)

In this passage, Paul gives us a long list of things related to righteous living. Here are some of the highlights that will help us "to walk in a manner worthy of the calling to which you have been called" (Ephesians 4:1 - ESV), and "to put on the new self, created after the likeness of God in true righteousness and holiness" (Ephesians 4:24 - ESV).

Fruit of personal godliness
We are to:
• Be completely humble and gentle;
• Be patient;
• Always give thanks to God;
• Be without stain or any other blemish; be blameless;
• In our anger we are not to sin (James 1:20 says "human anger does not produce the righteousness that God desires" - ISV).

General principles of godly living
We should:
• Be made new in the attitude of our minds;
• Be imitators of God, as dearly loved children;
• Live a life of love;
• Live as children of light (the fruit of the light consists in all goodness, righteousness, and truth);
• Find out what pleases the Lord;
• Be wise and very careful how we live;
• Make the most of every opportunity;
• Understand what the Lord's will is.

Fruit of justice and just relationships
We are told to:
• Bear with one another in love;
• Cultivate unity of the Spirit and in the faith;
• Speak the truth in love;
• Speak truthfully to your neighbor;
• Be kind and compassionate to one another;
• Forgive each other (just as in Christ God has forgiven us);
• Expose the fruitless deeds of darkness.

Specific family and work relationship principles
Righteousness in community living means:
• We are to submit to one another out of reverence for Christ;
• Wives, submit to their husbands as to the Lord;
• Husbands love their wives just as Christ loved the church;
• Children obey and honor their parents in the Lord, for this is right;
• Fathers don't exasperate their children but bring them up in the instruction of the Lord;

- Slaves obey their earthly masters just as they would obey Christ;
- Masters treat their slaves well and do not threaten them.

Negative principles

These are things to avoid when striving for righteous living.
We are **not** to:

- Live as the Gentiles do, in the futility of their thinking;
- Lose all sensitivity;
- Give ourselves over to sensuality, impurity, lust;
- Give the devil a foothold;
- Steal;
- Hold on to falsehood;
- Be sexual immoral or impure (these are improper for God's holy people);
- Be greedy;
- Get drunk;
- Let any unwholesome talk come out of our mouths;
- Hold on to bitterness, rage, anger, brawling, slander, malice;
- Engage in obscenity, foolish talk or coarse joking.

The role of the Holy Spirit and more fruit of righteousness

The Holy Spirit and righteousness

Jesus told His disciples that when the Holy Spirit came He would "convict and convince the world and bring demonstration to it about sin and about righteousness (uprightness of heart and right standing with God)" (John 16:8a - AMP). Only the Holy Spirit can convict and convince the unrighteous of their need to be made righteous through Jesus. To have a performance or work-based approach to being righteous before God is not only futile, it's dangerous. Paul warns that "if you seek to be justified and declared righteous and to be given a right standing with God through the Law, you are brought to nothing and so separated (severed) from Christ. You have fallen away from grace (from God's gracious favor and unmerited blessing)" (Galatians 5:4 - AMP).

As those made righteous are "filled with the Spirit" (Ephesians 5:18b), they are led to produce "fruit of righteousness" (Ephesians 5:9). Now, since the fruit of righteousness comes as a direct result of the work of the Holy Spirit, we may truly call them the "fruit of the Holy Spirit." Paul's list of the fruit of the Spirit, found in Galatians 5, reads like a summary of what he wrote in Ephesians 4:1-6:9. The negative aspects he calls "the work of the flesh" (compare to Ephesians 5:3-14), and the positive he calls "the fruit of the Spirit." (See Kingdom Values, numbers 9 through 17, under *The Fruit of the Spirit Kingdom Values*, in chapter 4).

At the end of this list, there is a concluding statement: "against such things there is no law" (Galatians 5:23). This is because those who live by the Holy Spirit conduct themselves righteously in their daily lives. This pleases the Father, making rules and regulations unnecessary. Righteous living fulfills not just the letter of the law but the spirit of the law as well.

More fruit of righteousness in Scripture

Paul prays for the Philippians, that they "approve what is excellent, and so be pure and blameless for the day of Christ, filled with the fruit of righteousness" (Philippians 1:9-11 - ESV). Sin, on the other hand, will "turn justice into poison and the sweet fruit of righteousness into bitterness" (Amos 6:12b - NLT).

Besides the fruit of the Spirit, what else does the Bible have to say about the fruit or result of righteousness in the life of those who faithfully follow the Lord? These are some of the fruit produced by righteous living:

• Life. The end result of righteousness is life. Literally, "The fruit of the righteous is a tree of life" (Proverbs 11:30a - ESV).
• Peace, quietness and confidence (Isaiah 32:17).
• An environment of peace. "And the fruit of righteousness is sown in peace by them that make peace" (James 3:18 - KJV 2000). "The peaceful fruit of righteousness" is yielded by God's discipline in our lives (Hebrews 12:11 - ESV).
• Love. "I said, 'Plant the good seeds of righteousness, and you will harvest a crop of love. Plow up the hard ground of your hearts, for now is the time to seek the LORD, that he may come and shower righteousness upon you'" (Hosea 10:12 - NLT).

The Sermon on the Mount

After all we have seen about the importance of this subject, it should come as no surprise that the central themes of the greatest sermon ever delivered, found in Matthew chapters 5, 6 and 7, are the Kingdom of God and righteousness. If we were to give Jesus' Sermon on the Mount a title, it could be "The Heavenly Father's requirements for Kingdom living," or "What it means to live righteously in the Kingdom." If it were a magazine article, the title might be "Jesus' guidelines for Kingdom living;" or perhaps this one: "Want to be righteous? Here's what to do in practical situations."

The Sermon on the Mount has been compared to the *Magna Carta* and to the Constitution, yet both of these originated from the need to curb the government's authority in an attempt to protect citizens from the abuse of power. That is simply not an issue when it comes to God's Kingdom. Quite the opposite. God is in His very nature a just King and Judge; and all His laws and ways are righteous, as seen repeatedly in Scripture. He is the One Who instills in us the burning desire to see righteousness triumph and justice prevail.

Some argue the Sermon on the Mount lays down the ideal ground rules for the Millennial Kingdom. That may be so, but they certainly apply to the here and now as well, because what Jesus has to say addresses very practical, day-to-day issues.

Hungry, thirsty, lost and needing to be rescued
Imagine you have been cruising on a transatlantic only to awake one day to a sudden outburst of fire on board. Everyone is ordered to abandon ship. The following events develop over the next few days:

Day one: It all happened so suddenly you cannot remember how you ended up all alone on a lifeboat. You look around and all you can see is deep blue water in every direction. You have no idea where you are. You search inside the raft and find there are some small packages of food and a few bottles of water.

Day two: There is no dry land in sight. You hope you are drifting in the right direction, to the nearest shore. You figure you should slow down on the food consumption just in case.

Day three: You're lonely and starting to get worried – really worried. Your food rations will not last much longer and your water is almost gone. You are not as confident in your own abilities to survive as you were on day one.

Day four: The water is gone and there are just a few crumbs left from your rations.

Day five: It occurs to you how ironic your situation really is. Here you are just dying for some water and yet you are completely surrounded by it – it just happens to be the wrong kind. And food! There it is, swimming all around you, and yet you don't stand a chance of catching a single fish.

Day six: You would give anything for a glass of water and some bread. Quenching your thirst and satisfying your hunger has become the driving motivation and purpose of your life.
Day seven: It has become obvious to you that you do not have the resources to make it on your own. You realize that if you are to survive you must be rescued. You must be *given* water and food. Being found and delivered from your terrible hunger and thirst has now become an obsession.

26

The beatitudes are Jesus' way of telling us that when something like this story happens in our lives spiritually, we are finally in a position to find the help we so desperately need from God. For He can only help us if we realize we cannot help ourselves. And we will only allow Him to rescue us from our sea of rebellion and sin if we truly hunger and thirst for His righteousness.

Just as the lifeboat was surrounded by salt water, we are surrounded by the world system and all that it has to offer. Yet the "water" the world offers us is not fit for consumption. And its "food" is elusive. So our spiritual hunger drives us to seek the Living Water (John 4:10) and the Bread of Life (John 6:35) with all our heart, soul, mind and strength (Mark 12:30). That's being hungry and thirsty for righteousness. And when we find our righteousness in Jesus, we will truly be filled and satisfied (John 10:10; Philippians 3:9).

If the Sermon on the Mount is the code of conduct of the Kingdom, then the beatitudes are like introductory remarks which explain what God's requirements are for entering and living in the Kingdom. (Since the beatitudes are covered individually as Kingdom Values in chapter 4, here they will be seen only as they relate to righteousness).

Righteousness and the beatitudes

Jesus constantly surprised His audience with unexpected parables and principles. He often used "shock therapy" to shake them out of their spiritual paralysis. Case in point: Jews of Jesus' time considered the rich and the powerful to be blessed by God. The poor and the weak were deemed to be lacking God's favor or seen to be under His curse. Isn't this the popular view still held today? Yet Jesus said the latter, not the former, were the blessed ones. I'm sure Jesus' listeners, including His closest disciples, were stunned to hear this.

But the blessing comes from the fact that it is precisely these three attitudes that lead a person to righteousness, the fourth Beatitude:
1. Being poor in spirit (being humble and recognizing your need);
2. Mourning (being sorry for your sins and repenting);
3. Being meek (being self-emptied and God-controlled).

Jesus then spoke of three attitudes which *result* from righteousness (fruits of righteousness):
1. Being merciful (being willing to forgive others);
2. Being pure in heart (having integrity and being sanctified);
3. Being peacemakers (or reconcilers, as seen in James 3:8).

In his excellent book about the Beatitudes, titled **Kingdom Living Here and Now**, John MacArthur, Jr. explains:

> The first three [Beatitudes] lead up to the fourth, to hunger and thirst after righteousness, which seems to be a kind of apex. You begin with a beggarly spirit, and out of that comes a mourning over sin. When you see yourself as a total sinner, you become humble and meek before God. At that point you cry out for righteousness. Then God acts and you find His mercy, purity of heart and the gift of peacemaking.[13]

Although the first three attitudes initially **lead** to righteousness, they are traits which, like the last three, are supposed to continue to characterize the life of every believer.

Blessings and rewards

Jesus tells those who come under His code of conduct for the Kingdom and are persecuted for taking it seriously – to "be glad and rejoice," and promises "your reward is great in heaven" (Matthew 5:12). Those who live out the Kingdom Values described in the Beatitudes have every reason to rejoice, because "the kingdom of heaven is theirs" (v.v. 3, 10), "they will be comforted" (v. 4), "they will inherit the earth" (v. 5), "they will be filled" (v. 6), "they will be shown mercy" (v. 7), "they will see God" (v. 8), and "they will be called sons of God" (v. 9).

Jesus' sermon on righteousness: the rest of the message

After showing the way to enter the Kingdom by being "filled" with righteousness, Jesus' sermon continues describing how we are to live in His Kingdom. He taught about dealing with persecution (Matthew 5:11, 12), how we must influence an insipid and dark world as salt and light (Matthew 5:13-15), and the importance of practicing and teaching His commands (Matthew 5:17-20).

As far as our relationships go, He told us to avoid angry bickering and name-calling; to settle differences and seek reconciliation (Matthew 5:21-26). Jesus commanded us to avoid sexual lust at any cost, taking decisive steps to control eyes and hands (Matthew 5:27-30). He taught there should be no divorce, except in cases of sexual immorality, most likely referring to infidelity (Matthew 5:31, 32). We are not to swear but to just say "yes" or "no" (Matthew 5:33-37). We are to deal with violent and oppressive evildoers in a non-aggressive manner (Matthew 5:38-42). This way we will be like God by loving our enemies and praying for our persecutors (Matthew 5:43-48).

We are to keep from being self-righteous show-offs, but do good deeds in secret

(Matthew 6:1-4). This includes our private prayer life (Matthew 6:5-8). Jesus modeled how His disciples are to pray by sharing "the Lord's prayer" (Matthew 6:9-13). His only commentary on the prayer was sharing the Kingdom Principle of forgiveness: forgive others if you want to be forgiven by the heavenly Father (Matthew 6:14). Jesus said to stop putting on a sad face when fasting but instead to keep it between ourselves and our Father (Matthew 6:16-18).

The Kingdom Principle which applies to these teachings is this: if you do good things to receive the applause of others, their recognition will be the extent of your "reward." In that case, you will forfeit your reward from the heavenly Father. If you do good to please God, "your Father who sees in secret will reward you" (Matthew 6:1-3; see 5-8; 16-18). It's a choice between the applause of people or the approval of heaven. It's the "*you either work for God and receive His reward or show-off to get popular recognition*" *Kingdom Principle*. You can't have both.

We should not accumulate treasures on earth but in heaven because we can't serve both God and money (Matthew 6:19-24). We are prohibited from worrying about life – what to eat, drink and wear, since God knows about all our needs (Matthew 6:25-32). Jesus said to give God's Kingdom and His righteousness our priority; then our needs will be provided for (Matthew 6:33). We are not supposed to worry about the future but live one day at a time (Matthew 6:34). We are not to judge others. If we do we will be judged by the same criteria we used towards others. We shouldn't dwell on the defects of others while ignoring our own (Matthew 7:1-5). And we must not waste what is holy on "dogs" or offer pearls to "pigs" (Matthew 7:6).

Instead, we need to keep asking, searching and knocking on the door, in order to receive, find and see the door being opened. Because our Father in heaven gives good things to those who ask Him (Matthew 7:7-11). Jesus expects us to treat others like we would like to be treated – which is what is referred to as "the golden rule" by many today, and is a great Kingdom Principle to live by (Matthew 7:12).

Demonstrating just how high the stakes are, Jesus said we must avoid the wide gate and broad road that leads to destruction. We must enter "life" through the narrow gate, while treading the difficult path (Matthew 7:13-14).

How do we recognize false prophets? Jesus instructed His disciples to do so by inspecting their fruit (good trees produce good fruit, bad trees, bad fruit) (Matthew 7:15-20). He warned that calling Him "Lord" is not good enough to enter the Kingdom; we must *do* the Father's will (Matthew 7:21-23). This involves hearing and acting on His teachings, which is like building on a rock as a firm foundation which the storms of life will not be able to destroy. Those who merely hear and do nothing about it are building on the sand (Matthew 7:24-27).

Much of what Jesus taught is counter-intuitive to fallen human nature. That is probably why He anticipates persecution for those who take His teachings seriously and begin to incorporate them into their daily lives. And, what an incredible world this would be if we everybody followed our Lord's teachings! How different even our homes, churches and Christian organizations would be if we would take the Sermon on the Mount to heart!

The danger of self-righteousness

Our righteousness comes from the Lord. *He* is our righteousness. That means we start out humble (poor in spirit) and that means we stay humble throughout our whole life. When we lose sight of this Kingdom Value, when we start comparing ourselves to others and not against the standards of the Kingdom, we risk becoming proud. Since pride cannot build a righteousness of its own, it becomes legalistic and emphasizes form over content (*how* we do things instead of *what* we do), the superficial over the internal, rules and regulations over fellowship and relationships. Soon we are trying to criticize others down to our level of spiritual mediocrity.

Self-righteousness simply has no place in the Kingdom of God.

The difference righteousness can make

Can you imagine what a different world we would live in if righteousness prevailed in society as a whole? We could go back to leaving our doors unlocked; gentlemen would open doors for the ladies; the young would help the elderly cross our busy streets. Scams would be no more, domestic violence would a thing of the past, robberies and murders would be confined to old documentaries, road rage would take an exit, adultery would be unheard of, gossip and slander would be unfashionable, the old terrorist would be the new pacifists, and liars would be out of business. Some revivals in the past produced similar results. But nothing compares to the time when righteousness will be the law of the land (see chapter 6, on *The Millennial Kingdom*, in *The Secret of the Kingdom*, volume one in this series).

Five steps to righteous living

Knowing about holiness and righteousness makes no difference unless we learn how to allow God to put this knowledge to work in a practical way in our daily lives. I have noticed in my own life and in the experience of others, that negative emotions are one of the main factors that bring us down or cause of to stray from the path of righteousness. (By negative emotions I mean our selfish felt needs, our desire for more or better things, but in a self-centered way. We give into sin so much easier when we *feel* down, stressed, worried, anxious, or in need of attention).

As Christians, we want to do God's will – and we usually have the head knowledge of what that will is. But the heart has a hard time getting on board. As we strive to live righteously we are thrown against trials and temptations which try to tear us apart; we continue to *believe* in doing right, but we *feel* like doing something else.

Our emotional state is key to a righteous life. Satan knows that so he targets us where it hurts. He tells us we are losers who will never make it, who will never amount to anything. When we get discouraged he can then more easily lead us to fret, get worked up or be overcome by depression.

This experience is not unique to Christians today. King David faced uphill emotional battles his whole life, as reflected in his desperate call for God's help and intervention in several Psalms. "Answer me when I call, O God of my righteousness! You have relieved me in my distress; be gracious to me and hear my prayer," he cried out on one occasion (Psalm 4:1 - NASB). "Heed the sound of my cry for help, my King and my God," he penned in one of his heartfelt psalms (Psalm 5:2a - NASB). "Have mercy on me, O Lord, for I am weak," he would confess as he pleaded for God's assistance (Psalm 6:2 - NKJV; see also Psalm 13).

As one who struggled with his emotions, David has a lot to share with us on the subject. There is one passage in particular which has spoken to me over the years. We could say David hit upon the solution to this problem and delivers it to us almost as a formula. In Psalms 37 he lays out five practical steps for conquering your emotions and living a righteous life before the Lord. They are just the opposite from the steps we naturally take when we try to live for God in our own strength. The following is usually how we react when faced with trials and temptations. They usually happen in rapid succession or simultaneously.

How *not* to react when faced with trials and temptations:

Fret. Our first reaction is to worry: "I can't handle this! This is just too much for me! Doesn't God know I can't face this and come out a winner?" We feel overpowered and at a loss.

Doubt. As soon as we fret, our trust runs out the door. We begin to question God and His promises. We figure He cannot accomplish His will and we cannot follow His way in our lives after all.

31

Get Discouraged. Now we feel like losers. We allow Satan to remind us just how much we have already failed in similar circumstances and that this is just going to be another one of those unfortunate situations.

Compromise. Since we feel there is nothing we can do about it, we give up and give in – at least to a certain degree. But we've crossed that line and feel miserable for it.

Struggle. At this point we get into a vicious cycle: we have allowed ourselves to compromise our walk with God but want to go back and make it right. We find ourselves in a descending spiral yet struggle to get back on our feet. It is the struggle of the double-minded: we love and hate our sin at the same time. We want release from it but aren't sure if we are willing to pay the price.

Unrighteousness. The consequence of this experience is living in disobedience and, therefore, in unrighteous behavior.

God's way to righteous living (*He* is our righteousness!)

The Bible shows us the way to live a righteous life before the Lord. It is based on what the Lord does for us and on our confidence in Him to bring it all about in our lives.

As we were studying about righteousness as it relates to God's Kingdom at the church I attended at the time, Mrs. Betty Jean Billingsley, our pastor's wife and truly one of the godliest women I know, shared with us a principle that the Lord had taught her. She said, "I am convinced that Jesus wants us to take our eyes off ourselves and focus on Him. So many are tired of trying to be righteous. We need to remember that *He* is our righteousness. We just need to accept it. He's already done it. He's died for us and so we've died to sin as well."

Which brings us to Psalm 37:1-7. Coincidently, it was Betty Jean's husband, pastor Bill Billingsley, who preached on this passage and alerted me to its deeper meaning and importance. Below are some insights inspired by that sermon. Notice the key words (highlighted) and the explanations below.

Psalm 37, verses one through seven, mentions the following:
1 - **Do not fret** because of evildoers; do not envy wrongdoers.
2 - For they will wither quickly like the grass and fade like the green herb.
3 - **Trust** in the Lord, and do good. Dwell in the land and cultivate faithfulness.
4 - **Delight** yourself in the Lord and He will give you the desires of your heart.

5 - Commit your way to the Lord, trust in Him, and He will make it happen.
6 - He will bring forth your **righteousness** as the light and your judgment as the noonday sun.
7 - Rest in the Lord and wait patiently for Him. Do not fret because of those who prosper while carrying out wicked schemes.

Applying the key concepts:

The following is an ideal case scenario. Unfortunately, our negative emotions will many times try to sabotage the process. Learning to "live by faith, not by sight" (2 Corinthians 5:7) is one of the most difficult lessons Christians must learn. But if we can take this Psalm to heart, we will be well on our way to living righteously and pleasing our Lord.

Don't fret. When trials and temptations hit, we resist the urge to throw up our arms in despair and complain. We realize there is a purpose for being tested (James 1:2-4; Romans 5:3,4), and submit our lives to God. We don't worry – we pray (Philippians 4:6).

Trust. We remember that our righteousness comes from God and that He is the one Who accomplishes His work in us, not our own efforts (Philippians 2:13). Just as we were saved by receiving His grace by faith, we understand we must live that way as well (Colossians 2:6).

Delight. Instead of concentrating on the problem, we concentrate on our Lord. Tony Evans, one of my favorite preachers, once said on his radio program: "Don't tell God how big your problem is; tell your problem how big your God is!" We do not fight darkness with our effort, sweat, intelligence or insight; we simply turn on the Light. We come to Him and find refuge in His loving arms. We delight in our relationship with Him. And we reflect on all He has in store for us in His Eternal Kingdom.

Commit. This is a key concept in this process. The Hebrew word actually means to "roll away, up, down or off on to." When we "roll" our journey over onto the Lord and trust Him with our life and problems, He will take it from there and do the rest: He will act to accomplish what needs to be done. We can take advantage of the difficult situation and reconfirm our allegiance to Him, telling Him that although we are weak and vulnerable to trials and temptations we commit our lives to Him again.

Rest. Once we have placed our trust in God, are delighting in Him and have committed our lives to His care we can stop struggling and enter into His rest,

34

"for anyone who enters God's rest also rests from his own work" (Hebrews 4:10a - NIV). We can *let go and let God*. Peace now reigns freely in our hearts (Colossians 3:15).

Righteousness. The result is that God's will is accomplished in our lives and we are enabled to follow His ways. God's righteousness becomes our righteousness and shines through our lives! We "become blameless and harmless, children of God without fault in the midst of a crooked and perverse generation, among whom you shine as lights in the world" (Philippians 2:15 - NKJV). Set free from the tyrannical dominion of unrighteousness and "having been liberated from sin," we now have become "enslaved to righteousness" (Romans 6:18 - HCSB). Now righteousness sets the rules and we follow it as our guide. A friend once said: "the train's freedom is to run on the tracks." Think about it. It makes sense.

Why does God allow us to go through difficult trials and temptations in the first place? It is part of our training in God's school of discipline. "He does it for our benefit, so that we can share His holiness." And though "no discipline seems enjoyable at the time," after awhile "it yields the fruit of peace and righteousness to those who have been trained by it" (Hebrews 12:10, 11 - HCSB).

In the next chapter we will see how righteousness lays the groundwork for Kingdom Values.

Chapter

2

**Righteousness:
the Foundation for
Kingdom Values**

Righteousness and justice are the foundation of your throne.
Unfailing love and truth walk before you as attendants.
Psalm 89:14 - NLT

Shower, O heavens, from above, and let the clouds rain down righteousness;
let the earth open, that salvation and righteousness may bear fruit; let the
earth cause them both to sprout; I the LORD have created it.
Isaiah 45:8 - ESV

Righteousness is central

Everything that leads to or flows from righteousness is a value in the Kingdom
of God. For this reason, some of the values mentioned in the next chapters may
coincide with certain features of righteousness or its "fruit." The fact that Kingdom Values and principles are grounded in and built upon the foundation of
righteousness cannot be overemphasized. Nor can the truth that righteousness is
the standard of the Kingdom of God.

The author of Hebrews tells his readers that Christians who are immature do not
know much about the concept of righteousness while the mature have learned to

discern right from wrong. He said: "Now everyone who lives on milk is inexperienced with the message about righteousness, because he is an infant. But solid food is for the mature–for those whose senses have been trained to distinguish between good and evil" (Hebrews 5:13-14 - HCSB). One of the best ways to recognize if something is good or evil is to be well acquainted with Righteousness in general and Kingdom Values specifically. That's what this book is all about.

True and lasting value

Rocks. They're everywhere. A dime a dozen. Or even less. You may even pay someone to get rid of those in your front yard. Pebbles, rocks, and stones come in all sizes, weights and shapes – many considered to have no value at all. But among them are those which reflect light in a special way and, when cut and polished by experts, are considered "precious." A rare pink diamond, just shy of 25 karats, was purchased by Laurence Graff for $45.6 million, the highest bid ever on a gem.[1] The money paid for that solitary stone would be enough to purchase 225 homes at $200,000 each – that is, a whole neighborhood. It would take the average middle-class worker, earning $50,000 a year, more than 900 years to earn enough to purchase this rare gem.

While a canvas, two dozen tubes of oil paint, brushes and a nice frame should cost you less than $1,000, Vincent van Gogh's *Portrait of Dr. Gachet* "was sold within three minutes for $82.5 million U.S. at Christie's, New York" and is now valued at $146.5 million. *The Card Players* by Paul Cézanne is the most expensive painting ever sold, coming in at $254 million.[2]

To me, attributing millions of dollars to an object that just sits there and looks pretty is ludicrous. I'd rather just take a picture of it and refer back to the image whenever I want to. Of course, the rich collect art and jewelry as an investment because they have evidence these will hold and even increase in value over time. But who sets the price of things? Who determines their worth? Who establishes what is really valuable?

Oh, but how our priorities change in the face of a crisis! If the owner of a multi-million dollar precious stone were marooned on a deserted island and offered a week's supply of food in exchange for her treasure, what do you think she would do?

Diamonds are **not** forever, circumstances change, fads and fashion come and go. And, for this reason, there is no comparison between temporal and eternal values and treasures. Jesus warned us not to "store up treasures here on earth" but to "store your treasures in heaven" (Matthew 6:19, 20 - NLT). Possessions here can be stolen or destroyed. Everything we have is on loan until we die – and we can't take it with us. "For what is seen is temporary, but what is unseen is eternal" (2 Corinthians 4:7, 16-18 - HCSB). It follows, as Jesus pointed out, that "wherever your treasure is, there the desires of your heart will also be" (Matthew 6:21 - NLT).

The question we are faced with is how can we invest our lives in that which has eternal value? How do we accumulate treasures in heaven? By directing our interest, energy and dedication towards Kingdom Values and adjusting our behavior accordingly. Our focus turns from ourselves to God. When we serve in the Kingdom, our good deeds follow us to eternity (Revelation 14:13) and we are rewarded (2 Corinthians 5:10), because our "labor in the Lord is not in vain" (1 Corinthians 15:58 - NIV).

So, what do we truly value? Where will we decide to invest our time, talents and treasure? In personal interests or in Kingdom priorities? Jesus asked: "What profit will a person have if he gains the whole world, but destroys himself or is lost?" (Luke 9:25 - ISV).

Jesus taught "the kingdom of heaven is like treasure, buried in a field, that a man found and reburied. Then in his joy he goes and sells everything he has and buys that field." Jesus went on to compare the Kingdom to "a merchant in search of fine pearls. When he found one priceless pearl, he went and sold everything he had, and bought it (Matthew 13:44-46 - HCSB).

Just as there are those who are fascinated with the beauty and value of art and gems – and are willing to pay just about any price for them – Jesus taught we should value the Kingdom above everything, sacrificing all else in order to possess it. Call it having a Kingdom obsession.

And yet the Kingdom is hidden from the view of most people. It simply is not on their radar. There are just too many distractions in life (Mark 4:19; 1 Timothy 6:9). But those who realize what Jesus is offering find that its value exceeds everything else in life. For them, the Kingdom is priceless.

The Kingdom is so valuable because it reflects God's character and is the vehicle for accomplishing His will. As any kingdom, the Kingdom of God has laws and regulations. As seen in the preceding chapter, they can all be summed up in the word "righteousness." But righteousness is a very broad term which can be divided into personal godliness and social justice. We can further break these down into values and principles. These are as immutable and eternal as the Kingdom itself. They hold true and lasting value.

The Values of the Kingdom

On March 27, 2004, Cathleen Falsani, at the time a religion reporter for the Chicago-Sun Times, interviewed the then-State Senator Barack Obama about his faith. Among the many questions put forth, Falsani asked: "do you believe in sin?" Obama answered "yes." "What is sin?," Falsani persisted. "Being out of alignment with my values," came the answer. Falsani then asked, "what happens if you have sin in your life?" Obama, referring to a previous question about his belief in the afterlife, responded: "I think it's the same thing as the question about heaven. In the same way that if I'm true to myself and my faith that that is its own reward, when I'm not true to it, it's its own punishment."[3]

On the surface, the discrepancy between Obama's answer and the traditional Christian view may seem subtle. But there is a profound difference between recognizing that sin is breaking *God's* laws and defining sin as being out of alignment with one's own values; between believing that we are accountable to God and will be punished for breaking His commandments (if there is no repentance), and stating that if we are inconsistent with what we value, that this is its own punishment. One focuses on God – His values and laws – and the other on personal values and beliefs.

Just as citizens of the United States do not make up their own speed limits or laws in general, citizens of the Kingdom of God must abide by the laws and values of the Kingdom, not their own. Of course, God's values should *become* their own, but they are always cognizant of their divine origin. Mike Huckabee believes "there has to be an immovable standard. A solid foundation. A moral thermostat whose setting is not subject to the whim of personal opinion."[4]

In the Kingdom, God holds the highest position in the judicial, legislative and executive branches of His government, "for the LORD is our judge, the LORD is our lawgiver, the LORD is our king; it is he who will save us" (Isaiah 33:22). Being true to "my values" and "my faith" is highly subjective as it will vary from individual to individual. This can easily lead to chaos. Being true to Kingdom Values is an objective endeavor which brings clarity and leads to order. Abraham Lincoln once said, "Sir, my concern is not whether God is on our side; my greatest concern is to be on God's side, for God is always right."[5]

40

There are Kingdom Values and there are worldly values, and they stand opposed to each other in essence and outcome. The first are synonymous with Christian virtues (as in 2 Peter 1:5), the second with carnal vices. In Scripture the first is often referred to as "wisdom" and the latter as "foolishness." Read James 3:13-18 and you will notice that "bitter envy and selfish ambition" are values or "wisdom" which "does not come from above but is earthly, unspiritual, demonic." We may gather from this that the values of the fallen world system are demon-inspired. The fruit or consequence of such earthly values "is disorder and every kind of evil." Life just doesn't work out like it's supposed to when everything we do is self-centered and self-serving. The common, greater good is impossible to achieve if everyone is pulling in a different direction – their own. When "me, myself and I" are sitting on the throne, everybody loses (including "me, myself and I").

In order for Kingdom Values to be accepted and incorporated into our lives, we must be humble enough to recognize God's sovereignty and wisdom. Arrogance and the desire to indulge in sinful behavior are two of the main reasons people do not wish to submit to God's authority and guidance. They either believe they know what's best for "number one," or feel God's commands are too restrictive and old-fashioned. This leads to an awful lot of rationalizing and excuses.

Whether or not a society holds fast to the values of the Kingdom is one of the surest ways to evaluate its spiritual condition. These values act as a barometer, showing if society is moving closer or further away from God. It is no secret that when what God values is not important to a society, and moral or family values go down, crime and violence go up in the same proportion.

What a difference it makes when Kingdom Values prevail. Kingdom Values are peace-loving, gentle, encouraging, full of mercy and good fruits, without favoritism and hypocrisy. Does this describe your workplace? Your church? Your home? It should.

How different our world would be if only we took the Kingdom's values seriously. Divorces would be virtually unheard of. Church splits and pastoral burn-out would be at an all-time low. Wars? Not happening anymore. Peace would prevail. Truth would win out. Love would triumph. People would honor God and respect each other. But, alas, we live in a fallen world with fallen beings. Got people? Got problems! But we are not called to change the whole world. Our responsibility is to allow God to change our own lives. If we let Him, He will change our attitude, outlook, actions and relationships. As we learn and apply His Kingdom Values in our lives, teaching them to our families and communities of faith, things will begin to change.

In 1930 Harry E. Fosdick penned these words as part of what became a hymn, still sung in our churches today, under the title "God of Grace and God of Glory." This is the third stanza of that hymn:

> Cure Thy children's warring madness,
> Bend our pride to Thy control.
> Shame our wanton selfish gladness,
> Rich in things and poor in soul.
> Grant us wisdom, grant us courage,
> Lest we miss Thy kingdom's goal,
> Lest we miss Thy kingdom's goal.[6]

A list of Kingdom Values

At the end of each Kingdom Value, there is a scale for your consideration, to help you evaluate how you are doing in that particular area. As you notice strong areas you may wish to express your thanksgiving to the Lord. As you encounter areas of weakness or inconsistency, you may wish to pray, focus your attention on these and set personal goals in that area. The chart below explains how the scales work. Check the box in each scale which best describes how you are doing when it comes to that particular Kingdom Value.

There are 70 Kingdom Values that are considered in the following chapters – a large number yet far from complete. But I believe the list is representative and includes some of the most fundamental values of the Kingdom. All values and principles mentioned are based on Scripture verses. Some of these values have their own principles or an attached promise or condition. These principles will be included either throughout or at the end of some of the value sections.

The values list is organized by category. Although some of the values could go under multiple categories, I had to arbitrarily decide which seemed to be the best fit in order to avoid repetition. No matter which category these values have been placed under, it is important to stress that every single value applies to every Kingdom citizen.

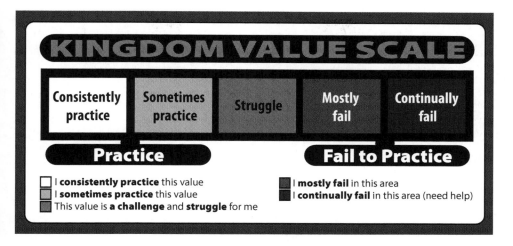

The Ground Zero Kingdom Value

Kingdom Value #0: Knowledge

This Kingdom Value is so obvious I almost missed it. In fact, it was only after compiling the whole list and adding some thoughts to them that "knowledge" kept jumping off the pages in different passages I was reading during my devotionals. So I came back and added this basic Kingdom Value as "number zero" because it precedes all others in the sense that we would not even *know* about the others – much less understand how to apply them to our lives – if we did not first have the knowledge of God and of His word.

Ignorance of God's revelation has been a primary source of misery, hopelessness, purposelessness, and sinfulness. The Lord has strong words for those who do not know Him by choice. He warns: "My people are destroyed for lack of knowledge. Because you have rejected knowledge, I also will reject you from being My priest. Since you have forgotten the law of your God, I also will forget your children" (Hosea 4:6 - NASB).

God does not want anyone to lack the necessary information about Him. He stated this purpose clearly when He said, "For I desire loyalty and not sacrifice, the knowledge of God rather than burnt offerings" (Hosea 6: 6 - HCSB). Unfortunately, some know about God and still reject Him. The New Testament speaks of those who, "though they knew God, they did not glorify Him as God or show gratitude" (Romans 1:21 - HCSB). Instead, they "by their unrighteousness suppress the truth, since what can be known about God is evident among them, because God has shown it to them" (Romans 1:18, 19 - HCSB). Mark Twain once said, "It ain't those parts of the Bible that I can't understand that bother me; it is the parts that I do understand."[7]

For those who know the Lord and follow Him there is the great need for humility and caution because mere "knowledge inflates with pride" (1 Corinthians 8:1 - HCSB). Life is complicated, human behavior is bewildering, and the Lord's ways are mysterious. So "those who think they know something do not yet know as they ought to know" (1 Corinthians 8:2 - NIV). Besides, Christians should be seeking knowledge which not only *in*forms but ***trans*form**s. Paul confronted the believers in Rome with this very problem. He told them, "You think you can instruct the ignorant and teach children the ways of God. For you are certain that God's law gives you complete knowledge and truth. Well then, if you teach others, why don't you teach yourself?" (Romans 2:20-21a - NLT). The problem is possessing purely theoretical knowledge instead of applying that knowledge to good use.

Knowledge of God must include a better understandion of His will and the wisdom to put it into practice via a life of obedience. Paul told the Colossians he was "asking that you may be filled with the knowledge of His will in all wisdom and spiritual understanding" (Colossians 1:9-11). He said he was praying for this so that their conduct would be worthy and pleasing to the Lord, so they would bear fruit and be empowered.

Peter writes to those who have come to faith "through the righteousness of our God and Savior Jesus Christ" and wishes: "May God give you more and more grace and peace as you grow in your knowledge of God and Jesus our Lord." He goes on to explain that God supplied all they needed to live a godly life "through the knowledge of Him who called us," and discusses the values (literally *virtues*) that should be added to faith, including knowledge, to which self-control should be added as well (2 Peter 1:1, 3, 6 - HCSB; 1:2 - NLT). Clearly, knowledge was an important issue for Peter.

But for Peter, knowledge was not to remain simply theoretical. It should involve the intellect, emotions, and actions: head, heart, and hands. Knowledge should lead to self-control and ultimately to love (2 Peter 1:7). I love the theory but struggle with the practice. I want all the Biblical knowledge I can get. But I have a lot to learn about putting all of this knowledge into practice on a consistent basis.

It is a good thing Peter later, in the same letter, tells his readers to "grow in the grace and knowledge of our Lord and Savior Jesus Christ" (2 Peter 3:18a - NASB).

If we have any hope of adding self-control to our knowledge we will have to grow just as much in grace. To grow in grace is to become more and more dependent on God's power and less and less on our own. That's why Peter began by praying God would give his fellow believers more grace as they grew in knowledge. This may sound like circular reasoning, but only because both or so closely intertwined.

It is true that "God's riches, wisdom, and knowledge are so deep that it is impossible to explain his decisions or to understand his ways" (Romans 11:33 - GW). We can never fully understand God because "the LORD our God has secrets known to no one. We are not accountable for them, but we and our children are accountable forever for all that he has revealed to us, so that we may obey all the terms of these instructions" (Deuteronomy 29:29 - NLT).

We may not be held accountable for the unsearchable mysteries of the Lord but those He has revealed in His word we have a responsibility to know and obey. I remember riding a subway with my brother Bill who lives in Paris. Bill told me we had to hang on to our tickets for the duration because the controller could come by at any moment. And if we did not present the tickets to him he could fine and kick us off the train. I asked him about the tourists who don't know any better or can't read the instructions in French. He told me, "they're expected to know." God's Word is more available than ever. And He expects us to know what He has revealed to us.

Proper knowledge of God's Word is vital because it prevents: deception by "persuasive arguments" (Colossians 2:4); the destruction of God's people (Hosea 4:6); and nonsensical and darkened thinking (Romans 1:21-22). On the other hand, "The discerning person acquires knowledge, and the wise person seeks knowledge" (Proverbs 18:15 - NET Bible). This was Paul's desire and prayer for believers in the churches he planted: "How I long for you to grow more certain in your knowledge and more sure in your grasp of God himself. May your spiritual experience become richer as you see more and more fully God's great secret, Christ himself! For it is in him, and in him alone, that men will find all the treasures of wisdom and knowledge" (Colossians 2:2-3 - PHILLIPS).

We usually think of the Old Testament prophet as being the mouthpiece of God, the one chosen to teach the way of the Lord to the people of Israel. And this is true. But we are told priests had this responsibility as well. "For the lips of a priest should preserve knowledge, and people should seek instruction from his mouth, because he's the messenger of the LORD of the Heavenly Armies" (Malachi 2:7 - ISV). Jesus warned the religious leaders of His day because not only were they

45

not properly instructing the people, they were hindering them! "What sorrow awaits you experts in religious law! For you remove the key to knowledge from the people. You don't enter the Kingdom yourselves, and you prevent others from entering" (Luke 11:52 - NLT).

God has a special treat for those who seriously seek Him and study His Word. There is much wisdom and knowledge on the surface but much more beneath. A casual reading of the Bible brings blessing, but digging deeper shows just how God is in the details and everything is connected. I believe God has hidden this deeper understanding of His truths because He wants us to eagerly pursue Him. He rewards those who sincerely seek His presence with the wonderful secrets of His Kingdom.

Christ Himself is the key to the treasures of wisdom and knowledge.

How much knowledge to you have of God? Do you know Him personally? Are you getting to know Him better each day? What difference has this knowledge made in your decision-making, your priority-setting and the way you conduct yourself at home, at church and in society?

Chapter

3

The Beatitude Kingdom Values

*Blessed are the **poor in spirit**, for theirs is the kingdom of heaven.*
*Blessed are **those who mourn**, for they shall be comforted.*
*Blessed are **the gentle**, for they shall inherit the earth.*
*Blessed are those who **hunger and thirst for righteousness**,*
for they shall be satisfied.
*Blessed are **the merciful**, for they shall receive mercy.*
*Blessed are **the pure in heart**, for they shall see God.*
*Blessed are **the peacemakers**, for they shall be called sons of God.*
*Blessed are **those who have been persecuted** for the sake*
of righteousness, for theirs is the kingdom of heaven.
Matthew 5:3-10 - NASB

Kingdom Value #1: Humility

Humility relates to the first beatitude, "blessed are the poor in spirit" (Matthew 5:3). Why is this Kingdom value so crucial? Because we can easily miss the right path to God on account of our own pride. Pride, the attitude which led to the first sin and the fall of the first couple, blinds us to our true condition. It insists we do not need God. It sets itself up as a substitute for God and sees itself as its own final authority. Pride is at the center of all rebellion against God because sin is rejecting God's right to reign over our lives. It's the "I'll do it my way" philosophy of life.

C. S. Lewis was concerned with the problem of pride. He understood pride to be the worst form of sin, a vice in its own category, far more dangerous than carnal sins, including greed. There would be no devil were it not for pride. Pride, in fact, is what leads to all other vices.[1]

We know that God's forgiveness and salvation are dependent upon a person's faith and repentance. Yet, many argue this is too simplistic, just "too easy." Not really. Because both go to the heart of humanity's sin problem by requiring humility and the abandonment of pride. Faith involves confessing God as the center of life (as opposed to self) and acknowledging the need for a Savior. Repentance presupposes admission of failure and confession of sin, as well as the willingness to change course. In a very real way, then, faith and repentance require a person to give up their pride, one of the main obstacles to inheriting eternal life.

Again, commenting on the danger and ugliness of pride, C. S. Lewis wrote that pride is the main source of misery, all the way from family units to entire nations.[2] He lamented that this most terrible of vices found its way into the heart of religious life. Lewis believed that, while other vices are promoted by Satan via our "animal nature," pride is more direct, as it inspired in – and comes directly from – Hell, making it more subtle and lethal.[3] This is a surprising concept, since we tend to equate the grossest sins with carnal sin.

Those who are able to overcome the pride barrier and recognize they are indeed "poor in spirit" are most fortunate because they can see themselves as God sees them. They are blessed because humility opens the way to true repentance, without which there can be no forgiveness of sins or salvation. Humility is the antidote to pride just as repentance is to sin (Revelation 2:5, 16, 22; 3:3, 19; see the next Kingdom Value).

The Apostle Paul had every right, humanly speaking, to be spiritually proud. But after listing his credentials, he says he "wrote them off as a loss for the sake of Christ" in Whom he found "the righteousness of God that is based on faith" (Philippians 3:7, 9 - CEB).

King David united and ruled over all the tribes of Israel. He was a visionary, a military strategist, a builder, and a composer. He made things happen. Most of the time he was very popular. Most importantly, he was usually on good terms with the Lord. He became wealthier as his kingdom took hold. And yet, at least four times he described himself to the Lord as being "poor and needy" (Psalms 40:17; 70:5; 86:1; 109:22). David understood what many successful people today do not: it all comes from and belongs to the Lord.

The prophet Micah summed up Kingdom Values beautifully when he declared: "He has shown you, O man, what *is* good; and what does the Lord require of you but to do justly, to love mercy, and to walk humbly with your God?" (Micah 6:8 - NKJV). There is no other way to draw close to and connect with God than with a humble attitude. God "gives grace to the humble"(Proverbs 3:34; James 4:6 - HCSB). It is a Kingdom Principle that "a man's pride will bring him low, but a humble spirit will obtain honor" (Proverbs 29:23 - NASB).

Humility Kingdom Principles:
1. Pride goes before a fall, humility before honor (Proverbs 16:18; 18:12).
2. "But those who exalt themselves will be humbled, and those who humble themselves will be exalted" (Matthew 23:12 - NLT).
3. "Blessed are the poor in spirit, for theirs is the kingdom of heaven" (Matthew 5:3 - NASB).
3. Humble yourself before God and He will lift you up when the time is right (1 Peter 5:6).
4. "God opposes the proud but favors the humble" (James 4:6b - NLT).
5. If you are humble, God can teach you. "He leads humble people to do what is right, and he teaches them his way" (Psalm 25:9 - GW).

Where are you on "the humility scale"? (Careful with false humility...)

Kingdom Value #2: Repentance

Scripture passages like 2 Chronicles 7:14 and James 4:6-10 show the vital role being humble plays in getting to a place of genuine repentance. There is simply no way one can truly repent if first a sorrowful humbling does not occur. This is why it is assumed that when Jesus taught in the second beatitude that "blessed are those who mourn" (Matthew 5:4), He was referring to those who weep over their behavior and come to repentance.

Repentance is the only proper response to God's grace and free offer of salvation (see *Grace – Kingdom value #41*). It is only through repentance that we can see the light of God's truth (see *Truth – Kingdom value #60*). There can be no fellowship with God if there has been no initial repentance, followed by subsequent repentance when sin is found in our daily lives (see *Fellowship – Kingdom value #19*). Repentance is so foundational for salvation that Peter equates the two when he says that God "is patient with you, not wanting any to perish but all to come to repentance" (2 Peter 3:9b - HCSB).

Although repentance and regret may easily be confused, and although true repentance may include some elements of regret, the two are quite different. And that difference determines contrasting outcomes: forgiveness or condemnation, fellowship or alienation, friendship or antagonism, life or death.

The Easton's Illustrated Bible Dictionary can help us understand the difference between repentance and regret, as it explains "there are three Greek words used in the New Testament to denote repentance." The first is *metamelomai* which "is used of a change of mind, such as to produce regret or even remorse on account of sin, but not necessarily a change of heart. This word is used with reference to the repentance of Judas (Mat 27:3)."[4]

The second and the third words are similar and signify true Biblical repentance. They are "*metanoeo*, meaning to change one's mind and purpose, as the result of after knowledge" and *metanoia*, which "is used of true repentance, a change of mind and purpose and life, to which remission of sin is promised."[5]

This change of mind brought on by repentance leads to agreeing with God that we have sinned, we were wrong, and we are guilty. It is seeing life from God's perspective and aligning our personal values with His Kingdom Values. Because, when God says a sin is a sin, it *is* – no matter how loud the world shouts that it isn't and despite how convincing its arguments may seem.

Repentance is a change of heart and of purpose because God is now the center of our universe. We live for Him and for His purposes. He is the love of our life. It is His will we seek to do, His way we endeavor to follow.

At its root regret is self-seeking. Regret, not repentance, is what Judas experienced. Whether he was trying to force Jesus to save Himself by using His supernatural power, as some have suggested, or just wanted the reward money, or wanted to see Jesus eliminated, the fact remains that Judas had not submitted his will to that of the Lord's. He was out of line with Jesus' leadership. When he took the 30 pieces of silver from the religious leaders and saw what happened to Jesus, he still did not humble or submit himself. He was filled with remorse and regret and felt tremendous guilt. Still, this did not lead him to confess, ask for forgiveness and change his heart and mind. Regret and remorse are always too little and usually too late.

Humility is the first Kingdom value in this list. Humility is the fertile ground the seed of repentance requires to germinate. If arrogance includes the notion that we are self-sufficient and do not want or need God in our lives, humility is the acknowledgment that we are nothing and can do nothing good aside from Him. If pride comes before a fall, humility is the first step in the right direction if we recognize why we fell in the first place.

Repentance is absolutely vital for entering the Kingdom and for "getting right" with the Lord when there are failures in the Christian's walk. Repentance leads to justification and restoration. (For a more in-depth look at repentance, please refer to chapter 3, *Access to the Kingdom of God*, of **The Secret of the Kingdom**, the first volume in this series).

- Repentance Kingdom Principles:
1. When you mourn in repentance, God Himself will comfort you. "Blessed and enviably happy ... are those who mourn, for they shall be comforted!" (Matthew 5:4 - AMP).
2. When the Kingdom of God is near, you must repent and believe the Good News (Mark 1:15); because unless seekers repent, they will perish (Luke 13:5).
3. If Christians and churches stubbornly refuse to repent, God will take His hand of blessing from them (Revelation 2:5).
4. "If we confess our sins, he is faithful and just to forgive us our sins and to cleanse us from all unrighteousness" (1 John 1:9 - ESV).
5. When we repent, our sins are wiped away and the Lord provides times of refreshing (Acts 3:19).

As you consider where you are on the "repentance scale," remember there are two different situations where repentance is needed: 1) The repentance that leads to salvation; and 2) The repentance, after salvation, that leads to forgiveness and restoration.

51

Kingdom Value #3: Meekness

Meekness relates to the third beatitude, "blessed are the meek" (Matthew 5:5). Meekness has been described as power under control. More contemporary versions use the term "gentleness." "Biblical meekness is not weakness but rather refers to exercising God's strength under His control – i.e. demonstrating power without undue harshness."[6] If self-control is the ability to keep one's weakness under control then meekness is the ability to keep one's strength under control.

"Power tends to corrupt, and absolute power corrupts absolutely,"[7] Lord Acton would write in 1887. Unfortunately, history has proven him correct over and over again. On the other hand, only God actually possesses absolute power, and He knows how to use it in an absolutely righteous manner. And that is how He desires we use the authority He delegates to us as well. For this reason, only the meek are promised possession of the earth (Matthew 5:5b; see chapter 12 on the Millennial Kingdom). God is not interested in tyrants or those who abuse the power they have received (Romans 13:1). God can't stand bullies on any level.

Notice in the Bible the kind of people God chose to use in special ways. With very few exceptions (Samson comes to mind), they were not conceited and were not the kind to abuse their power. Take Moses, a great leader who had been given impressive power to perform miracles and with whom God would speak in an audible voice (Numbers 7:89). In fact, "the LORD would speak to Moses face to face, as a man speaks with his friend" (Exodus 33:11a). How easy it would have been for him to become puffed up with spiritual pride and abuse his position and power. And yet we are assured, "the man Moses was very meek, more than all people who were on the face of the earth" (Numbers 12:3 - ESV). Moses was remembered as "the servant of the LORD" (Joshua 1:1), and the evidence shows this is how he viewed himself as well. His greatest honor was not being a tremendous leader who made history by delivering a whole nation to their promised land. His highest honor was being recognized as the Lord's servant.

And yet it is our Model in all things, Jesus, Who is the meekest Person Who ever lived. He was keenly aware that "all authority in heaven and on earth" had been given to Him (Matthew 28:18). This unequaled authority and power never drove Him to pride or to being a show-off. On the contrary, "Jesus, knowing (fully aware) that the Father had put everything into His hands, and that He had come from God and was [now] returning to God, got up from supper, took off His garments, and taking a [servant's] towel, He fastened it around His waist" (John 13:3, 4 - AMP). He then proceeded to wash His disciples' feet, the lowliest of services performed by house servants. Jesus used His authority and power to benefit others by serving them. And He wanted His disciples to do the same.

Jesus described Himself as meek and humble of heart and told His followers to learn from His example (Matthew 11:29). Whether dealing with the poor and outcast, the religious leaders of the day or those in the highest authority over Israel, Jesus was always meek and humble.

Think of it! Here was the King of kings in the form of a lowly itinerate preacher, with no show of power – except when benefiting others through the miracles He performed. He never used His powers to serve Himself, refusing even to command stones to become bread (Matthew 4:3). And He never used His power to hurt or destroy.[8]

When it came time for His triumphal entry into Jerusalem, He did not come on a white horse, used to symbolize a conquering king. Rather, He came on a lowly donkey, signifying one who comes in peace, just as prophesied (Zechariah 9:9; Matthew 21:5).

You will not find "tips for becoming a meek leader" in secular media. Meekness is not something to which those in power aspire. Meekness is a Kingdom Value, and you can see some of its related principles below.

Meekness Kingdom Principles:
- The power and authority God has given us is to be used to benefit others (see *Kingdom Value #66*, in chapter 10). When we do so we are being meek. When we are meek we are "blessed (happy, blithesome, joyous, spiritually prosperous–with life-joy and satisfaction in God's favor and salvation, regardless of their outward conditions)" (Matthew 5:5a – AMP).

- One of the biggest blessings is future: "but the meek will inherit the land and enjoy great peace" (Matthew 5:5b; Psalm 37:11).

- The meek (not the fittest) will survive and remain. While the rebellious, disobedient, unfaithful, treacherous and arrogant people will be removed from God's holy mountain (Jerusalem). "The righteous LORD," Who "does no wrong" but "applies His justice morning by morning" promises: "I will leave a meek and humble people among you" (Zephaniah 3:1-5; 11, 12 - HCSB).

- The meek are teachable and are therefore the best equipped to live out the Mirroring Principle, which involves reflecting Jesus (see **The King of the Kingdom**, the fourth and final book of this series). "The meek will he guide in justice: and the meek will he teach his way" (Psalm 25:9 - KJV 2000).

- If anyone is going to be spared the Lord's anger, it will be the meek – those who are humble, who seek the Lord and His righteousness (Zephaniah 2:3).

How meek are you in your daily relationships and dealings with others? Is there room for improvement?

Kingdom Value #4: A burning desire for righteousness

This value relates to the fourth beatitude, "blessed are those who hunger and thirst for righteousness" (Matthew 5:6). Notice that Jesus did not say "blessed are the righteous," which would be more consistent with the way He presented all the other beatitudes. Possibly because He wanted to emphasize that short of being *made* righteous (justified) by God, there are none who would qualify.

Jesus was emphasizing righteousness as the driving motivation for His followers. In this same sermon, Jesus told us to "seek first His kingdom and His righteousness" (Matthew 6:33). Hungering, thirsting and seeking all imply an intensity, craving and focus bordering on obsession. The kind a famished person would have, as in the story about the man lost at sea for days on end. One of the psalmists expressed his desire for God poetically: "As the deer longs for streams of water, so I long for you, O God. I thirst for God, the living God. When can I go and stand before him?" (Psalm 42: 1-2 - NLT). David described this driving force this way: "O God, You are my God; I shall seek You earnestly; My soul thirsts for You, my flesh yearns for You, In a dry and weary land where there is no water" (Psalm 63:1 - NASB).

We have seen how all Kingdom Values flow from God's righteousness. Here, the emphasis is on the hunger and thirst for that righteousness. This burning desire to be right with God and walk in fellowship with Him leads to a deep interest in seeing His plans being accomplished, His Kingdom advancing against the forces of darkness, and waiting expectantly for the day when His will is done on earth just as it is in heaven (Matthew 6:10).

Jesus, as our supreme model in all things, was all about seeing righteousness being fulfilled. When John was hesitant about baptizing Him, "Jesus answered him,

54

'Allow it for now, because this is the way for us to fulfill all righteousness.' Then he allowed Him to be baptized" (Matthew 3:15 - HCSB). Fulfilling righteousness means accomplishing God's purpose by doing things according to His plan. At age 12, Jesus asked His mother when she was looking for Him and found Him in the Temple, "knew you not that I must be about my Father's business?" (Luke 2:49b - KJV 2000).

Jesus claimed that "My Father is still working, and I am working also" (John 5:17 - HCSB). He pointed to His work as proof of His identity as Messiah. "The proof," He said, "is the work I do in my Father's name" (John 10:25b - NLT). He also referred unbelievers to His works as proof of His Sonship. When Jewish leaders wanted to stone Him for claiming to be God's Son, "Jesus said, 'At God's direction I have done many a miracle to help the people. For which one are you killing me?'" (John 10:32 - TLB). He told them, "Don't believe me unless I carry out my Father's work" (John 10:37 - NLT). As He prayed to the Father when His time on earth was quickly coming to a close, He said, "I brought glory to you here on earth by doing everything you told me to" (John 17:4 - TLB).

The question we must all answer, is: "What am I here for?" Am I here to satisfy my own desires? Build my own little kingdom? Please others and seek their applause? Am I propelled by selfish desires for selfish gain? Or am I driven by a passion for doing God's will, fulfilling what I was destined for, accomplish the mission I was given, go about God's business, promote His agenda, proclaim His glory, announce the Good News of the Kingdom, serve others and do good to all I can? If we live out the latter, then we are hungering and thirsting for God's righteousness and seeking His Kingdom.

Now, all of this can become tricky when we put these concepts into practice because our fallen human nature is highly deceitful. We can convince ourselves we are seeking God's will and Kingdom while playing office politics, maintaining hidden agendas, practicing backstabbing, and throwing our colleagues under the bus. That is why it is vital to consider the means as being just as important as the end: because the means will *determine* the end.

For instance, I may feel tempted (literally) to badmouth my pastor with the excuse of attempting to make the church more efficient, instead of going directly to him to voice my concern. Or, I may feel that it's okay to withhold information from a colleague, go behind his back, keep him out of the loop, criticize him in his absence, and then pretend all is a-okay when meeting with him again. I may try to convince myself I must do this for the greater good, to be able to achieve an important Kingdom goal I have set. But we must understand there is no right reason to use deceit, slander, or any other form of unrighteousness. Unrighteous means do not lead to righteous ends.

Instead, "flee from these things, you man of God, and pursue righteousness, godliness, faith, love, perseverance and gentleness" (1 Timothy 6:11 - NASB). There it is again: pursue righteousness. Summing it up: seek God, His righteousness, and His Kingdom. Seek to do His will, His way. But do this with all your heart, with a burning desire, with a deep and pure motivation. Do it for God's sake and for God's glory.

A burning desire for righteousness Kingdom Principles:
- The *being fulfilled by righteousness* Kingdom Principle. When we seek righteousness with all our heart we are blessed by being "completely satisfied!" (Matthew 5:6b - AMP). How many of us have sought fulfillment in our work, hobbies, sports, ministry, relationships or in other people? We soon discover our parents, children, spouse and friends cannot fill our inner emptiness or satisfy our deepest existential longings. We usually learn the hard way that only God can do that. Ultimately, we were made for Him!

- The *well-balanced life* Kingdom Principle. When we focus on being right with God, balance is brought into our lives. Once "we have been justified through faith, we have peace with God through our Lord Jesus Christ" (Romans 5:1). This peace with and from God "will guard your hearts and your minds in Christ Jesus" (Philippians 4:7; see *Peace – Kingdom Value #11*, below). Peace (*shalom*) conveys the idea of well-being, harmony, and balance.

How strong is your desire for righteousness? Does it lead to righteous activity?

Kingdom Value #5: Mercy

The fifth beatitude says "blessed are the merciful for they will be shown mercy" (Matthew 5:7). My wife and I were living in Santiago, Chile, when our daughter Melissa came to spend her college summer break with us. Time had flown by very quickly and it was time to take her to the airport to catch her plane back to the states. I could see her at the immigration booth and was wondering why things were taking so long when the officer made his way back to me with Melissa. "This can't be good," I thought. I was upset, imagining what in the world could be wrong. The officer was young and very courteous. He told me that unfortunately Melissa had overextended her tourist visa by a week and that he would have to take the case to his supervisor.

The supervisor came over, looked at Melissa's passport, and told us we would have to go downtown the following day, pay a fine, get the proper permit, and that if all went well, she could leave the following night. I explained that this was an honest error, that I had no idea this had happened, and if she could reconsider her decision. She was adamant: "There is no way she will be leaving this airport tonight on an airplane." I knew this would be a great setback because Melissa didn't have an extra day to get back to college and this would mean getting there late. So I very humbly said, *"con mucha humildad pido que, por favor, tenga misericordia y permita que ella se vaya"* (I would humbly like to ask that you have mercy and please allow her to go). The supervisor asked if she was coming back anytime soon because this would go on her record. I said no. She handed the passport to the officer and walked away without saying another word. "What just happened?," I asked the officer. "She's going to let your daughter catch her plane," he said.

Mercy is a very powerful thing. It can forgive sin, wipe away guilt, forgive a debt, eliminate the need for punishment, release from shame, and provide a second chance. It promotes healthy relations, draws people near, extends grace, walks the second mile, allows for failure while sending the message: "your faults do not define you; you can get up, try again and do better next time."

To ask for mercy you must recognize the authority invested in the person who is to dispense this favor. This requires humility. It means you must understand that you are, quite literally, at that person's mercy. In relation to peers or spouses, the issue may not be one of authority, but the right the one offended has to demand some form of explanation, recompense or, at least, the stated request for forgiveness. When we fail others we are in their debt. And it is up to them to release us from that debt ... or not. Of course, the One Who forgave our debt requires we forgive the debt of others (see Matthew 6:15; 18:35; and *Forgiving – Kingdom Value #23*).

The Global Kingdom could not function without the Kingdom Value of mercy. First, in relation to God, there would be no hope for the sinner (that would be all of us), were it not for His willingness to forgive and extend mercy. Second, human relations would be an endless ocean of grief, conflict, legalism, and accusation which would make fellowship and intimacy an impossible proposition. Bullies are not limited to grade school. There are bosses, family members, and even pastors who constantly deny mercy to others.

You have probably heard of people, as have I, who suffer a constant barrage of verbal and emotional abuse from their spouse. At the sign of the tiniest "failure," they are reprimanded, berated, and humiliated. There is no margin for error. There is no room for imperfection. And yet we are instructed to live with an entirely different set of values and attitudes. "Most important of all, continue to show deep love for each other, for love covers a multitude of sins" (1 Peter 4:8 - NLT; see also Colossians 3:13).

Asking for mercy seems to be one of my favorite prayers. "Have mercy, Lord," I often say under my breath, when facing personal trials and temptations, or when interceding for family members and friends. Just how much I ask the Lord for mercy became obvious to me while writing this section. I noticed it almost seems to be a habit of mine. But it is a genuine cry from the heart, because living on a fallen planet, with a fallen human nature, with fallen people, and a formidable enemy has made it abundantly clear I cannot make it through the day without God's intervention, protection, guidance, power, and care. That's where His grace and mercy come in. If He does not "overlook" my imperfections then there is no reason to take another step. "It is of the LORD'S mercies that we are not consumed, because his compassions fail not" (Lamentations 3:22 - KJV). And, once forgiven, He does not keep score: sins forgiven are sins forgotten. That's why we can join Jeremiah and declare, "Great is his faithfulness; his mercies begin afresh each morning" (Lamentations 3:23 - NLT).

Someone has defined grace and mercy in a very clever way: grace is getting what I do **not** deserve, while mercy is **not** getting what I deserve.

As people blessed with mercy, we must now extend mercy to those around us.

Mercy Kingdom Principles:
- The *what goes around comes around* Kingdom Principle: we receive mercy from God; we show mercy to others; because we show mercy to others, God shows mercy to us. Mercy is cause and effect.
- On the other hand, there is **the there will be no mercy for those who have not shown mercy to others Kingdom Principle**. This verse comes with the reminder: "But if you have been merciful, God will be merciful when he judges you" (James 2:13 - NLT).
- This principle is dramatically exemplified in the story of the compassionate king and the wicked servant. When the king saw that his servant could not repay his

58

debt, he "was moved with compassion, and released him, and forgave him the debt" (Matthew 18:27 - KJV 2000). But when that same servant went out and ran into a fellow servant who owed him some change (compared to his own recently forgiven debt), he showed him no mercy. This caused the king to call him back in, revoke his pardon and act with swift judgment.

- This brings us to a sobering Kingdom Principle: ***God can reverse His forgiveness towards those who refuse mercy.***

- The ***mercy triumphs over judgment*** **Kingdom Principle** (James 2:13b) can be turned on its head and became "judgment triumphs over mercy" if we do not mirror our King's action and show mercy to others.

Check the box that best describes where you are on the mercy scale.

Kingdom Value #6: Purity

The sixth beatitude tells us that "blessed are the pure in heart" (Matthew 5:8). Only after tasting of the Lord's credited righteousness can we be declared not guilty and have our slate wiped clean. This brings about a new beginning, a new life, new goals and a new hope. We discover "how very much our Father loves us, for he calls us his children." Because of His love and because He will take us to be with Him one day, "all who have this eager expectation will keep themselves pure, just as he is pure" (1 John 3:1-3 - NLT).

Being made pure depends on God's work in our lives but we are still responsible for remaining pure. This does not mean we do it on our own power. We are intentional about allowing God's grace and God's Spirit to take over and fight our battles (see *Grace – Kingdom Value #41* and *Spirit Controlled – Kingdom Value #52*).

Both the adjective "pure" (Greek *katharos*, as in Matthew 5:8) and the verb "purifies" (*hagnizó*, as in 1 John 3:3) speak of the same idea of cleansing: unstained, being free from contamination; possessing something in its pure state, without mixture and free from defilement.[9] The English dictionary also agrees with this definition. Pure, it states, means "not mixed or adulterated with any other substance or material."[10]

Paulo, a friend of our family in Brazil, went into the coffee business years ago and shared an insider's secret with me. He discovered that when companies select coffee from suppliers, they are led to an area where the different grades of coffee are lined up, from the superior beans (most expensive), all the way down to the inferior ones (least expensive). It is up to each company with its distinctive blends to select and mix the grades according to the quality and pricing of their particular brand. But not only are there bags of inferior coffee which can be added to the mix. Bags of roasted twigs and leaves and even ground corn are made available for the cheaper brands that wish to add volume to their final product.

Nobody wants twigs in their coffee. Adding foreign ingredients destroys the purity of the product. What people want is coffee that is in its pure state, with no contamination and without mixture. And that is what the Lord wants from us as well.

We could say purity deals with the ethical and moral aspects of our sanctification process. One of the main goals of this process is to keep us free from the contaminating effects of the world while we wait for Christ's return, and nurturing our unadulterated faithfulness and love for the Lord (Matthew 22:37 - ISV). That is being pure in heart. It means our heart is not contaminated with sin or other "gods" and is not torn between other loyalties. Our heart is pure because our motivation is pure (see *Integrity – Kingdom Value #55*).

How do we keep ourselves pure?
When we enter the Kingdom, we are forgiven and cleansed from every sin. From then on out, how to we stay clean? What exactly are we to do in order to achieve this permanent goal? Jesus prayed that the Father would, "Sanctify them in the truth; your word is truth" (John 17:1 - ESV). Peter reminded his readers that, "Having purified your souls by your obedience to the truth for a sincere brotherly love, love one another earnestly from a pure heart" (1 Peter 1:22 - ESV).

We purify our souls by obeying the truth (see *Obedience – Kingdom Value #37* and *Truth – Kingdom Value #60*). According to our Lord's priestly prayer, God's Word *is* truth. We remain pure by obeying God's Word. It brings us the truth about ourselves, the world, God's will, His purpose, and His values for our lives. We begin to fall away from purity as soon as we allow ourselves to listen to the lies the world spreads about what is important, or the lies Satan tells us about God, such as that He is not really interested in our happiness and success (see Genesis 3:4-5). Lies that tell us we can do better than God in taking care of ourselves and getting what we want out of life.

When a person is described as "pure," the first thing that would probably come to mind is that they are morally or sexually pure. And that makes perfect Biblical sense. Because we are told to "flee from youthful passions, and pursue righteousness, faith, love, and peace, along with those who call on the Lord from a pure heart" (2 Timothy 2:22 - HCSB). If we want to approach God with a pure heart, we must run *from* lust and instead run *after* righteousness and all the Kingdom Values that come with it. This can be a daily struggle, given society's fascination with – and promotion of – all things "sexy." Life tests us in all areas yet sexual purity is for many the main battleground (see *Overcoming – Kingdom Value #62*).

We must always remind ourselves and each other that remaining pure in heart is an essential Kingdom Value because our King deserves and demands our undivided loyalty. Jesus commanded His disciples to "keep watching and praying that you may not enter into temptation; the spirit is willing, but the flesh is weak" (Matthew 26:41 - NASB). Peter told his fellow believers, whom he called "aliens and strangers" in relation to this world, of the need "to abstain from fleshly lusts" because they "wage war against the soul" (1 Peter 2:11 - NASB). (*See Holiness – Kingdom Value #53; and Self-denial – Kingdom Value #54*).

Purity Kingdom Principles:
The *blessed are the pure in heart because they will see* God Kingdom Principle. This is one of the greatest rewards of being justified and purified by the Lord: we will get to see Him!

The *seeing God and becoming like Him* Kingdom Principle. When we "see Him as He is" then "we will be like Him" (1 John 3:2). This brings us to the next principle.

The *imitating God now means being like Him forever* Kingdom Principle. If we make it our aim to be like God now, He will make us like Himself in eternity.

Are you pure at heart? Are your intentions and motivations pure? Have you kept yourself pure from the polluting forces in this fallen world?

Kingdom Value #7: Reconciliation

In the seventh beatitude, Jesus teaches that "blessed are the peacemakers" (Matthew 5:9). We could also say that those who are involved in the ministry of reconciliation are blessed. Being a peacemaker or reconciler means helping two or more parties overcome their differences, forgive each other and mend their relationship. It also includes the idea of helping people get right with God.

We can help people make peace with God by sharing the Good News which says we can be "made right in God's sight by faith" and "have peace with God because of what Jesus Christ our Lord has done for us" (Acts 10:36 and Romans 5:1 - NLT). Though it is God Himself Who takes the initiative to draw the world back to Himself through His Son, He "gave us the ministry of reconciliation," making us representatives of His Kingdom as "ambassadors for Christ," so that, as Paul the apostle and missionary, we also "plead on Christ's behalf" with those God places before us, inviting them to "be reconciled to God" (2 Corinthians 5:18-20 - HCSB).

Brazilians have a saying: "if one does not want to, two do not fight." Even if others want to pick a fight, we should do our best to avoid vicious confrontations and spiteful arguments. Believers should be able to settle issues – even legal disputes – among themselves and certainly out of court. But even if we find ourselves in a win-loose situation, for the sake of harmony and a good testimony before the world, it is preferable to "put up with injustice" and be the losing party (1 Corinthians 6:1-8 - HCSB). It's better to lose the case than lose the brother or our credibility before the lost.

When someone wrongs us, what is the right way to respond? Should we repay "evil for evil"? Should we take justice into our hands and show them just how wrong they are? What if we were to take revenge? The Bible says "if it is possible, as far as it depends on you, live at peace with everyone" (Romans 12:18; see verses 17 and 19).

Keeping the peace, however, does not mean compromising on truth or throwing out other Kingdom Values just to keep people happy. We want to be at peace with God and with people, but if we can't have both, our priority should always be to side with God – with His will and values. Remember there is the conditional "if it is possible" to the imperative "live at peace with everyone."

Another reason reconciliation becomes an impossibility is when one of the parties refuses to be reconciled. I once was going to work with an aspiring Brazilian pastor in South Florida who had become disgruntled with the pastor of the last Brazilian church in the area, with which he had served. He thought that pastor had dragged his feet on his ordination and had decided to leave that church and seek another route to his goal. In the process, they decided to cut ties with each other. I imagined that if I could just get them together over a meal, they could mend the relationship. I spoke with the pastor and he agreed to the meeting. But when I spoke with the aspiring pastor, he categorically refused. "There is nothing to talk about," he told me. "I wanted him to ordain me and he kept putting it off and giving me excuses. That's it. He's not going to change his mind and neither am I."

Nobody said being a peacemaker would be easy. Sometimes it's as hard as forgiving those who have offended us and whom we feel do not deserve our forgiveness. Of course they don't! That's what forgiveness is all about, isn't it?

Principles related to being a peacemaker:
If you are a Christian, you have been called to be a peacemaker. Your main assignment is helping people get right with God. The Bible calls that the ministry of reconciliation.

When we fulfill our ministry of reconciliation and "are the makers and maintainers of peace," then we are blessed. By definition, that means "enjoying enviable happiness, spiritually prosperous–with life-joy and satisfaction in God's favor and salvation, regardless of their outward conditions." Reconcilers "shall be called the sons of God!" (Matthew 5:9 in the Amplified Bible).

We will be called "sons of God" because we will be following His lead and acting like Him, "For God was in Christ, reconciling the world to himself, no longer counting people's sins against them. And he gave us this wonderful message of reconciliation" (2 Corinthians 5:19 - NLT).

Are you a peacemaker? Do you promote forgiveness and reconciliation among those you know who have held back their friendship from each other? Rate yourself on the "Reconciliation scale."

Kingdom Value #8: Being Persecuted

The last Beatitude is "blessed are the persecuted." More and more Christians are being persecuted around the world. More are being targeted, confronted, ridiculed, scorned, sued and thrown in prison in the United States because they hold fast to Kingdom Values. On the other side of the globe, things are much worse. What Islamic terrorist groups are doing to our brothers and sisters is horrifying! When I hear about Christians being targeted over here and about the literal warfare "over there," my blood boils and I become greatly upset.

However, when I read my Bible I get a very different perspective. I'm told not to be surprised, but to "rejoice as you share in the sufferings of the Messiah," and that "if you are ridiculed for the name of Christ, you are blessed, because the Spirit of glory and of God rests on you" (1 Peter 4:12-14 - HCSB).

In the Beatitude we are examining, Jesus declares blessed those who "have been persecuted for righteousness' sake" and promises their reward is "the kingdom of heaven" itself (Matthew 5:10 - ASV). The persecution, Jesus adds, includes verbal abuse and false accusations because of *Him*. His people represent Him and become easy targets. If you examine some of the slanders slung against faithful Christians who hold on to their Kingdom Values today, you will see they are over the top vicious and utterly false.

What, then, should be our response? Or, at least, how should we *feel* about this? King David's ancient advice fits like a glove. He said:

> Do not fret because of those who are evil or be envious of those who do wrong; for like the grass they will soon wither, like green plants they will soon die away. Trust in the Lord and do good. Be still before the Lord and wait patiently for him; do not fret when people succeed in their ways, when they carry out their wicked schemes. Refrain from anger and turn from wrath; do not fret—it leads only to evil. For those who are evil will be destroyed, but those who hope in the Lord will inherit the land. (Psalm 37:1-3, 7-9 - NIV)

Not only are we not to fret, Jesus tells us to *celebrate*! He says we are to "rejoice, and be exceeding glad" and gives us two reasons: "for great is your reward in heaven" and because "so persecuted they the prophets that were before you" (Matthew 5:12 - ASV).

This Kingdom Value is directly related to the Faithfulness value (*Kingdom Value #15*), because the faithful are easily identified as holding beliefs contrary to those of the persecutors. Those who hold loosely to their faith usually are not very vocal and are more easily swayed by peer pressure and current cultural values. If you are being persecuted it probably means you are standing up for your faith and being bold enough about it to evoke a contrary response. If that is the case, then you are happy and fortunate, because you are suffering for the sake of righteousness.

Jesus did not mean we are to go around bashing other people's values. Much less that we should be arrogant and legalistic. Remember that we should speak about our faith "with gentleness and respect." And here is a Kingdom Principle: "For it is better to suffer for doing good, if that should be God's will, than for doing evil" (see 1 Peter 3:15-17 - HCSB). It's better to suffer for presenting the Gospel in love than suffering because you treated others with disrespect and tried to bully them into believing like you do.

Persecution has a way of uniting the family of faith. Have you noticed how families leave their own bickering behind when there is an outside threat? It also forces half-hearted Christians off the wall: either they will decide to stand with God or deny Him and stand with the status quo. Either way, there is a heavy price to be paid. The Church has grown healthier and larger under persecution throughout the centuries. Cuba is a good example of this today.

If we can pull back from our comfort zone, our natural fear of suffering and our instinct of preservation and see life from God's perspective, then we will more clearly see that "blessed are the persecuted." Because it is easier for God to bring about Kingdom Values in the lives of those who suffer persecution than it is for Christians who are comfortable, over-indulged and over-entertained, and who live in a persecution-free environment. "Therefore, since Christ suffered in the flesh, equip yourselves also with the same resolve—because the one who suffered in the flesh has finished with sin— in order to live the remaining time in the flesh, no longer for human desires, but for God's will" (1 Peter 4:1, 2 - HCSB).

My former Brazilian pastor, Pr. José Maria de Souza, preached on the Beatitudes at our church in Rio de Janeiro. In his last sermon in the series, he concluded by listing four reasons why we are blessed when we suffer persecution:

1) Because the Holy Spirit becomes evident in your life.
"If you are insulted for the name of Christ, you are blessed, because the Spirit of glory and of God rests on you" (1 Peter 4:14 - BSB).

2) It means God can trust you.
"The apostles left the high council rejoicing that God had counted them worthy to suffer disgrace for the name of Jesus" (Acts 5:41 - NLT).

3) Suffering is temporary; it's a passing reality.
"For this light momentary affliction is preparing for us an eternal weight of glory beyond all comparison" (2 Corinthians 4:17 - ESV).

4) You will be richly rewarded.
"And since we are his children, we are his heirs. In fact, together with Christ we are heirs of God's glory. But if we are to share his glory, we must also share his suffering" (Romans 8:17 - NLT).

It's not easy being a Christian. Yes, but neither is it easy *not* being a Christian. I'd rather suffer for being a Christian than to suffer for not being one.

Have you suffered persecution because of your faith or what you stand for? How did you hold up? Did you get mad or sad or did you find cause for celebration – knowing that you are in good company and suffering for a great cause and a great Person?

KV8 – **BEING PERSECUTED**				
☐ Consistently practice	☐ Sometimes practice	☐ Struggle	☐ Mostly fail	☐ Continually fail

We will now move on to other Kingdom Values, mentioned elsewhere in Scripture.

Chapter

4

The Fruit of the Spirit Kingdom Values

*But the fruit of the Spirit is **love, joy, peace, patience, kindness,**
goodness, faith, gentleness, self-control.
Against such things there is no law.*
Galatians 5:22-23 - HCSB

Before listing the components of the fruit of the Spirit, Paul furnishes an ugly list of unacceptable human behavior, at the end of which he declares "that anyone living that sort of life will not inherit the Kingdom of God" (Galatians 5:21 - NLT). If those are the practices that characterize the life of people who are not entering the Kingdom, then the fruit of the Spirit is what distinguishes those who have entered the Kingdom. Their life is under the influence and control of the Holy Spirit, and it is He Who produces these wonderful qualities, against which there are no "thou shall not" commands (Galatians 5:23).

Kingdom Value #9: Love

Without love all else is useless

"Can our hearts break?" My daughter Melissa sprang this question on me when she was only five. Before I could figure out where she was coming from, she answered her own question. "No, only when somebody doesn't love us and we love **them.**"

The number one thing our King wants from us is to return His love in kind. That

67

is the essence of seeking first the Kingdom of God. It means seeking first the God of the Kingdom. Out of pure love. Seeking God for God's sake, not for some self-ish agenda.

As the "love chapter" (1 Corinthians 13) makes abundantly clear, without love every other virtue – or Kingdom Value – is meaningless. In that chapter, the apostle Paul mentions "prophecy" (see *Proclamation – Kingdom Value #21*); "knowledge" (see *Knowledge – Kingdom Value #0*; **and** *Wisdom – Kingdom Value #61*); "faith" (*Kingdom Value #39*); giving all one's possessions to feed the poor (see *Benevolence – Kingdom Value #51);* and surrendering one's body to be burned (see *Kingdom Values #54, #57, and #64*). But Paul is clear: to have all of these and lack love "profits me nothing" (1 Corinthians 13:2-3 - NASB).

Next (1 Corinthians 13:4-7), Paul describes love as being, among other things, "patient" (*Kingdom Value #12*); "kind" (*Kingdom Value #13*); as not being arrogant (*Kingdom Values #1*). Love "is not self-seeking" (see mutuality values #23 through #34); "does not rejoice in unrighteousness" (all Kingdom Values are based on righteousness); "but rejoices with the truth" (*Kingdom Value #60*); and "bears all things" (see *Perseverance – Kingdom Value #58*).

I mention all of these Kingdom Values in relation to love to make two points: Kingdom Values are interconnected and dependent on each other; and without love all other values become hollow, insignificant and ineffective. Love is a Kingdom core value because it should be the motivation behind every other value. Love is not a means to an end. Love is the end of all righteous means.

Is it any wonder that after listing several Kingdom Values in a different letter, the Apostle Paul says, "And over all these virtues put on love, which binds them all together in perfect unity" (Colossians 3:14)?

In love with the Lord

King David was certainly not perfect, but he deeply loved the Lord. Serving God and enjoying fellowship in His presence was his passion. That's what he lived for. "I love the LORD because he hears my voice and my prayer for mercy," expresses that passion (Psalm 116:1 - NLT). In some ways it seems his sins were of a more serious nature than that of his predecessor. "But God removed Saul and replaced him with David, a man about whom God said, 'I have found David son of Jesse, a man after my own heart. He will do everything I want him to do'" (Acts 13:22 - NLT). This is how Jesus defined loving God: "If you love Me, you will keep My commandments" (John 14:15 - NASB).

The church in Ephesus was doing really well in their evaluation until the Lord got to the part about love. Jesus told them: "nevertheless I have this against you, that you have left your first love" (Revelation 2:4 - NKJV). Similarly, God asked unfaithful Israel: "what can I do with you, Ephraim? What can I do with you, Judah? Your love is like the morning mist, like the early dew that disappears" (Hosea 6:4 - NIV). The solution was to repent and go back to the way they were before – or face swift judgment.

Love is the "more excellent way" (1 Corinthians 12:31). It comes down to this: "he who does not love does not know God, for God is love" (1 John 4:8 - NKJV). Love is one of God's most prominent attributes.

When asked which is the greatest commandment, Jesus replied: "you shall love the Lord your God with all your heart and with all your soul and with all your mind (intellect)." He emphasized that "this is the great (most important, principal) and first commandment;" the second most important being "you shall love your neighbor as [you do] yourself." So fundamentally important is loving God and others that "these two commandments sum up and upon them depend all the Law and the Prophets" (Matthew 22:37-40 - AMP).

In his book, "On Loving God," Bernard of Clairvaux (1090-1153 A.D.) considers four degrees of love, each purer and more mature than the previous one. Although Bernard did not use this exact terminology, pastor John Claypool once preached on the subject and described these four stages of love as the love of self for self's sake; the love of God for self's sake; the love of God for God's sake, and the love of self for God's sake. Much like the prodigal son (Luke 15:11-32), our love begins in a very self-centered and self-serving way. But, hopefully, it will mature, passing through the next three stages.

One would think that love of God for God's sake would be the ultimate goal of the Christian life. But learning to love ourselves for God's sake (accepting who and how we are and where we came from with a thankful heart), and dedicating ourselves fully to God for His glory, is our highest calling.[1]

Remember how, even when the prodigal son "came to his senses," instead of thinking about just how much he hurt his father, his initial motivation was "how many of my father's hired hands have more than enough food, and here I am dying of hunger!" (Luke 15:17 - HCSB). The son, in a sense, loved the father for his own personal sake. Even so, the father, in an example of unconditional love, accepted him back with open arms. This is a portrait of our Heavenly Father, Who loves us no matter in what stage of spiritual maturity we find ourselves. And His desire is to help us grow to love Him for His sake and server others without selfish motivations.

In his book, **Life Together**, Dietrich Bonhoeffer talks about human love as opposed to God's love. Human love is the natural way of loving ourselves through others, instead of loving others for who they are. When we express our love to someone and it is not corresponded in a manner that serves us, if we then deny them any more of our "love," this is proof that we are simply using them for our own benefit. That is why serving others (*Kingdom Value #30*) is a good indication that our love is the God-type: because it seeks the benefit of others, even though it costs us something.

Love Kingdom Principles:
1. Jesus said the greatest command is "you shall love the Lord your God with all your heart and with all your soul and with all your mind and with all your strength" (Mark 12:30 - ESV).
2. Jesus said the second greatest command is "you shall love your neighbor as yourself" (Mark 12:31 - ESV).
3. Without love, every other Kingdom Value is useless.
4. Real love proves itself by serving God and others.
5. We should learn to love God for God's sake.
6. We should learn to love ourselves for God's sake.
7. God loves us no matter what stage of love we are in, but wants us to grow.

Do you love God with all your heart? Do you love others as much as you love yourself? How would you rate your love for God and others?

Kingdom Value #10: Joy

When my wife Monica was a teenager, she received Jesus as her Savior. She had been carrying a heavy load of doubt and discouragement and was seeking answers about God and what He had to offer. When a friend's sister sat down and shared from God's Word with her, then asked her if she would like to submit her life to Him, she saw Jesus with outstretched arms inviting her to Himself. She said "yes," and felt joy rush into her life. The dark cloud which seemed to be hanging over her head had been lifted. As she walked home she felt like she was walking on air. When she arrived, her mother said, "What happened to *you*? Your face looks like it's glowing. Have you been doing drugs or something?"

When Jesus comes in, He brings His joy with Him.

Joy is a fruit of the Spirit (Galatians 5:22): He produces it in the lives of those He fills and controls. While people search for happiness in all the wrong places and as an end in itself, the Bible is clear that joy is generated by the Holy Spirit, comes as the result of God's presence, forgiveness and favor, and spontaneously occurs when we live according to God's Kingdom Values. Joy is not an end in itself, but the result of righteous living. It is God's reward.

When Hurricane Wilma hit South Florida in October of 2005, our family was left without electricity for 23 days. Things were hot, muggy, dark and difficult. Imagine what joy filled our lives when the lights came back on! Now imagine how much more joy is generated when God shows up and frees His people from misery, bondage, oppression, and darkness. The relief, the peace, and the hope which take place produce abundant joy.

An appropriate response to God's intervention is to "Rejoice in the LORD, righteous ones; for the praise of the upright is beautiful" (Psalm 33:1 - ISV; see *Thanksgiving - Kingdom Value #42*). The whole world has received one blessing after another from above. An appropriate response to all of God's benefits is to "Shout for joy to the LORD, all the earth, burst into jubilant song with music" (Psalm 98:4 - NIV).

There are many dimensions to joy. Joy is what we feel when we have done the work Jesus has assigned to us. "The seventy-two returned with joy and said, 'Lord, even the demons submit to us in your name'" (Luke 10:17). Joy is what we experience when deliverance brings about great relief. Such as when those condemned to suffer and die have their fortune reversed. When Queen Esther, guided by her cousin Mordecai, was able to persuade her husband, King Ahasuerus, to save the Jews in the Persian empire from certain genocide, the Jewish population established the Feast of Purim, in which there was "feasting and rejoicing" (Esther 9:18, 28).

Joy is what a whole nation felt when 33 miners, who were trapped in a copper mine which had caved in, were rescued after 69 days of intense rescue efforts. The mine, which became their "prison," is located in Chile's Atacama Desert. The whole world watched in suspense, from August 5 to October 13, 2010, until they were rescued, one-by-one, through a narrow vertical tunnel carved out in order to set them free. The joy the miners, their families, workers, authorities, and TV and Internet spectators felt was indescribable! My wife and I lived in Chile at the time, and the emotion, anticipation, the hope that just would not relent, was almost palpable during those days. When they were finally rescued, the whole country let out a huge sigh of relief and began to rejoice. It was a momentous and joyous occasion for Chile and for the watching world.[2]

There is definitely "a time to laugh" (Ecclesiastes 3:4), especially after someone has suffered long and hard and is now out of trouble. The population in Jerusalem during the days of Nehemiah had experienced their share of hardship and frustration. But now it was time to regroup, restore and rebuild. So Nehemiah **told** them to "go and celebrate with a feast of rich foods and sweet drinks, and share gifts of food with people who have nothing prepared. This is a sacred day before our Lord. Don't be dejected and sad, for the joy of the LORD is your strength!" (Nehemiah 8:10 - NLT).

Joy is God's antidote to one of Satan's most frequently used weapons: discouragement. Perhaps that's why Paul's imperative for the followers of Christ is to "always be joyful" (1 Thessalonians 5:16 - NLT). He repeats the same charge to others on his list: "always be full of joy in the Lord. I say it again—rejoice!" (Philippians 4:4 - NLT).

Jesus wants our joy to be complete, as we remain connected to Him in vital union, bear much fruit and understand the Father's deep love for us (John 15:11). God is the One Who gives us joy, and this should lead us to rejoice and celebrate (Nehemiah 12:43). Our brothers and sisters – fellow citizens in the Kingdom – also bring us joy (1 Thessalonians 3:9); as do those who love us (Philemon 1:7). Joy is given by the Holy Spirit to those who welcome the Word of God (1 Thessalonians 1:6).

And, finally, joy is the eternal reward for a life well lived. "His master said to him, 'Well done, good and faithful slave. You were faithful with a few things, I will put you in charge of many things; enter into the joy of your master'" (Matthew 25:21-NASB).

Experiencing Kingdom joy
Every time the Kingdom bursts on the scene, God shows up or people turn from their sins, there is joy and rejoicing! It is the natural response: when the weight of sin is lifted, the "joy of the Lord" comes rushing in.

For this reason, joy is a key component of worship. When we see people worshiping the Lord, invariably they are doing so with a heart that is overflowing with joy. Jesus knew how the Father had kept Kingdom secrets from those who were wise in their own eyes "and revealed them to little children," which caused Him to be

72

"full of joy through the Holy Spirit" and exclaim, "I praise you, Father, Lord of heaven and earth" (Luke 10:21 - NIV).

Joy, more intense and pure than what we experience on this side of eternity, will follow us to the afterlife as God is able "to present you before his glorious presence without fault and with great joy" (Jude 1:24, 25).

Joy Kingdom Principles:
1. We are **commanded** to "rejoice in the Lord!" (Philippians 3:10; see *Rejoicing in the Lord – Kingdom Value #44*).
2. Sadness and anxiety sap our energy, but the joy of the Lord is our strength (Nehemiah 8:10).
3. God **wants** us to be full of joy. He designed us to be joyful and to celebrate fellowship with Him an life with others (see *Celebrating – Kingdom Value #33*).

With true joy comes genuine peace. How's your supply of joy doing these days?

Kingdom Value #11: Peace

"Peace of mind wherever you are." The promise is made in an ad for a home security system which feeds video to your smartphone. But it's not like that's going to cancel out all your other worries. Jesus promises a different kind of peace. "I am leaving you with a gift–peace of mind and heart. And the peace I give is a gift the world cannot give. So don't be troubled or afraid" (John 14:27 - NLT).

It's not a peace without problems but a peace in spite of problems. Jesus provides the perfect balance: He acknowledges living in this world is difficult, but tells us to maintain a positive attitude and joyful outlook because He is in control. He said: "I've told you this so that my peace will be with you. In the world you'll have trouble. But cheer up! I have overcome the world" (John 16:33 - GW). "Cheer up" also means taking heart and being courageous.

Right before going through the ordeal of the cross, Jesus told His disciples about a special kind of peace He was going to give them. After His resurrection, the very first thing He tells His disciples, when He appears to them was "peace to you!" (John 20:19). How appropriate and needed this message was! Because this "peace"

73

had a double meaning: He had just paid for their sins, "making peace through the blood of His cross," which would reconcile them to God (Colossians 1:20); and He was encouraging by demonstrating that He was indeed in control of the situation. They needed no longer cower behind closed doors. Nor run from the authorities. Or fear for their lives. He was alive! And He was ready for them to get up, go out and be on mission!

True peace is something only God can give. "The wicked are like the tossing sea, which cannot rest" (Isaiah 57:20a). There "is no peace for the wicked" (Isaiah 48:22a - NLT). But "the Lord blesses His people with peace" (Psalm 29b - HCSB). Jesus offers: "Come to Me, all of you who are weary and burdened, and I will give you rest" (Matthew 11:28 - HCSB). Peace means being able to rest in the Lord or, to enter the Lord's rest (Hebrews 4). It is a result of being forgiven, saved and living in harmony with God. "Therefore, since we have been justified through faith, we have peace with God through our Lord Jesus Christ" (Romans 5:1). "Rest" and "peace" are used interchangeably in the Bible.

What does the term "peace" or *shalom* mean to the Jewish people today? Anyone who has been around Jewish families knows they use this term quite often. My friend Ana Willis, who for five years lived in Jerusalem, told me what Jewish people mean when they wish each other *shalom*.

> *Shalom* is not the absence of problems in our life," she explained, "but the peace of God that surpasses all understanding. It keeps us calm and confident in God no matter what happens around us. I just love to hear people greeting each other with *shalom*, because there is no doubt this is what the world needs more than ever: the peace that comes from knowing God and knowing He is in control over everything, even when things seem completely out-of-control down here. In Hebrew, when we ask each other "how are you?," we literally say "how is your peace?" My question for us, Christians, is how is our peace when troubles come? If we believe the Prince of Peace lives in us, then His *shalom* must be a reality in our lives.

That reminds me of the promise that "the peace of God, which transcends all understanding, will guard your hearts and your minds in Christ Jesus" (Philippians 4:7 - NIV).

Inner peace is achieved when other Kingdom Values come together, such as when we are reconciled with God and live in harmony with others (Kingdom Values #7 and #25), when we follow God's Spirit instead of our lower nature (#37 and #52), and when we live a life characterized by mercy and love (#5 and #9). Peace comes into focus when we have a solid hope for the future (#40), enjoy fellowship with those we love (#19), and live a life of service (#30), that is, a life invested in others instead of a life focused on our own problems.

Peace Kingdom Principles:
1. Jesus is the Prince of Peace. As the bumper sticker says, "Know Jesus, know peace; no Jesus, no peace."
2. Like joy, peace is the result of being reconciled with God and others.
3. Peace happens where other Kingdom Values meet.
4. *Shalom* includes the notion of well-being, balance, harmony, contentment and fulfillment.

Is your life normally characterized by peace of mind and heart? Is your spirit at peace with God? Are you at peace with yourself and others?

Kingdom Value #12: Patience

Patience requires learning how to wait. Waiting for a problem to be solved or a difficulty to be overcome. Waiting for something that is irritating us to stop or go away. Waiting for people to arrive, change their behavior or leave. There was a sign on the office door of a former colleague, that read: "Everyone brings joy to this office. Some when they arrive; some when they leave."

Being born in Brazil to American parents means I've got a lot of the American *and* Latin culture. So I should be well equipped to handle either when the need arises. But I was reminded just how much I need patience when we were invited to a church farewell party by a pastor, while serving in Chile as missionaries. It was one hour before the get-together. "Just calling to confirm we are on for 8:00 PM," I told the pastor. He confirmed he'd be there. Although I usually run a little late, my wife Monica and I arrived at eight o'clock.

It was cold outside and the heater wasn't working inside. A table had been set and there were a few people there, but no pastor. More arrived and we just sat around, waiting for the pastor. Nothing would officially begin without him. But the clock was ticking and I was getting ticked off. Although we waited one hour and twenty minutes for him, no one seemed upset or offended. All were simply happy to be together. I, on the other hand, had reached my limit. If someone had asked me to fill out the patience scale right then, I would have flunked the test!

Patience also has a lot to do with learning how to wait for God.

This Kingdom Value is about "active patience." It is a deliberate choice. Reinhold Niebuhr's Serenity Prayer helps us to understand this issue. You've heard it before: *God grant me the serenity to accept the things I cannot change, courage to change the things I can, and wisdom to know the difference.*

"The serenity to accept the things I cannot change" requires an abundant supply of patience. Especially if we are dealing with conditions which last for years or a lifetime.

Most patients have to wait for long periods in waiting rooms (no wonder they call them "patients"). Many of us have been waiting for people we love to change, for circumstances to get better, for God to answer a specific request we made years ago. We are in *God's* waiting room. But why do we have to wait and what are we waiting for? The short answer is God's timing (as in 2 Peter 3:9). And His timing is aimed at bringing about good fruit, better character, and the best outcome, for His glory.

Our character does not grow over night. It takes time for God to bring us to the place He wants us to be. And only He knows when trials, temptations, and testing have been enough and it is time to stop waiting because He is ready to intervene and bring about the solution we have so often prayed and hoped for.

When we suffer we especially need patience (see **Enduring Suffering – Kingdom Value #57**). Even Job became exasperated with all the suffering he had to endure, and he has been considered the most patient person every to live. He asked, "With my strength gone, I have no hope to go on living. With nothing to look forward to, why should I be patient?" (Job 6:11 - ERV).

The Apostle John identified himself as "your brother and your partner in suffering and in God's Kingdom and in the patient endurance to which Jesus calls us" (Revelation 1:9a - NLT). Every single human being on earth is destined to suffer adversities. But we are called to be patient during the process. When predicting severe suffering in the book of Revelation, the announcement is made that "this calls for patient endurance and faithfulness on the part of the saints" (Revelation 13:10; 14:12). Patience and suffering are supposed to go hand-in-hand.

James tells us to be patient while we wait for the Lord's return. He wrote, "Be you also patient; establish your hearts: for the coming of the Lord draws near" (James 5:8 - AKJV; see v. 7). Paul told the Romans to "be joyful in hope, patient in trouble, and persistent in prayer" (Romans 12:12 - ISV). Knowing what awaits us in eternity helps us to be patient as we face difficulties, trials, and temptations on earth. We can more easily practice patience when we know our problems are temporary.

One of love's characteristics is that it is "patient and kind" (1 Corinthians 13:4). If we are smart we will be patient. "Whoever is patient has great understanding, but one who is quick-tempered displays folly" (Proverbs 14:29 - NIV).

The wear and tear of life can make us weary, "but they who wait for the LORD shall renew their strength; they shall mount up with wings like eagles; they shall run and not be weary; they shall walk and not faint" (Isaiah 40:31 - ESV).

We have come to a point where we expect instant solutions. Got a question? Google it. Want to purchase something right now? Go on Amazon.com. Need to talk to someone across the globe? Just call them via What'sApp. But some problems are more complicated or refuse to go away. They take time and patience. When it comes down the pesky small stuff or life-changing situations, how does your patience hold up?

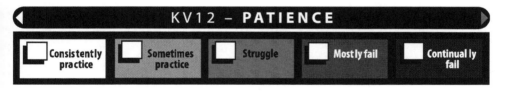

Kingdom Value #13: Kindness

"But the fruit of the Spirit is... kindness" (Galatians 5:22 - ISV).

In my teen years, every time I would leave the house, without fail, my mother would give me a kiss and say "be sweet." She was the kindest person I have ever known.

"Since God chose you to be the holy people he loves, you must clothe yourselves with ... kindness" (Colossians 3:12a - NLT). Our kindness should be as evident to others as the clothes we wear. I just read how a Muslim and a Jew both surrendered their lives to Christ, at different times and in different places, because of the kindness of Christians with whom they came in contact. Their kindness was living proof that what they were saying was true and had made all the difference in their own lives.

There are reports that indicate many Muslims have become disillusioned with their religion because of the violence they have witnessed – including against other Muslim groups. And, when they become aware of the kindness offered by Christians, several of them have decided to follow Jesus instead. "We prove ourselves by our... kindness, by the Holy Spirit within us..." (2 Corinthians 6:6b - NLT).

Unfortunately, kindness is getting rarer by the day. Just read the comments at the end of articles posted on the web. Shocking. Even some who identify themselves as Christians on these online discussions will, many times, resort to shameful put-downs and be exceedingly rude in their remarks. It's easy to understand how one's blood can boil when faced with sarcasm and stinging remarks from others, but when Christians resort to the same, they are defeating the purpose of defending Christian values and the faith.

It is very important to state that the Kingdom has no place for bullies. Quite the opposite. This is such a big issue today that I have preferred to add both Meekness and Gentleness as separate Kingdom Values instead of trying to bring them together under one title, though they are admittedly very similar (see *Meekness – Kingdom Value #3* and *Gentleness – Kingdom Value #16*).

What is kindness? Kindness is a command, a fruit, an aspect of love. It is imperative to "be kind to one another, tenderhearted, forgiving one another, as God in Christ forgave you" (Ephesians 4:32 - ESV). Kindness is a portion of the fruit of the Spirit, the result of His indwelling and being in control. And, kindness is included in the definition of love, in Paul's love chapter. "Love is kind," he wrote (1 Corinthians 13:4 - NIV).

Kindness means treating others with respect – even when they do not deserve it. "Random acts of kindness," a popular notion, means being nice to others and doing something special for them, "just because." Being kind sometimes involves walking the second mile (Matthew 5:41). Have you ever had the satisfaction of seeing someone's face glow because you gave them an unexpected tip – or a disproportionately large one? Or, because you gave something you like to someone who needed it more than you? We are usually kind to others when we are overflowing with joy (another portion of the fruit of the Spirit). There should be a deliberate decision to make this a lifestyle (see *Benevolence – Kingdom Value #51)*. Civility is a term which has practically taken the place of "kindness" in politics and social engagement. The dictionary defines civility as "formal politeness and courtesy in behavior or speech."[3] We need more of that not just "out there" in the public square, but behind closed doors: in the workplace, at church, and in our homes. It is sad to hear about all of the verbal abuse which occurs even in Christian families today.

A sad – yet interesting – thing happens with people who practice verbal and emotional abuse as a lifestyle. They seem to be divided into at least three groups: a) First, there are some who are nice to everyone at work, at church, or in public in general, but who are just the opposite at home. These usually fool everybody except their own family. b) Second, there are those who are nice at home but abusive everywhere else. c) And thirdly, there are those who are abusive *everywhere*, to *everybody*. I am not a psychologist, but I've lived long enough to know that usually aggressive behavior stems from frustration with self. Which means telling a frustrated person to be nice is not going to be enough. Other Kingdom Values must come into play, especially that of living a life which is controlled by the Holy Spirit (see *Being Spirit Controlled – Kingdom Value #52*).

Jesus modeled exemplary kindness. But, unfortunately, there are too many rude Christians today who do not take Kingdom Values into consideration. Jesus, on the other hand, was always respectful and kind even when His opponents were slandering and blaspheming Him. He was firm but never disrespectful though He had all the right to be. When the religious leaders of the day called Him a "Samaritan" (for them a derogatory term) and accused Him of having a demon, this is how He responded: "'I do not have a demon,' Jesus answered. 'On the contrary, I honor My Father and you dishonor Me'" (John 8:49 - HCSB). He could have shredded them to pieces, yet responded with restraint. He was able to love even His fiercest enemies.

Jesus showed compassion and kindness when dealing with the outcast and notorious sinners. He did not accuse them publicly, condemn them directly, put them down, or shame them. He was gentle and kind.

Observe how Jesus dealt with the Samaritan women at the well. He approached her and interacted with dignity, knowing full well who she was, even though Jews did not speak with unknown women, much less Samaritans, and even less with those society frowned upon. As He spoke, He shared hope and wisdom. Then, He honored her by sending her as a missionary to her people (John 4).

Jesus' kindness transcended cultural and religious barriers. He, as a Jewish man, had shown genuine interest in communicating with a Samaritan woman. Then He spoke of her need for living water and the true Messiah, and saved her and many from her town. There is no greater kindness than to point people to the way of salvation.

God is kind. Psalm after psalm declares that God's "lovingkindness is everlasting," and Psalm 136 (NASB) repeats this truth at the end of every verse. The Hebrew term means "favor" and relates to God's covenant loyalty.[4] The greatest act of kindness God has performed for us was sending His Son to bear our sins and save us from an eternity of suffering. "But when the kindness of God our Savior and His love for mankind appeared, He saved us, not by the righteous deeds we had done, but according to His mercy..." (Titus 3:4-5a - BSB).

God's lovingkindness is so good it "is better than life" (Psalm 63:3). That's why we should think about it all the time (Psalm 48:9). King Solomon expressed his gratitude to the Lord saying, "You have shown great kindness to your servant, my father David, because he was faithful to you and righteous and upright in heart. You have continued this great kindness to him and have given him a son to sit on his throne this very day" (1 Kings 3:6 - NIV).

However, it is important to "notice how God is both kind and severe. He is severe toward those who disobeyed, but kind to you if you continue to trust in his kindness. But if you stop trusting, you also will be cut off" (Romans 11:22 - NLT; see Psalm 89:31-33).

We should imitate God and be kind to others. Being kind does not mean compromising truth or Kingdom Values. On the contrary, being kind is dependent on these values. Where are you on the "kindness scale"?

Kingdom Value #14: Goodness (doing good)

Goodness is the sixth mentioned aspect of the fruit of the Spirit (Galatians 5:22). Doing good is also a mutuality principle. We are to "see that no one repays anyone evil for evil, but always seek to do good to one another and to everyone" (1 Thessalonians 5:15 - ESV). We cannot do good to others without, in some form, serving them (see *Serving one another – Kingdom Value #30*). Doing good is also part of what it means to bear fruit (see *Fruitfulness – Kingdom Value #45*). It's easy to see how Kingdom Values are interconnected. Each part helps to form a whole, a value system.

God expects everyone to *be* good and *do* good. But the expectation seems to be even higher for the rich. Paul told Timothy to "[charge them] to do good, to be rich in good works, to be liberal and generous of heart, ready to share [with others]" (1 Timothy 6:18 - AMP; see *Benevolence – Kingdom Value #51*).

Evil is conquered with good. The Kingdom way involves reconciliation, seeking peace, working through problems and finding the best solutions. If a conflict is inevitable, if a Kingdom citizen is insulted, treated unfairly or even attacked, revenge is not an option. This does not mean there aren't times one must *defend* himself or his family. But you don't fight fire with fire. There are honor cultures which strongly believe they must protect their family's "honor" by seeking revenge. When insulted or attacked, they quickly devise how to up the ante, which in turn leads to a further escalation of the conflict. Things get very ugly in a hurry and stay that way for a very long time. Sometimes for several generations.

You protect your honor by being honorable. After repeating his instructions to "never pay back evil with more evil," Paul instructs the Christians in Rome, the seat of an empire that was beginning to seriously persecute Christians, to "do things in such a way that everyone can see you are honorable. Do all that you can to live in peace with everyone." He tells them to "never take revenge," but to "leave that to the righteous anger of God," the One Who has promised, "I will take revenge; I will pay them back" (Romans 12:17-19 - NLT). Paul concludes by sharing the secret to defeating violence. "Don't let evil conquer you, but conquer evil by doing good" (Romans 12:21 - NLT). Only doing good can break the vicious cycle of violence and aggression.

It is only fitting that "doing good" be a portion of the fruit of the Spirit. Because, when we are not being controlled by the Holy Spirit, we are controlling ourselves, which is another way of saying we are out of control. And when that happens we "bite and devour one another" (Galatians 5:15 - HCSB) – even family members and brothers and sisters in Christ. That is the antithesis of the "one another" Kingdom Values (see the *Mutuality Kingdom Values*, numbers 23 through 34).

Jesus, our King, set the example in doing good. Just as we are to be filled and controlled by the Spirit, "God anointed Jesus of Nazareth with the Holy Spirit and with power, and ... He went about doing good and healing all who were under the tyranny of the Devil, because God was with Him" (Acts 10:38 - HCSB). Doing good meant giving people real hope, healing their bodies and setting them free from the oppression of the evil one.

Doing good according to God's book of values is not always perceived as "good" by the school system, in the workplace or in society at large. Standing up for good is getting harder by the day, but God promises to reward those who do:

> Turn away from evil and do good. Usually no one will hurt you for wanting to do good. But even if they should, you are to be envied, for God will reward you for it. Do what is right; then if men speak against you, calling you evil names, they will become ashamed of themselves for falsely accusing you when you have only done what is good. So then, those who suffer according to God's will should commit themselves to their faithful Creator and continue to do good.
> 1 Peter 3:11a, 13-14, 16 - TLB; 1 Peter 4: 19 - NIV

What does doing good look like in our world today? There are specific attitudes and actions we should take as individuals to bless our family members, neighbors, the community of faith and those in need of salvation or care. And this effort should be multiplied through the church and Christian agencies. It's as simple as offering to wash the dishes at home, being there for your neighbors, giving your tithe, being available to use your spiritual gift at church. Or it can be as complex as getting shoe boxes to needy children across the globe and planting churches in hostile territories. Whatever the case may be, God is calling us to do good, just as Jesus did.

The Salvation Army's slogan is "Doing the Most Good™." That's a good motto to live by. But doing good all the time runs the risk of wearing one down. You've heard of "compassion fatigue." If not empowered by God's Spirit we will very quickly conclude that it's just not worth doing good to those who are non-responsive or antagonistic. As can menial, repetitive work – such as cleaning the house. How appropriate, then, is this scriptural reminder: "dear brothers and sisters, never get tired of doing good" (2 Thessalonians 3:13b - NLT).

Kingdom Principles related to doing good or goodness:
1. Goodness refers to "the Golden Rule:" "Do to others whatever you would like them to do to you. This is the essence of all that is taught in the law and the prophets" (Matthew 7:12 - NLT).
2. True and lasting goodness has its source in God.
3. Only when we are controlled by the Holy Spirit are we able to sustain an attitude of doing good to others and not become weary in doing good.
4. "It is better to suffer for doing good than for doing wrong!" (1 Peter 3:17 - TLB).

When it comes to doing good, where do you usually find yourself on the Goodness scale?

☐ Consistently practice	☐ Sometimes practice	☐ Struggle	☐ Mostly fail	☐ Continually fail

Kingdom Value #15: Faithfulness

I still remember the day I was sharing with my father some of the struggles I was having at work. I was in my twenties and felt I was not being given a chance to achieve my full potential. And I was wondering if what I was doing was really counting for the Lord. I earnestly wanted to make a difference but doubted that I truly was. Dad was not a man of many words, but what he said made a deep impression on me. He said: "John, God hasn't called us to be *success*ful; He's called us to be *faith*ful." That stuck with me to this day.

I believe that more than anything else, the trials and temptations we face each day are designed to test our faithfulness (see ***Overcoming – Kingdom Value #62***). Will we defy or obey God's will? Will we do it our way or His way? Will we try to get the credit or give God the glory? This is what God wants: "for I desire loyalty and not sacrifice, the knowledge of God rather than burnt offerings" (Hosea 6: 6 - HCSB). Faithfulness is what our rewards will be based on because faithfulness is a very accurate way to measure our love for the Lord.

What earthly king would demand anything short of absolute loyalty? Why would the King of kings? And yet, when it comes to faithfulness, God cannot be out-done. He is the supreme example of faithfulness. He is trustworthy and faithful to those who put their trust in Him – to those whose allegiance is with the Lord. He will never let them down. His word promises: "but the Lord is faithful; He will strengthen and guard you from the evil one" (2 Thessalonians 3:3 - HCSB; see also 1 Thessalonians 5:24). The Lord is faithful and works to make us faithful as well.

When this verse says the Lord will "strengthen" us, it means God will "firmly establish" and "solidly plant" us, "which eliminates vacillation."(@5) I find that in those areas where I struggle the most, one of my biggest problems is precisely vacillation or wavering. This is a verse I want to claim each day so that I don't end up like Charlie Brown in the scene below:

> **Charlie Brown:** I've decided next year, I'm going to be a changed person.
> **Lucy van Pelt:** Oh, be serious, Charlie Brown.
> **Charlie Brown:** No, I mean it. I'm going to be strong and firm.

Lucy van Pelt: Forget it, Charlie Brown. You'll always be wishy-washy.
Charlie Brown: Why can't I change just a little bit? I've got it! I'll be wishy one day, washy the next.[6]

When our love is lacking, our zeal will be tepid and our faithfulness will waver and wane. The northern kingdom of Israel, just before its fall and demise as a sovereign nation, became extremely unfaithful to God. Its slide down the slippery slope of unfaithfulness, one of the main topics in the book of Hosea, became so treacherous that the people of Israel began to completely ignore their God. They wouldn't admit their guilt (Hosea 5:15), acknowledge God (Hosea 6:3, 6), call on Him (Hosea 7:7), and return to or search for Him (Hosea 7:10, 16). They strayed and rebelled against Him (Hosea 7:13), without ever looking back.

There is an old joke about a person who decided to swim across the Atlantic, from Europe all the way to Brazil. When he could see Rio de Janeiro at a distance, he was so tired that he told himself: "I just can't go any further!" So, he turned around and swam all the way back! How tragic for Christians who have remained faithful all their lives, only to slip and fall in the last days of their earthly pilgrimage.

How much better to hear the Master say "well done, good and faithful servant. You have been faithful over a little; I will set you over much. Enter into the joy of your master" (Matthew 25:21 - ESV). The commendation comes from a parable Jesus told close to the end of His life on earth and is aimed at two servants who had been faithful with what they had received – the third was not (Matthew 25:14-30). Jesus has also given abilities and resources to each one of us and expects us to be productive in their use for the furthering of His Kingdom. One day Jesus is coming back and we will have to give an account of what we have done with our lives. "No creature is hidden from Him, but all things are naked and exposed to the eyes of Him to whom we must give an account" (Hebrews 4:13 - HCSB). Were we faithful to Him? Were we faithful in our relationships? Were we faithful in our Kingdom work?

The first and fundamental test of faithfulness is this: what will we do with Jesus? The third servant, who buried his talent, most likely represents those who fail to entrust their lives to the Lord. They have turned their back on every opportunity afforded them, claimed all the excuses in the book, put the decision on hold as long as they could, and have never gotten around to repenting and believing. The master called this person a "wicked and lazy servant!" and gave the order: "Now throw this useless servant into outer darkness, where there will be weeping and gnashing of teeth" (Matthew 25: 26a, 30 - NLT).

A promise to some, a threat to others, Jesus said, "Look, I am coming soon! My reward is with me, and I will give to each person according to what they have done" (Revelation 22:12 - NIV). For the faithful it will be a time for rewards; for the faithless it will be a time for payback. The stakes could not be higher, nor the consequences more extreme (see Revelation 21:7-8; 22:12-15). That is why we must choose Jesus without delay and follow Him closely each and every day.

One day you will be evaluated by your Creator. But right now you can examine your life and evaluate yourself: how faithful are you?

Kingdom Value #16: Gentleness

Are you married? Do you work in an office with other people? Do you attend a church? Do you go out in public (like to the supermarket)? Wherever you go, with whomever you relate, you have probably come to see how important gentleness is.

The words meekness (***Kingdom Value #3***) and gentleness share the same root: meekness from *praus* and gentleness from *prautés*, both from *pra*. Yet the attitudes of meekness and gentleness are so Christ-like and so necessary, it is well worth examining their different nuances. Meekness has been seen (above) in the context of the beatitudes and now we will look at gentleness in the context of the fruit of the Spirit.

You've seen the sign, "fragile, handle with care." People are also fragile and should be treated with gentleness. What is so special about gentleness and what does the Bible say about it?

> "Gentleness" (*prautes*) describes the person who is so much in control of himself that he is always angry at the right time and never angry at the wrong time (Aristotle, Nicomachean Ethics, IV, 5, 1-4), just like Moses, who is praised for being the gentlest or meekest among his contemporaries (Num 12:3). This is the spirit in which to learn (James 1:21) and in which discipline must be applied and faults corrected (Gal 6:1). It is also the virtue for meeting opposition (2 Tim 2:25) and giving a Christian witness (1 Peter 3:15, 16).[7]

What a difference gentleness can make in relationships and life in general! "A gentle answer deflects anger, but harsh words make tempers flare" (Proverbs 15:1 - NLT). To be gentle is to be like Jesus, which should be every Christian's goal. Jesus said we should "learn from me, because I am gentle and humble. Then you will find rest for yourselves" (Matthew 11:29 - GW). The King James version has it as "meek and lowly in heart."

Jesus had all the power and authority in heaven and on earth (Matthew 28:18), and yet He was humble and gentle, even when dealing with those who were resisting and accusing Him. He always treated women with respect and dignity. He always dealt with the sick, poor and needy with compassion. This flowed from His gentle attitude and humble character.

Proportionally speaking, when considering His magnificent glory and unlimited power, Jesus was the most humble and gentle Person Who ever walked the earth. It is depressing to see how celebrities, owners of great corporations and successful politicians quickly leave their humble beginnings behind and become big-headed when they sense how much power and influence they now have. Many become rude, abusive, competitive and even ruthless. This is a far cry from being "gentle and humble."

Each one of us should, "as a person dedicated to God... pursue... gentleness" (1 Timothy 6:11 - NET Bible).

Even when engaging unbelievers, we are instructed to do so with gentleness. Scripture tells us to "in your hearts honor Christ the Lord as holy, always being prepared to make a defense to anyone who asks you for a reason for the hope that is in you; yet do it with gentleness and respect" (1 Peter 3:15 - ESV). Nothing turns non-Christians away faster than an arrogant, holier-than-thou attitude and an aggressive approach. We sometimes seem to forget that we too were saved by grace, by no merit of our own.

We should avoid those things which provoke unnecessary conflicts because, "The Lord's bond-servant must not be quarrelsome, but be kind to all, able to teach, patient when wronged, with gentleness correcting those who are in opposition, if perhaps God may grant them repentance leading to the knowledge of the truth" (2 Timothy 2:22-25 - NASB). This same approach and attitude also apply when dealing with Christians who have fallen into sin. "Brothers and sisters, if someone is caught in a sin, you who live by the Spirit should restore that person gently. But watch yourselves, or you also may be tempted" (Galatians 6:1 - NIV).

Whether it be relating to others, witnessing, correcting, and restoring others who have slipped or fallen, all should be done with a gentle spirit. When wronged, confronting opposing views and dealing with others in day-to-day relationships, how consistent are you in practicing gentleness?

Kingdom Value #17: Self-Control

One thing is clear to those who take following Christ seriously: *self* is incapable of controlling itself. I suspect most if not all Christians have come to realize that we only have "self-control" when we are Spirit-controlled. That is the underlying theme of this section: the fruit of the Spirit's control in the lives of believers.

What most contemporary versions call self-control, the King James calls "temperance" (Galatians 5:23). The Greek *egkrateia* means "self-mastery, self-restraint," and "the virtue of one who masters his desires and passions, especially his sensual appetites."[8]

The wisest man on earth once said that "a man without self-control is like a city broken into and left without walls" (Proverbs 25:28 - ESV). Before modern technology, walls were essential to the protection of cities. And since there were usually no centralized governments that could muster troops in time, walled cities and towns were mostly on their own. And enemies abounded. Therefore, it was unthinkable not to have walls around the city.

The comparison is striking: people who have no self-control open themselves right up to attacks. Once attacked they are left with no defense against future assaults. They might as well paint a target on their heart.

In an almost reverse illustration, Proverbs also states it is "better to have self-control than to conquer a city" (Proverbs 16:32b - NLT). How many army officers can command thousands of troops with a high degree of success, only to lose control of their own behavior as they try to relate to their spouse and children. One of the highest ranking American generals was, not too long ago, relieved of duty because he was trusting confidential information to the woman with whom he was having a hidden, adulterous affair.

Celebrities have learned how to woo crowds and wow fans, only to crash and burn when dealing with their own inner demons. It is more important to master anger management than professional management; or to rule over your emotions than to govern a whole nation.

Samson, a Judge over Israel for 20 years (Judges 15:20), comes to mind. He was set apart for the Lord from birth for a special mission, God blessed him as he grew up, and God's Spirit began to work mightily in his life (Judges 13:5, 24, 25). But he had a self-control issue. He had a weakness for beautiful young women. And they all just happened to be Philistine (Philistia was Israel's greatest enemy at the time).

Though Samson had tremendous physical strength, and though many times the "Spirit of the Lord came upon him in power" (Judges 14:19), he still could not control his sexual urges. "One day Samson went to the Philistine town of Gaza and spent the night with a prostitute" (Judges 16:1 - NLT). Then, "some time later Samson fell in love with a woman named Delilah" (Judges 16:4a - NLT). The rest is history (see more under *Self-denial – Kingdom Value#54*).

Peter taught that knowing is not enough. "To knowledge," he said, we must "add self-control" (2 Peter 1:6 - GW). That is the sticking point. Christianity is not that complicated in theory. It's where the rubber meets the road that things can get messy. Because the problem usually is not that we do not know enough, it is that our emotions get in the way, our fleshly desires are ever clamoring to be met, the world is constantly trying to entice us, and the enemy is vigorously tempting and attacking us. To forever be on guard gets tiring if we do not learn to rest in the Lord's strength and allow Him to fight the battle. Of course sometimes we do... and sometimes we don't. It's something each believer must learn to deal with and overcome (see *Overcoming – Kingdom Value #62* and *Being Spirit Controlled – Kingdom value #52*).

Paul preached "about righteousness and self-control" (Acts 24:25). He taught that there is no law against self-control (Galatians 5:23). He warned that in the last days people would be "without self-control" (2 Timothy 3:3). He believed that if singles "cannot exercise self-control, they should marry" (1 Corinthians 7:9 - ESV). He felt we should be highly motivated to live a life of self-control and reminded us that "every athlete exercises self-control in all things. They do it to receive a perishable wreath, but we an imperishable" (1 Corinthians 9:25 - ESV).

James taught that being self-controlled includes controlling the tongue. He admits "we all stumble in many ways" but discovered that "if anyone does not stumble in what he says, he is a mature man who is also able to control his whole body" (James 3:2 - HCSB; see verses 3-12).

Paul encouraged Timothy by saying that "God gave us a spirit not of fear but of power and love and self-control" (2 Timothy 1:7 - ESV). And church leaders, he said, must be "self-controlled" and "disciplined" (Titus 1:7, 8 - ESV; see also 1 Timothy 3:2). He advised Titus to "teach the older men to exercise self-control, to be worthy of respect, and to live wisely. They must have sound faith and be filled with love and patience" (Titus 2:2 - NLT). This is great advice for everyone who follows Jesus, regardless of their gender, age, or position.

Where are you on the self-control scale?

Chapter

5

The Five Purposes of the Church Kingdom Values

*They devoted themselves to the apostles' **teaching** and to the **fellowship**, to the **breaking of bread** and to **prayer**. A sense of awe came over everyone, and the apostles performed many wonders and signs. All **the believers were together** and had everything in common. Selling their possessions and goods, they shared with anyone who was in need. With on e accord they continued to meet daily in the temple courts and to **break bread** from house to house, sharing their meals with gladness and sincerity of heart, **praising God** and enjoying the favor of all the people. And **the Lord added** to their number daily **those who were being saved**.*
Acts 2:42-47 - BSB

The Church is the Kingdom's agency or "official representative" in the world today. There are many "in the church" who are not "in Christ." They go to church and may have been accepted as members, but they have not repented and believed in the King of kings. The redeemed, those who are members of the Body of Christ, compose the true Church. And it is the true Church we are addressing when we say that to be in the Church is to be in the Kingdom. And to be in the Kingdom is to be in or belong to the Church.

We cannot bypass the Church and decide simply to "be in the Kingdom." If we have been redeemed, the Holy Spirit has given us one or more spiritual gifts, ministries and activities (1 Corinthians 12:4), to be used in the local church, to serve God and others. Doing so is a very large part of what it means to be fruitful.

For this reason, Church and Kingdom Values coincide. Keep this in mind as we take a look at the five-fold purpose or ministries of the universal Church.

Kingdom Value #18: Worship

There is a sense in which the whole notion of worship eludes me. I realize we were created with the purpose of bringing glory to God and worshiping Him. I accept the fact that we owe our existence to God and He is absolutely deserving of our adoration. I just have a hard time understanding why *God* would be interested in our worship. And yet He is.

So, I have sought to understand this issue a little better and this is what I have learned. It came to me that worship is the only thing we can give to God which has not first come to us from Him. Everything else we offer **back** to Him, as it came from Him in the first place. Why, He Has given us our very lives!

We can dedicate our time, talents and treasures to God, but that is more like a child offering her mom a bite of her food. Like when my granddaughter Heidi would claim her toys, clothes, and food are "mine"– a word she employed daily with strong conviction. Yet I know they are only hers because her parents gave these things to her in the first place. But when she spontaneously surprises her mom with a kiss, her mother melts in sweet satisfaction, because that is something that comes from her heart, from her own initiative.

It is true that worshiping God is the only appropriate response from us. He is so superior to us that we can scarcely imagine His magnificence, power, authority, and glory. There is a fact which will forever make all the difference between God and us: He is the Creator, we are the created. That is a fundamental and essential difference. And that will never change. As the Creator, God is the only One Who deserves and is permitted to receive our worship. Unless you are God, accepting worship is strictly forbidden, no matter how glorious and powerful you are (Jeremiah 25:6; Acts 12:22, 23; Revelation 14:11; 19:10; 20:4; 22:9). The very first of the Ten Commandments is, "Thou shalt have no other gods before me" (Exodus 20:3 - KJV). The second command forbids making idols and warns: "You shall not bow down to them or worship them; for I, the LORD your God, am a jealous God" (Exodus 20:5a - NIV).

Worship involves praising God for Who He is and what He has done, and sanctifying His name by keeping it holy – separate from the vulgar and mundane. True worshipers seek the Lord with all their hearts and worship Him in spirit and truth. That is because worship is a spiritual connection with God which can only take place when we are completely honest and open with Him.

God told the people of Israel they were not to bow down to any other "gods" (or idols) because He is "a jealous God" (Exodus 20:5). God told Moses to tell the people, "Hear, O Israel: The Lord our God, the Lord is one! You shall love the Lord your God with all your heart, with all your soul, and with all your strength" (Deuteronomy 6:4, 5 - NKJV). God demands our complete devotion and exclusive adoration.

God is not the only one who wants our worship. Satan has been trying to steal humanity's devotion away from God from the beginning. In an insolent act of presumption, he even requested to be worshiped by our Lord! But Jesus responded, "Get out of here, Satan,' Jesus told him. 'For the Scriptures say, 'You must worship the LORD your God and serve only him'" (Matthew 4:10 - NLT).

Worship is the outpouring of reverent love, deep respect, and an intense desire to honor, exalt and praise the God of Creation. It is not merely a feeling. It is a lifelong commitment to surrender, submit, obey, enjoy fellowship with and serve the King of kings. This commitment is what the Bible calls a covenant.

First, God's love captivates us and "Christ's love compels us" (2 Corinthians 5:14 - HCSB). "We love him, because he first loved us" (1 John 4:19 - KJV). We then voluntarily surrender our will and our life to God by relinquishing the control and full rights over our lives by handing them over to Him (Galatians 2:20). Then, as imitators of Christ, we submit our life plan entirely to the Father (Psalm 37:5; John 5:19). We follow His guidance and fit into His plans.

Consequently, we live a life of obedience to our Lord. Jesus said that to love Him equaled obeying Him. He told His disciples that, "If you love Me, you will keep My commands" (John 14:15 - HCSB). A natural outcome of obedience is service, which results in producing much fruit, by which we glorify the Father (John 15:8). This, in turn, creates joy in the heart of the believer: "Serve the LORD with gladness! Come into his presence with singing!" (Psalm 100:2 - ESV).

Worshiping and serving God are sometimes synonymous in the Bible (see Daniel 7:10). One of the most tangible ways we can serve God is by serving others – serving them as an offering to God. That is why "if anyone boasts, 'I love God,' and goes right on hating his brother or sister, thinking nothing of it, he is a liar. If he won't love the person he can see, how can he love the God he can't see? The command we have from Christ is blunt: Loving God includes loving people. You've got to love both" (1 John 4:20, 21 - MSG; see also verses 11 and 12; see also James 2:8-15).

Worshipers show devotion by approaching God with genuine faith, sincere humility, profound respect, and the highest admiration. This flows spontaneously from those who are thankful to God and love Him passionately with all their heart, soul, mind and strength (Hebrews 11:6; James 4:10; Luke 11:2; 1 Chronicles 29:17; Deuteronomy 6:9). Worshiping the Lord is a spiritual experience which requires openness and honesty. Jesus explained that "God is spirit, and those who worship him must worship in spirit and truth" (John 4:24 - ESV).

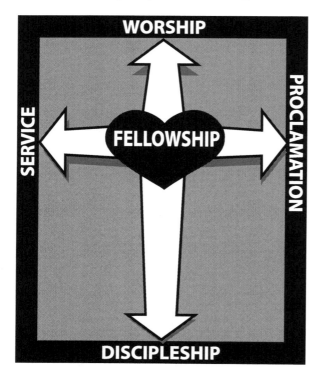

Sometimes our emotions have been so battered by life's struggles that we have a hard time expressing our worship – especially in public. That may be one reason God gave us music because it has the special ability to aid us in our worship: it puts us in the right "mood" or mindset and helps us to express our deepest feelings. Music draws out those deep feelings we haven't been able to outwardly express. Psalms, hymns, and choruses have the words that sometimes escape us and allow us to participate in corporate worship that is harmonious, pleasing, and meaningful.

A couple of days after writing the above paragraph I went to preach at a little country church my father had pastored years ago, in the state of Rio de Janeiro, Brazil. To my surprise, they had invited a group of singing men from a nearby city to come and help with the worship. To hear them singing in perfect harmony and to see the enthusiasm radiating from their facial expressions, lifted my spirit and created an environment of true worship for the whole congregation.

Worship is an act of faith and flows from the heart, so we may not be able to grasp its deepest meanings or logic. But that should not inhibit our heartfelt practice and expression of grateful praise and adoration. After all, "Our Lord and God, You are worthy to receive glory and honor and power, because You have created all things, and because of Your will they exist and were created" (Revelation 4:11 - HCSB).

Where do you stand when it comes to your personal worship of God?

Kingdom Value #19: Fellowship

"Where is everybody?!" The commercial showed a man running frantically through a downtown street in a large metropolitan area. With the wind blowing and papers flying, no one responded because there was no one to be found. The streets were deserted. This solitary man was desperate to find somebody – anybody. This commercial and movies with this reoccurring theme show how eerie it would be to wake up one day and be the last person alive on planet earth. Or, to be stranded for years without any form of human contact, on a deserted island, on the backside of nowhere. Such as in the 2000 movie "Cast Away," starring Tom Hanks.

"The LORD God said, 'It is not good for the man to be alone. I will make a companion for him who corresponds to him'" (Genesis 2:18 - Net Bible). Although the immediate context of this verse is that of man and woman, husband and wife, we can extrapolate on the principle and apply it to human relations in general. We were not made to be alone. We were wired for fellowship.

We crave finding those with whom we can relate and with whom we might participate in some meaningful way. Teens long to be accepted by their peers and will do almost anything to fit in. Youth who have all but been discarded by their parents are easy prey to gangs who lend them worth and meaning, even if they have to break the law and risk their lives to be accepted.

Research has shown that being accepted is what most people are seeking when they search for a church home.

Fellowship, in the Biblical sense, is one of those unique features of life which are not a means to an end, but an end in themselves. Fellowship is a key component of worshiping and to glorifying God (see *Worship – Kingdom Value #18* and *Glorifying God – Kingdom Value #35*). We were *created* to worship, glorify and enjoy fellowship with God. Those are our end goals, our very core purpose.

But we were also created to have fellowship with one another, in the Body of Christ. I like the graphic which shows the five purposes of the Church, which appears in the form of a cross, having the vertical pole relate to God with "worship" at the top and "teaching" or "discipleship" at the bottom; then the horizontal pole which has "service" on one side and "evangelism" or "proclamation" on the other side. Right in the middle, where both poles converge, there is the word "fellowship." That is so apropos because fellowship is the only one of the five purposes that is an end-goal for **both** our relationship with God and with "one another."

Notice in the following verse how the purpose of proclamation has the end goal of fellowship – with other believers and with God the Father and the Son. John said that "what we have seen and heard we proclaim to you also, so that you too may have fellowship with us; and indeed our fellowship is with the Father, and with His Son Jesus Christ" (1 John 1:3 - NASB). We share the Good News as a means to the end that people will be saved and enter into fellowship with God and with others who have also been saved.

Fellowship has the purpose of drawing us together in unity and harmony (*Kingdom Value #25*), so we can adequately function as the Body of Christ. Fellowship means enjoying – not just tolerating – our brothers and sisters in Christ. Learning more about them, what part they are playing in the Kingdom, and perhaps how we can join or support them. Fellowship is what families do.

96

In the parable of the Prodigal Son (Luke 15:11-32) there are three main characters, each with a different set of values and priorities. The youngest son's core value was *having* (money and pleasure). The eldest's son's core value was *doing* (accomplishing and self-realization). But the father's core value was *relating* (nurturing fellowship). As such he was not focused on possessions or accomplishments, but on his sons themselves. He loved *them*. And this led him to desire fellowship with them – and that they enjoy fellowship with each other.

I once participated in a meeting at a national mission board, where a colleague who had recently returned to the field asked for input about becoming a member at a certain church. He was told that it would be best not to join the church he had mentioned because it was in a turf war with a couple of other churches, and many churches in the city had taken sides with one or the other. So, he was informed, if he were to become a member there, "certain doors would close" when he visited other churches to promote his work. Other similar cases were discussed on a national level, as politics and power struggles were causing dissension among fellow Christians, their churches or whole associations of churches. And this national mission board had to navigate this minefield as they tried to put their plans together.

Paul had to deal with similar issues in his day (see 1 Corinthians 3).

The lack of love and harmony (see *Love – Kingdom Value #9*) directly impact fellowship and damage the witness of churches and Christians before an observing world. Jesus told His disciples plainly: "This is how everyone will know that you are my disciples, if you have love for one another" (John 13:35 - ISV). How much stronger and effective would churches be if there were a true fellowship *in* and *among* them!

Communion and communication come from the same Latin root, meaning to make something common among those who share (as in common knowledge or common possession). Nothing promotes fellowship (*koinonia*) like an activity which is almost synonymous with fellowship in the Bible: "breaking bread" together. It is during meals that we best share our lives and take the time to enjoy each other.

Besides the rich symbolism behind the Lord's Supper, the very fact that believers came together to share a special meal was a testimony to the fact that they held the most important beliefs and values in common. That they loved each other and wished to be together. That they enjoyed sweet fellowship as the Body of Christ.

In the early church breaking bread may have taken place every Sunday, along with teaching and preaching (Acts 20:7; 11). Shortly after Pentecost, believers new and old "devoted themselves to the apostles' teaching, to the fellowship, to the breaking of bread, and to the prayers" (Acts 2:42 - HCSB).

When Jesus invited a lukewarm church to return to fellowship with Him, here is how He expressed Himself: "Behold, I stand at the door and knock. If anyone hears my voice and opens the door, I will come in to him and eat with him, and he with me" (Revelation 3:20 - ESV).

We were created for fellowship – with God and with each other. And since fellowship with each are so closely related, indicate below how you're doing in this area.

Kingdom Value #20: Discipleship

Little kids like to step in their father or mother's footprints in the snow or sand. It's a heartwarming scenario. In the same way, discipleship means following and stepping in the footprints of our Master. Learning from His example. Imitating or mirroring His character, attitude and actions (see "The Son of God and the Mirroring Principle" in *The King of the Kingdom*, volume four of this series).

In that spirit, Ruth told Naomi, "Do not urge me to leave you or to return from following you. For where you go I will go, and where you lodge I will lodge. Your people shall be my people, and your God my God" (Ruth 1:16 - ESV). Ruth was a radical follower. She liked being influenced by Naomi. She wanted to learn from her, become like her, live with or by her, and worship just like her.

We learn by observation and imitation. And most people learn by asking questions (instead of reading instructions). My granddaughter Heidi is like a sponge. Even as early as four years of age she would pick up everything the adults around her were saying. Frequently she will surprise those adults by asking them to clarify what they meant, sometimes hours later. "Oh, you were listening to *that*?" Yes, she sure was. Heard every word. Then there is Derek, my grandson. He's younger, and he is like a recorder: he repeats everything his sister says. It's his way of putting phrases together and trying out new vocabulary. That's how he explores and finds out about the world around him.

It's also how we learn more about God and His word. Not just by asking questions, but observing how the pastor, the Sunday School teacher, and the average member behave in the different circumstances of life. There is a strong argument for house churches because they are more like real life and can better teach new Christians how to apply Kingdom Values to their own lives. How the hosts welcome their visitors into their home, handle the kids, clean up after the guests, and relate to each other. In the artificial and even staged settings of most churches, this is an impossibility.

When Jesus invited people to "come, follow me," the invitation usually came with a specific challenge. He called Peter and his brother Andrew to abandon their work as fishermen, and said, "Follow me, and I will turn you into fishers of people" (Matthew 4:19 - NET Bible). Jesus challenged the rich young ruler to leave his riches behind and, "Then come, follow Me" (Matthew 19:21 - HCSB). Even to His closest followers, to whom He had just shared about His impending suffering and death, Jesus said, "Whoever wants to be my disciple must deny themselves and take up their cross and follow me" (Matthew 16:24 - NIV).

Jesus' followers were called believers and later Christians, but while He was still with them they were mostly referred to as His disciples. The term is used throughout the Gospels of those who followed Him daily and more closely during His earthly ministry. Although "the Twelve," made up of His apostles, was a closed group, Jesus invited His audience to become His disciples as well. But He warned them as well: "Whoever doesn't carry his cross and follow me can't be my disciple" (Luke 14:27 - ISV).

He told his listeners, "Anyone who loves their father or mother more than me is not worthy of me; anyone who loves their son or daughter more than me is not worthy of me" (Matthew 10:37 - NIV). He also told them that "No one, after putting his hand to the plow and looking back, is fit for the kingdom of God" (Luke 9:62 - NASB). Being Jesus' disciple demands loving Him above all, never giving up, and never looking back.

As He was leaving and going back to the Father, Jesus left His disciples with the mission of making new disciples. Here are His instructions: "Therefore, go and make disciples of all the nations, baptizing them in the name of the Father and the Son and the Holy Spirit. Teach these new disciples to obey all the commands I have given you. And be sure of this: I am with you always, even to the end of the age" (Matthew 28:19, 20 - NLT; see *Proclamation – Kingdom Value #21* and *Missions – Kingdom Value #50*).

So much has been written about this, the Great Commission, but as a colleague of mine pointed out, we are not just to teach *about* Jesus' commands; we are to "teach these new disciples to *obey*" them. That means we should not dwell on the theoretical (as much as I love that), but the practical application of all that Jesus taught and commanded. By doing so, both discipler and disciple benefit, both growing stronger in their faith and walk. One realizes he or she must set the example and the other knows he or she must learn to follow it. And in the process both practice what is being preached.

In relation to the Church, discipleship includes the effort of teaching the Biblical truth; to *in*form in order to *trans*form. Jesus asked the Father for His disciples, that He would "sanctify them by the truth; Your word is truth" (John 17:17 - HCSB). Churches need strong teaching ministries and willing mentors who can disciple the newbies in the faith.

If we are following the Lord Jesus, then discipleship will necessarily include studying the life, teachings and character of Jesus, our King, Master and role model. To better appreciate God's Kingdom and plans through the ages, a good Bible overview will help us to better understand how things come together from Genesis to Revelation. Then we can better focus on understanding and applying Kingdom Values and Principles as well as the disciplines of Christian life, such as the practice of daily devotionals, a consistent prayer life, witnessing, contributing, and participating in local church life.

We will simultaneously need to discover in the Word, through prayer and a support group, how not only to survive spiritual warfare but to thrive under trials and temptations. Paul reminded Timothy, his disciple, to "be diligent to present yourself approved to God, a worker who doesn't need to be ashamed, correctly teaching the word of truth" (2 Timothy 2: 15 - HCSB).

There is a cost to discipleship and there are many challenges along the way. But could there ever be anything more meaningful and rewarding than following in the footsteps of the King of kings? Where are you on this journey? Has someone ever discipled you? Have you invested in someone's life by discipling them? What kind of follower of Jesus are you? There are always opportunities to grow!

KV20 – DISCIPLESHIP

| Consistently practice | Sometimes practice | Struggle | Mostly fail | Continually fail |

Kingdom Value #21: Proclamation

The Church is tasked with the mission to go to the whole world and preach the Gospel. This "Good News" is that God has paid our debt in full through His Son and, by His mercy and grace, offers forgiveness, salvation, eternal life and access to His Kingdom to those who repent and place their faith in Him as Lord and Savior. John the Baptist and Jesus both proclaimed: "Repent, because the kingdom of heaven has come near!" (Matthew 3:1-3 - HCSB; Mark 1:15).

The Apostle Paul defined "the ministry which I received from the Lord Jesus" as being "to testify solemnly of the gospel of the grace of God" (Acts 20:24 - NASB). He told the believers in Corinth that, "by this gospel you are saved, if you hold firmly to the word I preached to you. Otherwise, you have believed in vain" (1 Corinthians 15:2 - NIV).

Announcing the Good News to others is every believer's privilege and responsibility. King David said, "I have not hidden Your righteousness within my heart; I have spoken of Your faithfulness and Your salvation; I have not concealed Your lovingkindness and Your truth from the great congregation" (Psalm 40:10 - NASB). Another psalm invites us to "Sing to the LORD; praise his name. Each day proclaim the good news that he saves" (Psalm 96:2 - NLT).

Proclaiming God's grace, mercy and Kingdom is one of the most needed and positive things we can do. Isaiah exclaimed: "How beautiful on the mountains are the feet of those who bring good news, who proclaim peace, who bring good tidings, who proclaim salvation, who say to Zion, 'Your God reigns!'" (Isaiah 52:7 - NIV).

The full term used of the Gospel is "the Good News of the Kingdom," which appears in many New Testament passages. Let us take a look at a few of those.

Both in the Old and the New Testament times, God's message was proclaimed. However, there were differences, which Jesus summarized by explaining that, "Until John the Baptist, the law of Moses and the messages of the prophets were your guides. But now the Good News of the Kingdom of God is preached, and everyone is eager to get in" (Luke 16:16 - NLT).

In His own ministry Jesus "went to all the towns and villages, teaching in their synagogues, preaching the good news of the kingdom," because "He felt compassion for them." He told His disciples to "pray to the Lord of the harvest to send out workers into His harvest" (Matthew 9:35-38 - HCSB). But they were not only to pray; they were also to go. Jesus gave the Twelve – His inner circle – authority "and he sent them out to proclaim the kingdom of God and to heal" (Luke 9:1, 2 - ESV). Jesus told an individual who wanted to be His disciple to "go and proclaim the kingdom of God" (Luke 9:60b).

After sending the Twelve, Jesus sent out the seventy-two disciples to proclaim the Gospel with specific instructions, warning especially those who rejected the message "to be sure of this: the kingdom of God is near" (Luke 10:11 - NIV). Then He told them this ***proclamation Kingdom Principle***: "Whoever listens to you listens to Me. Whoever rejects you rejects Me. And whoever rejects Me rejects the One who sent Me" (Luke 10:16 - HCSB. This verse is a prime example of the Mirroring Principle, explained in volume four of this series).

Philip, "the first missionary named in Scripture and the first to be given the title 'evangelist,'" was one of the original seven deacons (Acts 6:5; 8:5; 21:8).[1] After severe persecution, masterminded by Saul, had broken out, many believers in Jerusalem had been scattered to other places. Philip had gone to the city of Samaria "and preached Christ to them." There he performed miracles, healed the sick and cast out demons. "But when they believed Philip as he preached the things concerning the kingdom of God and the name of Jesus Christ, both men and women were baptized" (Acts 8:5, 12 - NKJV).

After his conversion and being on three missionary journeys, Paul went to Jerusalem. Because he believed the Good News was also available to Gentiles, he was falsely accused and arrested (Acts 21:27-36). When the situation became precarious, Paul, being a Roman citizen, appealed to Caesar. When Paul arrived in Rome, he was placed under house arrest. He first called the local Jewish leadership. "They arranged to meet Paul on a certain day, and came in even larger numbers to the place where he was staying. He witnessed to them from morning till evening, explaining about the kingdom of God, and from the Law of Moses and from the Prophets he tried to persuade them about Jesus" (Acts 28:22, 23 - NIV).

Some accepted his message, but others did not. Paul remained there for two more years and kept an open door for all who were interested in the Gospel message. During that time, "He proclaimed the kingdom of God and taught about the Lord Jesus Christ—with all boldness and without hindrance!" (Acts 28:30, 31 - NIV)

We all need to be more like Paul in his zeal to proclaim the Good News! Despite the difficulties, we can be encouraged by Jesus' prophecy concerning the proclamation effort in the last days. He said that "this gospel of the kingdom will be proclaimed throughout the world as a testimony to all nations, and then the end will come" (Matthew 24:14 - ISV).

Proclamation Kingdom Principles:

1. Proclaiming the Kingdom involves calling for repentance and faith.
2. Proclamation is one of the main missions of the Church.
3. "Whoever listens to you listens to Me. Whoever rejects you rejects Me. And whoever rejects Me rejects the One who sent Me" (Luke 10:16 - HCSB).
4. It is an ideal situation when we can proclaim the Gospel "with all boldness and without hindrance!"
5. The Gospel of the kingdom will be proclaimed all over the world before the end (Matthew 24:14).

Where would you situate yourself on the proclamation scale?

Kingdom Value #22: Service

They say that "money makes the world go 'round,'" but, of course, that is not true. *Service* makes the world go 'round. Money just pays for it. It is someone's labor that puts the butter on the table. Well, actually, the work of a host of people, from the farmers to the dairy industry workers, the packaging company employees to the distributors, to the grocers and advertising and marketing staff. You get the idea. Service makes things happen.

Service is not only what moves society, it is the *modus operandi* of the Kingdom. Service is a means of blessing others – by providing such things as material help, physical care, spiritual encouragement and discipleship. Serving can be as simple as offering someone a cup of water (Mark 9:41). When we serve others, we are ultimately serving the Lord. Jesus Himself taught us this principle when He said that "the King will reply, 'I tell you the truth, whatever you did for one of the least of these brothers of mine, you did for me" (Matthew 25:40).

Service is key to many other Kingdom Values. We cannot love, for instance, without somehow serving the object of our love. We cannot bear fruit without serving God and people. And serving according to God's plan means using our gifts in the context of the church and our natural talents in society. Among the list of spiritual gifts is that of service itself. Paul says that "if your gift is serving others, serve them well" (Romans 12:7 - NLT). The Greek word for service or ministry is *diakonia*, from which we get "deacon." Paul also mentions the similar gift of helps or helping (1 Corinthians 12:28), which refers to one who aids others. We are all supposed to serve, but those with this gift are better equipped and more eagerly enjoy lending a helping hand.

As we think about the 5 purposes or missions of the church, it is important to stress that the church is responsible for ministering to its members, to its community and abroad. This usually takes on the form of caring for the poor, needy and discouraged. But the needs and opportunities are limitless. Some churches bless their communities by picking up the trash in parks and alongside highways. Others minister in nursing homes and hospitals.

Why is it so easy to talk about service and so hard to *just do it*? Because we are primarily concerned with our own interests, ministries and projects. To stop, listen and lend a helping hand requires time and effort. Especially when the service is recurring, like housework. We need to be reminded that even though we would personally prefer to crash on the sofa and watch TV instead of helping around the house, the Bible says we are to prefer... one another. That means putting the interests and needs of others first. That is the nature of true service (see *Serving one another, Kingdom Value #30*, below).

Here is an astounding Kingdom truth: even God the King serves! God has served us by giving us life and providing for us. He gave us the best He has and withheld nothing from us. "Since he did not spare even his own Son but gave him up for us all, won't he also give us everything else?" (Romans 8:32 - NLT). "Everything else" includes our eternal inheritance and reigning with Christ!

This is at odds with what the world system does. People usually employ their authority to be served, and power to be self-serving. God's Kingdom, on the other hand, is based on servant leadership. Power and authority equal being empowered to better serve and bless others.

Even Jesus, our ultimate model in all things, "did not come to be served, but to serve" (Matthew 20:28 - NIV). Although He is a mighty King, He came as the "Suffering Servant" or "the Servant of the Lord" (Isaiah 42:1-4; 49:1-6; 50:4-9; 52:13-53:12). He is our model because He served and died in our place and always put the Father's will and people's needs ahead of His own (Philippians 2:6, 7; John 13:13-15).

When God gives someone a position of authority – be it the CEO of a multibillion-dollar corporation or the father of a small family, He does it so the leader

104

may serve those under his responsibility. How refreshing to learn that great leaders like John Maxwell, Ken Blanchard and Chick-fil-A's Mark Miller coach other leaders by teaching them to serve – and to do so like Jesus (read *The Secret, What Great Leaders Know and Do*).

Even in the Eternal Kingdom, when we will reign with our Lord, our positions of authority will be given not so that we may be served but so we may minister to those under our care. This means everyone will be taken care of, there will be a tremendous amount of fellowship, and no one will have time to be selfish, whine or compare themselves with others.

Have you learned just how fundamental it is to serve God and others? Do you practice serving with a cheerful heart? Are there areas of service where you could improve?

Chapter

6

The Mutuality Kingdom Values

Do to others whatever you would like them to do to you.
This is the essence of all that is taught in the law and the prophets.
Matthew 7:12 - NLT

The mutuality values take into account the fact that "we, though many, are one body in Christ, and individually members one of another" (Romans 12:5 - ESV). As Christians and therefore Kingdom citizens, we were not meant to walk alone. It is essential that we "be mutually encouraged by each other's faith" (Romans 1:12 - ESV).

Kingdom Value #23: Forgiving *one another*

No earthly relationship can get very far if there is no forgiveness involved since we all sin and fail. We all make mistakes. Plenty of them. Even after entering the Kingdom. The Bible makes that clear when it says "we all stumble in many ways" (James 3:2a - NASB). Which is why we need the kind of love that "covers a multitude of sins" (1 Peter 4:8 - NASB). One of the most important lessons we can learn in life is how to forgive and how to *ask* for forgiveness (see James 5:16).

Forgiving is so much easier to handle as a concept. But when someone wrongs us, hurts our feelings, treats us unfairly, lies about us or harms one of our loved ones, our blood boils and we just want to get even. Many times something inside of us cries out and just wants to put the offender in his or her place. However, that is not our prerogative. "For we know the one who said, 'I will take revenge. I will pay them back.' He also said, 'The LORD will judge his own people'" (Hebrews 10:30

- NLT). Forgiving means no pay-backs. We must "see that no one repays anyone evil for evil, but always seek to do good to one another and to everyone" (1 Thessalonians 5:15 - ESV).

Now, as a side note, it is important to make a distinction between forgiving and trusting. We are commanded to forgive, but the offending party is responsible for regaining our trust. We forgive and treat the offender with dignity and respect, but we do not leave our wallet laying around a known kleptomaniac.

There is some motivation that will help us decide to forgive (forgiveness is both a command and a decision that doesn't always count on the support of our emotions). First, we must remember that the Lord set the example by forgiving us, and we are to mirror His spirit of forgiveness. Scripture commands us: "as the Lord has forgiven you, so you also must forgive" (Colossians 3:13b - ESV). It also says, "Be kind to each other, tenderhearted, forgiving one another, just as God through Christ has forgiven you" (Ephesians 4:32 - NLT).

Second, if you're still not motivated enough, consider this: if you do not forgive others, God won't forgive you. Forgiving is so important that it is the only part of the Lord's Prayer to receive further treatment by our Lord. He prayed: "And forgive us our debts, as we also have forgiven our debtors." Then He set forth a Kingdom Principle: "for if you forgive people their wrongdoing, your heavenly Father will forgive you as well. But if you don't forgive people, your Father will not forgive your wrongdoing" (Matthew 6:12; 14, 15 - HCSB).

The Lord also dedicated a whole parable (one of my favorite) to the concept of forgiving others or forfeiting God's forgiveness (Matthew 18:21-35). Jesus compared the Kingdom of Heaven to this king who forgave his servant an incalculable debt because he begged for mercy, only to see this same servant turn around and demand that a fellow-servant, who owed him infinitely less, pay on the spot or be thrown in jail.

When word of this found its way back to the king, he reinstated the debt and threw this wicked servant in jail until he could pay it all off. Of course, he never would be able to do so. Considering what he owed the king "could be over a billion dollars in today's currency"[1], it could easily take 25,000 years to pay off this debt. And to think his fellow servant only owed him an amount worth three-months salary! When Jesus finishes the story He says "that's what my heavenly Father will do to you if you refuse to forgive your brothers and sisters from your heart" (Matthew 18:35 - NLT).

Jesus told this parable in response to Peter's famous question "how many times could my brother sin against me and I forgive him? As many as seven times?" And, of course, Jesus' response was "not as many as seven... but 70 times seven" (Matthew 18:21, 22 - HCSB). We usually think of this as 490 separate offenses. But, as someone has suggested, it can also apply to the same offense which keeps coming back to mind. We've forgiven the person and tried to put it behind us, but something happens that triggers that memory again. Every time that happens, we need to decide all over again to forgive that same offense.

It also applies to separate offenses, as Jesus taught on a different occasion. He warned us to "be on your guard. If your brother sins, rebuke him, and if he repents, forgive him. And if he sins against you seven times in a day, and comes back to you seven times, saying, 'I repent,' you must forgive him" (Luke 17:3, 4 - HCSB). The value is forgiveness, the principle is forgiving whenever one repents. That is the secret to harmony in the church, success in marriage and peace in the family.

I grew up as a missionary kid (MK) in Brazil. Many of the MKs in our mission were caught up in the changing times and their parents were unable to understand or deal with them. It was the 70's. Missionary Robbie Ellis felt called to work with us; so she organized annual MK camps. I missed the first one, but at the annual mission meeting, the MKs who had gone to the camp were given the opportunity to share what happened there.

There were close to 200 missionaries in attendance and they were all intensely focused on the testimonies that were being given. God had shown up and had changed lives. Now He was moving in the hearts of the adults who were receiving the Good News of this breakthrough. Someone would stand, point to a fellow missionary across the aisle and say: "For years I have held a grudge against you. This stops here. I now want to ask you to please forgive me." The colleague would also stand up and promptly forgive and ask to be forgiven. Then they would give each other a big hug. There were misty eyes everywhere.

This went on spontaneously for close to an hour. You could feel the powerful and sweet presence of the Lord, touching lives, healing wounds, restoring relationships and bringing about a spirit of unity and harmony. This was so exciting it just had to be shared, so some went out to witness to the hotel employees. Incredible things happen when God shows up. But many times we keep that from happening simply because we refuse to forgive each other with our whole heart.

Forgiveness Kingdom Principles:
• When we forgive we act like our Heavenly Father and so become more like Him.

- When we forgive we make way for the Holy Spirit to act – to save, heal, restore and use lives.

- The Kingdom is like a King Who forgave an incalculable debt because His servant earnestly pleaded for His compassion (Matthew 18:26, 32).

- The Kingdom is like a King Who expects His servants to forgive each other (Matthew 18:33, 35).

- If we forgive others, God will forgive us.

- If we don't forgive others, God won't forgive us either.

- God has the right to revoke our forgiveness if, after forgiving us, we do not forgive others.

- We must forgive others when they repent, even if this happens several times a day.
- Revenge is not ours to take; that is God's prerogative. We are told, "Do not repay anyone evil for evil... live at peace with everyone. Do not take revenge, my friends, but leave room for God's wrath..." (Romans 12:17-20 - NIV).

How good are you at forgiving? Is there someone you need to forgive right now?

Kingdom Value #24: Honoring *one another*

Let's begin by stating what honoring one another is not. It is not playing politics. It is not patting each other on the back and putting each other on display or a pedestal. It is not making stars out of the brightest and most talented among us. It is not reproducing Oscar night among our partners in the Kingdom.

Jesus said, "I do not receive honor from men," or "human praise" (John 5:41 - NKJV; ISV). And He asked the Jewish leadership "how can you believe, who receive honor from one another, and do not seek the honor that comes from the only God? (John 5:44 - NKJV).

The kind of honor we are looking for is the kind that tries to please God first and foremost. And, as it relates to others, it is an attitude of respect and dignity, putting them before our own need for recognition. That goes against our human nature and is a tough thing to do. But we are encouraged to "be devoted to one another in brotherly love" and learn to "honor one another above yourselves" (Romans 12:10). This is a God thing and only He can produce this attitude in us.

Honor is different from glory. In Scripture, glory usually refers to the ultimate credit which is due only to God, as He is the source of everything (see *Glorifying God – Kingdom Value #35*). Honor, in its proper place, is the recognition we give to others for allowing themselves to be used by God, and for the accomplishments which have come through their instrumentality. As humans, one of our basic, legitimate needs is recognition.

Maslow's Hierarchy of Needs hints at the need for recognition when listing "belonging," "esteem," and "self-actualization" as motivating factors. Herzberg's Motivation-Hygiene Theory mentions "recognition" directly as one of the motivating factors (as opposed to the "hygiene" factors which simply maintain the status quo). Socially and emotionally mature people wish to contribute to a cause which is greater than themselves and feel the need to be recognized for their accomplishments. Recognition can range from a simple "thank you" or "good job!" to a full-fledged celebration.

Jesus spoke of this principle when He told the parable of the talents. The two servants who invested and earned more than they had been given, received recognition and honor from their master. "The master was full of praise. 'Well done, my good and faithful servant. You have been faithful in handling this small amount, so now I will give you many more responsibilities. Let's celebrate together!'" (Matthew 25:21 - NLT).

Notice that the master honors them with the recognition of a "well done," proceeds to say what they did that gained them this honor, then informs them about the promotion they would receive, as well as what it would entail. At the end, the master invites them to "enter into the joy of your master" (ESV), or "let's celebrate together!" (NLT), meaning that one of their greatest rewards would be to join his inner circle and enjoy his company.

Honoring one another flows from an attitude which says, "I will do what I can to be a blessing in your life, to help you grow and thrive, even if I don't get any personal gain out of this effort." In this sense, we are to "honor everyone. Keep on loving the community of believers, fearing God, and honoring the king" (1 Peter 2:17 - ISV). We are especially to "respect those who labor among you and are over you in the Lord and admonish you, and to esteem them very highly in love because of their work. Be at peace among yourselves" (1 Thessalonians 5:12-13 - ESV).

The opposite of honoring one another in this Biblical sense would be to disrespect, slander, criticize and put down one another. James says "don't speak evil against each other, dear brothers and sisters. If you criticize and judge each other, then you are criticizing and judging God's law. But your job is to obey the law, not to judge whether it applies to you" (James 4:11 - NLT).

When Paul wrote about family life, he reminded his readers about one of the 10 Commandments, saying, "Honor your father and mother." Then he struck a balance by saying, "Fathers, do not provoke your children to anger; instead, bring them up in the discipline and instruction of the Lord" (Ephesians 6:2-4 - BSB; see Exodus 20:12). These commandments are needed more than ever, as we see children disrespecting their parents and authorities in general. But untold harm has also been inflicted by fathers who do not honor their children. It has been discovered that both boys and girls get their sense of self-worth from their father. And, if the father never demonstrates love, affection, and acceptance – if he never says "well done!" – the child tends to grow up feeling like he or she will never measure up.

Kids should obey their parents while living at home, but they should honor them for life. And parents, likewise, should always honor their children, even after they have moved out. Whether in the family or in society, we are to show "respect to those you owe respect, and honor to those you owe honor" (Romans 13:7b - CSB).

Honoring Kingdom Principles:
• Only when we give glory to God above all, seeking to please Him in all things, are we willing and able to truly honor one another like we should.
• Honoring others is only genuine if we do not do so to gain favors.
• We are to honor one another in the Church, in the family and in society.

Have you been honoring those God has placed in your life?

KV24 – **HONORING** *One Another*

| Consistently practice | Sometimes practice | Struggle | Mostly fail | Continually fail |

Kingdom Value #25: Living in harmony with *one another*
I once went to the theater with my wife, Monica. This was many years ago and I do not remember what the play was about, because what really caught my at-

tention was the orchestra. Before the show, each musician began to warm up by playing his instrument in a random fashion and to no particular tune. The result was a cacophony of conflicting sounds. This went on for some time and one could scarcely imagine anything coordinated and beautiful coming from what seemed to be a band of madmen.

Until the *maestro* came on stage. The "tac, tac, tac" from his baton brought immediate silence to the auditorium. What came next was a harmonious piece of music, performed in perfect coordination, under the conductor's unquestioned leadership. To me, that is a picture of the Church. We all have different gifts – or instruments to play, if you will. But they all should harmonize and come together to produce something beautiful for the Kingdom and for the King's glory. Yet for that to happen, we all have to be looking at the Conductor, agreeing to follow His every command.

"Harmony" comes from the Greek word from which we get "symphony" and occurs only once in the New Testament, in 2 Corinthians 6:15, which says: "What harmony is there between Christ and Belial?" In this context harmony means "agreement." Yet there are several other verses in our English versions of the Bible which use the term "harmony." In those cases they are actually translating words that literally mean "single-minded" (1 Peter 3:8), "perfect unity" (Colossians 3:14), "united in soul" (Philippians 2:2), "to be of the same mind" (Romans 15:5 and Philippians 4:2), or something to that effect.

Living in harmony means having the same mind or thinking alike. Practicing harmony means agreeing to agree with each other. Paul explains: "I appeal to you, brothers, by the name of our Lord Jesus Christ, that all of you agree, and that there be no divisions among you, but that you be united in the same mind and the same judgment" (1 Corinthians 1:10 - ESV). It was vital for the new churches Paul was planting to stick together against a pagan and sometimes hostile society that knew nothing about Christianity. Yet, there is only one thing more dangerous to the Church (and families) than attacks from the outside and that is division on the inside.

There is no need to add a Kingdom Value of "Unity" because, as seen above, "harmony" fundamentally includes this notion. Harmony and unity are like heads and tails of the same coin. Both are essential for the well-being and good functioning of the Body of Christ. As with any organization, if the Church is to be productive and achieve what the Head of the Body desires, these qualities must be present.

Yet, harmony is not just about being productive. It's about fellowship – building and maintaining meaningful relationships with our brothers and sisters. God commands us to love one another and to live in harmony. This is pleasing to the Lord and enjoyable to the Body. "How good and how pleasant it is for brothers to dwell together in unity!" (Psalm 133:1b - NASB).

Living in harmony is not optional. To "live in harmony with one another" (Romans 12:16a - ESV) is imperative. Christ commanded us to "live in peace with each other" (Mark 9:50b - NLT). Only God can bring about harmony in human relations. He is the One Who grants us to "live in complete harmony with each other" (Romans 15:5 - NLT). The result is that "there should be no division in the body, but that its parts should have equal concern for each other" (1 Corinthians 12:25 - NIV).

Only when we are filled with and walking in the Spirit are we able to live in harmony with one another. Otherwise, we seek our own interests and not the greater good. We wish to be served instead of serving. We insist "our will be done," and rant and rave when it is not. The list of "the works of the flesh" include harmony and unity **busters**, like "hatreds, strife, jealousy, outbursts of anger, selfish ambitions, dissensions" and "factions." The result of being led by the Spirit includes such harmony and unity **boosters** as "patience, kindness, goodness" and "gentleness" (Galatians 5:20, 22-23 - HCSB).

"Finally," to "live in harmony" with one another requires us to "be sympathetic, love as brothers, and be compassionate and humble" (1 Peter 3:8 - ISV). On the flip side, it means we "do not grumble against one another" (James 5:9 - ESV), since complaining and fault-finding are sure ways to promote division and disharmony. Instead, "if one has a complaint against another" we should make it a habit of "forgiving each other" (Colossians 3:13 - ESV; see *Kingdom Value #23 – Forgiving one another*, above).

Harmony Kingdom Principles:
• Harmony results from agreeing with each other and following the same Leader. Instead of pulling in different directions, all unite and pull towards the same goal.
• The Harmony Value depends on other Kingdom Values, such as Humility (#1), Love (#9), Patience (#12), Kindness (#13), Gentleness (#16), Service (#22 and #30), and Compassion (1 Peter 3:8).
• Without harmony, Fellowship (#19) would be unattainable.
Have you been doing your part to "keep the peace" and live in harmony with others? At home and at church, have you actively pursued being like-minded with those with whom you live or work?

114

☐ Consistently practice	☐ Sometimes practice	☐ Struggle	☐ Mostly fail	☐ Continually fail

Kingdom Value #26: Hospitality for *one another*

Things have changed dramatically since Bible times, at least in our western society. Back then, "The reception and lodging of travelers was viewed in Bible lands as a binding obligation to be conscientiously fulfilled. The stranger was to be courteously treated as a guest. In fact, the facilities of the household were placed at his disposal. After eating food with his guest, the host considered it his duty to protect him during his stay."[2]

Were it not for this practice, it would have been very difficult for the Gospel to spread in Israel and throughout the Roman empire as it did (see Luke 10:1-12). "During the Apostolic Age, apostles and itinerant teachers were supported by the hospitality of Christian people while on tour (Acts 16:15; 17:7; 18:7; 21:4-8, 16; 28:7, 14; III Jn 5–8)."[3]

The practice of hospitality varies greatly from culture to culture and even in our own it has undergone great changes. There was a time when families would travel to visit and stay with relatives on a regular basis. Many salesmen or clergymen relied on the hospitality of others as they moved about. Today, this practice is sometimes frowned upon, except on rare or special occasions. Now, it seems, except for close friends and family members, passers-by are expected to stay in hotels and eat out when visiting. If they do stay, it better not be too long.

This does not mean there is no place for hospitality today. Especially because "hospitality" extends beyond the idea of having guests stay overnight. It includes inviting new church members over for refreshments or a meal, entertaining neighbors, enjoying the fellowship of a Sunday School class during a get-together or barbecue, inviting friends and family to sleep over when experiencing difficult circumstances (like being stranded, in danger, or passing by when the money is tight).

I believe hospitality would also include making people feel welcome in your church and in your social or work group. It would include such activities as inviting others – especially those who are new to the area or who usually get over-

115

looked, to join you, your family, or your group either at home or at social events, like going to the beach, a ball game, a concert, or a conference. While the world promotes an exclusive lifestyle, the Kingdom teaches an inclusive way of life.

In regard to fellow Christians, Paul instructed the Romans to "contribute to the needs of the saints and seek to show hospitality" (Romans 12:13 - ESV). As for people in general or strangers in particular, we are told, "Don't neglect to show hospitality, for by doing this some have welcomed angels as guests without knowing it" (Hebrews 13:2 - HCSB).

Hospitality must come from the heart. Although sharing one's home and meals is not always an easy or comfortable thing to do, we still should "offer hospitality to one another without grumbling" (1 Peter 4:9 - NIV). Or, The New Living Translation has it, "Cheerfully share your home with those who need a meal or a place to stay."

Pastors or "overseers" were to be "given to hospitality" (1 Timothy 3:2 - KJV). In selecting which widows would receive help from the church, one of the criteria was if they had "shown hospitality" to others while their husbands were still alive (1 Timothy 5:9-10).

There were those who were going out and spreading the Good News and teaching Kingdom truths. John said they were not receiving any outside help so, "We ought therefore to show hospitality to such people so that we may work together for the truth" (3 John 1:8 - NIV). Some local churches today offer mission houses to missionaries as they come back to the United States to rest and see family members, before heading back to the field. My family and I are grateful to those churches in Florida and Arkansas that have allowed us to stay in their mission houses. We felt loved and cared for. Jesus told His disciples, as He sent them out, "Don't hesitate to accept hospitality, because those who work deserve to be fed" (Matthew 10:10b - NLT).

On the other hand, those who go out or visit your church and promote heresy should not be welcomed. "If anyone comes to your meeting and does not teach the truth about Christ, don't invite that person into your home or give any kind of encouragement" (2 John 1:10 - NLT).

Hospitality is similar to being a good "neighbor" – one who is a concerned citizen who opens his or her heart to those in need. When asked to define "neighbor," Jesus told the story of the Good Samaritan (Luke 10:25-37). Notice that the Samaritan saw the man who had been assaulted and left for dead just like the priest and Levite had. The difference was that he felt compassion. "So he went to him and bandaged his wounds, pouring on oil and wine; and he set him on his own animal, brought him to an inn, and took care of him" (Luke 10:34 - NKJV).

The Samaritan paid the hotel manager what amounted to two days' wages. He told him he would come back and cover any other expenses incurred. This tells us the Samaritan was willing to use his resources freely to help others. And that he was going to check up on the person he helped by coming back by as soon as he could.

Being hospitable may take us out of our comfort zone (unless that happens to be our spiritual gift or specific calling), but all Christians are expected to "contribute to the needs of the saints and seek to show hospitality" (Romans 12:13 - ESV). One day we will be the ones needing to receive hospitality. Will we be treated as we treated others?

Where do you consider yourself to be on the hospitality scale?

Kingdom Value #27: Preferring *one another*

The hypothetical discussion came around to this: "I think if my wife and I were being held at gunpoint and it were between the assailant and my wife, I would rather he kill my wife than, if I had a way to do so, I kill him." The other two participants of the conversation looked at each other and gasped (at least on the inside). His reasoning? "Because the guy would certainly not be saved and, if killed, would go straight to hell. My wife would go to heaven." (The proponent of this idea was not married, while the other two in the discussion were).

The takeaway from this extreme example is that we should be careful not to put the unsaved first simply because they are unsaved. We should make every effort to lead the unsaved to Christ, but this should not lead us to neglect our responsibility towards our family and brothers and sisters in Christ.

Some pastors and missionaries spend all they have "to further the Kingdom," while spending little time with, or scarce resources on, their spouse and children. They win the world only to lose their family. Yet, after God Himself, their family

117

is their first priority. Ministry comes next. The Bible has strong words for such negligence: "If anyone does not take care of his own relatives, especially his immediate family, he has denied the faith and is worse than an unbeliever" (1 Timothy 5:8 - ISV).

We find a similar principle in what Jesus said when a women poured expensive perfume on His head. The disciples became indignant and considered it a waste. It could have been sold and the money given to the poor, they reasoned. Jesus, however, reprimanded them and said, "For the poor you always have with you, but not always do you have Me" (Matthew 26:11 - BLB). Jesus was not saying we should not care for the poor but that caring for the poor should not keep us from giving God our priority.

When Scripture tells us we are to "be kindly affectioned one to another with brotherly love; in honour preferring one another" (Romans 12:10 - KJV), there are at least two general applications: 1) This is the Bible's way of saying "put others first; give them the preference; honor them above yourself." And, 2) Taking similar verses into consideration, it is likely the idea here is also to prefer those in the family of faith over those who are not in the Kingdom.

Favoring or preferring Christians over non-Christians may seem limiting or selfish, yet the idea is not to exclude but to prioritize. Because while we are called to be witnesses and salt and light in the world, and to serve and love the needy around us, the following verse will show us that our priority should be to bless and do good to the family of faith: "So then, while we have opportunity, let us do good to all people, and especially to those who are of the household of the faith" (Galatians 6:10 - NASB).

The New Testament authors tell us to prefer our Christian family **and** to love everyone, even our enemies. Jesus told us to "love your enemies" and "do what is good" because God "is gracious to the ungrateful and evil" (Luke 6:35 - HCSB). There is a meaningful example of this from our day and time. An Islamic State fighter called Fadely confessed to killing Christians and to enjoy doing so. Until he started "having dreams of this man in white who came to him and said, 'You are killing my people.'"[4]

Fadely felt bad about what he was doing. One day he was about to kill another Christian who told him he was giving him his Bible. After killing him, he started reading it. Then, in another dream, Jesus invited Fadely to follow Him. Fadely began "asking to become a follower of Christ and to be discipled."[5] So, as we prefer each other, we ought not to forget to also reach out to the "others," the lost, even our enemies. That is what Jesus still does today!

While we should love our enemies and do good to them, our priority is still to demonstrate our love and support to our brothers and sisters. The idea behind "prefer" is to show favor without favoritism. That can be a difficult balancing act. But it will help to remember that we are to "do nothing out of selfish ambition or vain conceit, but in humility consider others better than yourselves" (Philippians 2:3). Not playing favorites means "there should be no division in the body, but that its parts should have equal concern for each other" (1 Corinthians 12:25 - NIV).

It may help if we compare the "Preferring" Principle to another Kingdom Principle which speaks about the Christian's priority and responsibility as being that of taking care of his own family. This principle states that "if anyone does not provide for his own, and especially for those of his household, he has denied the faith and is worse than an unbeliever" (1 Timothy 5:8 - NASB). If we can extrapolate and apply that to the believer's spiritual family, then individual Christians and the local church should first take care of the community of faith. This does not exempt Christians from doing "good to all people;" it means that other believers come first in line, before unbelievers.

Another way of advancing the same idea is the command to "*respect* everyone" but to "*love* your Christian brothers and sisters" (1 Peter 2:17 - NLT).

"Preferring one another" is a Kingdom Value which compliments and fits well with all the other mutuality Kingdom Values in this section. Because to prefer implies forgiving, honoring, living in harmony, submitting to, having brotherly affection for, serving, being tenderhearted towards, encouraging, celebrating with, and speaking scripturally with each other (see *Kingdom Values 23* through *34*). The opposite "values" would be "provoking one another, envying one another" (Galatians 5:26 - ESV; see also verse 15).

We must learn to defer to the needs of others, to humbly "consider others better than yourselves," and to bless and take care of the family of faith as a priority while also serving and blessing those outside the faith.

In what ways to you show your love to your brothers and sisters in Christ? Do you prioritize their needs? Are you considering them first, even before others who also need your service or care?

KV27 – **PREFERRING** *One Another*

Consistently practice	Sometimes practice	Struggle	Mostly fail	Continually fail

Kingdom Value #28: Submitting to *one another*

While compliance is sometimes compulsory and obedience mandatory, submission – although commanded in God's word – is, in its essence, voluntary. We must decide: will we have a spirit of submission or an attitude of rebellion?

"God does not give Kingdom Authority to rebels," but to "his children who have a *spirit of submission*."[6] Wise words from Adrian Rogers, who has a clever way of defining the Submission to Authority Principle. He says "we can never be *over those things* God has put *under* us until we are *under those things* that he has set *over* us."[7] It's the **you only have authority if you are under authority** Kingdom Principle (see Luke 7:7-8).

If nobody is following, the "leader" is not leading – a timeless truth which has found a new expression in social media. Following requires an attitude of submission. A kingdom only works if there is a respected hierarchy. Because human authority requires respect, it must be earned, not imposed.

You can force someone to obey by holding a gun to their head, but you cannot, in a Biblical sense, force someone to submit. Submission comes when we respect the other person's leadership and willingly come under their authority. It helps when both leader and follower understand that, in the Kingdom, leadership always has to do with service. Those in authority are placed there by God so they can serve, care for, nurture, encourage and empower those entrusted to them.

To whom should we submit?

1. To God
The Bible is clear that we should submit first and foremost to God. "Submit yourselves therefore to God. Resist the devil, and he will flee from you" (James 4:7 - KJV). God the Father is the final authority over all creation, which of course includes the spirit world and all celestial beings. We must first come under God's authority in order to defeat the devil's authority in our life.

Just as we submitted to our earthly fathers, we must also submit to our Heavenly Father. "Since we respected our earthly fathers who disciplined us, shouldn't we submit even more to the discipline of the Father of our spirits, and live forever?" (Hebrews 12:9 - NLT). We are to submit to the Father's authority and to His righteousness. Some independently rebellious people "disregarded the righteousness from God and attempted to establish their own righteousness" when they should have "submitted themselves to God's righteousness" (Romans 10:3 - HCSB).

When we submit to God's rules we discover He is the One Who has the only solutions that work.

2. To Christ as Head of the Church

God the Father gave God the Son "the highest position in heaven" and "He is far above all rulers, authorities, powers, lords, and all other names that can be named, not only in this present world but also in the world to come." Also, "God has put everything under the control of Christ. He has made Christ the head of everything for the good of the church" (Ephesians 1:20-22 - GOD'S WORD®).

It is clear that Jesus is the King of heaven and the Head of the Church. After "the resurrection of Jesus Christ" He went to "heaven and is at God's right hand" where "angels, authorities and powers" are all "in submission to him" (1 Peter 3:21, 22 - NIV). Now, if all of these heavenly authorities submit to Jesus, who are we not to live a life of submission to Him?

3. Authorities and rulers

As a general Kingdom Principle, "Every person must be subject to the governing authorities, for no authority exists except by God's permission. The existing authorities have been established by God" (Romans 13:1 - ISV). As corrupt as some authorities may be, if there were no authorities at all, utter chaos would ensue. We get a glimpse of this when there are riots of large groups who no longer acknowledge the government's right to rule over them. That's why it is good to be reminded "to be submissive to rulers and authorities, to obey, to be ready for every good work" (Titus 3:1 - HCSB).

Peter adds one or more caveats when he speaks of our submission to earthly authorities. He says to "be subject to every human ordinance" but adds "that is of the Lord." This applies to "whether it be to a king or to a superior, and unto governors" and we are to do so "as unto those that are sent by him for the punishment of evildoers and for the praise of those that do well." This, Peter teaches, "is the will of God." And he closes this subject by telling his readers to "honour the king" (1 Peter 2:13-17 - JUB).

4. Our bosses at work

According to the Bible, we don't have to agree with our bosses. While under their authority we need to submit to and honor them. But as we do, keep in mind that our "Ultimate Boss" is the Lord Jesus Christ.

Although given to slaves, the principles in these instructions apply to worker-supervisor relations: "Slaves must always obey their masters and do their best to

121

please them. They must not talk back or steal, but must show themselves to be entirely trustworthy and good. Then they will make the teaching about God our Savior attractive in every way" (Titus 2:9, 10 - NLT; check out Colossians 3:22-25 in "The Message" version).

5. Spiritual leaders in the church

If church members are always critical, second-guessing, over-analyzing, questioning, and being stubborn, relationships will be fractured and ministry will be severely hindered. Imagine if our own body were to act in that way.

The Bible instructs us to "obey your leaders and submit to them, for they are keeping watch over your souls, as those who will have to give an account. Let them do this with joy and not with groaning, for that would be of no advantage to you" (Hebrews 13:17 - ESV). In the local church, "young people must submit to the elders" and all "must clothe yourselves with humility for the sake of each other" (1 Peter 5:5 - ISV). Humility is a prerequisite to an attitude of submission.

In the Church we all have a role to play according to the spiritual gifts we have received. When we fulfill our role, we are in the position of leadership in that area. Others should submit to our leadership at that point (see 1 Corinthians 16:15-16).

6. Wives to husbands

First, we are to "submit to one another out of reverence for Christ" (Ephesians 5:21 - NIV). Another version has, "Place yourselves under each other's authority out of respect for Christ" (GOD'S WORD®). Submitting means being compliant in a positive – not passive – way. It is being willing to cooperate, not compete. It means voluntarily allowing ourselves to come under someone else's leadership.

When we see how Jesus submits to the Father, we better understand how the wife mirrors this relationship in terms of her submission to the husband. Just as the husband mirrors the Lord's sacrificial love for His Church, when the husband relates to his wife.[8] Scripture tells us that "the head of every man is Christ, the head of woman is man, and the head of Christ is God" (1 Corinthians 11:3 - NKJV).

The wife's submission to her husband should follow the biblical criteria, which includes the fact that **the order to submit is directed to the wife.** The order was not, "Husbands, see that your wife submits to your leadership." Since submission is voluntary, it must be the wife's decision. This is her responsibility. It also means **husbands are commanded to love their wives as Jesus loved His church, with unconditional *agape* love.** When the husband loves and cares for his wife with this quality of love, respect, and honor, submitting to his leadership should come naturally.

The husband is to be "understanding, giving honor to the wife," and to realize that he and his wife are "heirs together of the grace of life." Marriage is a partnership where there should be mutual respect. The husband should act on this so his "prayers may not be hindered" (1 Peter 3:7 - NKJV; on the wife's submission, see Ephesians 5:22-24; Titus 2:4-5; Colossians 3:18-19; 1 Peter 3:1).

7. Children to parents

Just as spouses and parents (Colossians 3:21) have their responsibilities, children must answer to their moms and dads. More than ever, the Biblical command needs to be heeded: "Children, obey your parents in all things, for this is well pleasing to the Lord" (Colossians 3:20 - NKJV). Adult sons and daughters no longer submit to their parents but owe them respect and honor till the day they die (Exodus 20:12; Ephesians 6:2).

This is what Jesus did: "And he went down with them and came to Nazareth and was submissive to them. And his mother treasured up all these things in her heart" (Luke 2:51 - ESV). The eternal Son of God submitting to mortal humans! He came to model true submission and to fulfill all righteousness (Matthew 3:15).

8. "One to another"

We have already seen the importance of "submitting to one another" in regards to married life and church life. But this command is broader and reaches into all aspects of life. There are times when even the most powerful CEO must submit to another's authority, such as when his doctor orders him to undergo life-saving surgery, or the policeman hands him a speeding ticket.

In the Global Kingdom there are people we must submit to on several levels – and each one of them does too. This calls for humility, patience, and an attitude of cooperation. When we submit to those God places over us we are saying, "Lord, I trust in Your provision and leadership. I'm doing my part to work with your will and cooperate as best I can with the authority over me, and am confident that your plan will be fulfilled for my life in the right way, at the right time."

Evaluate how you have been doing in the area of submission in the different areas of your life. Between husbands and wives, there is an added item where husbands can "grade" their love since this is the context in which the wife's submission is mentioned in a key passage.

SUBMISSION TO:	Consistently practice	Sometimes practice	Struggle	Mostly fail	Continually fail
GOD / JESUS	☐	☐	☐	☐	☐
AUTHORITIES	☐	☐	☐	☐	☐
BOSS(ES)	☐	☐	☐	☐	☐
CHURCH LEADERS	☐	☐	☐	☐	☐
HUSBAND LOVES WIFE	☐	☐	☐	☐	☐
WIFE TO HUSBAND	☐	☐	☐	☐	☐
PARENTS	☐	☐	☐	☐	☐
ONE ANOTHER	☐	☐	☐	☐	☐

◄ KV28 – SUBMITTING TO *One Another* ►

Kingdom Value #29: Brotherly affection; loving *one another*

We have seen love as part of the fruit of the Spirit (Kingdom Value #9). Now let's look at the action of loving one another as it relates to mutuality. When Jesus, John, and Paul say we are to love one another, they use the Greek verb *agapaó* (the noun being *agapé*), which is usually described as unconditional love. It also means focusing on preference. We are to prefer God and what He prefers. And He wants us to love one another.

Loving one another is a non-negotiable command, repeated several times by the Lord Jesus and likewise by the Apostle John. Jesus told the Twelve that "a new commandment I give to you, that you love one another, even as I have loved you, that you also love one another" (John 13:34 - NASB; see also John 15:12, 17; 1 John 3:11 and 1 John 3:23). To love others as He loves us is a challenging proposition. In order for this to take place we must allow Him to live and love through us.

Loving one another is a perpetual debt which we should pay out on a regular and consistent basis. Because of the Father and the Son's example and command, we owe it to each other. John writes: "dear friends, since God so loved us, we also ought to love one another" (1 John 4:11). And Paul says, "let no debt remain

124

outstanding, except the continuing debt to love one another, for he who loves his fellowman has fulfilled the law" (Romans 13:8).

Loving one another is proof we have been born again. John challenges his people: "beloved, let us love one another, for love is from God, and whoever loves has been born of God and knows God" (1 John 4:7 - ESV; see also 1 John 4:12). Once born again, we "must show sincere love to each other" and "love each other deeply with all your heart" (1 Peter 1:22 - NLT). Jesus explained to His disciples that "your love for one another will prove to the world that you are my disciples" (John 13:35 NLT).

Our love for one another should not be halfhearted, passive or static. Instead, it should continue to grow and mature (2 Thessalonians 1:3). "And may the Lord make your love for one another and for all people grow and overflow, just as our love for you overflows" (1 Thessalonians 3:12 - NLT). And, "above all, keep fervent in your love for one another, because love covers a multitude of sins" (1 Peter 4:8 - NASB).

Because we are dealing with fellow Kingdom citizens who have fallen human natures we must have an ever stronger love. All forms of human relationships require overlooking each other's faults and shortcomings. To do so we will need to add other Kingdom Values to the mix, such as Mercy (KV #5), Patience (KV #12), Forgiving (KV #23), being Tenderhearted (KV #31), and Compassion (KV #46).

It should go without saying that loving one another is central to Christianity. "Now concerning brotherly love you have no need for anyone to write to you, for you yourselves have been taught by God to love one another" (1 Thessalonians 4:9 - ESV; "brotherly love" is the Greek *philadelphia* and "taught by God to love" brings us back to *agapaó*).

Before becoming citizens of God's Kingdom "we lived in malice and envy, being hated and hating one another" (Titus 3:3b). Because God's love conquered our hearts and took hold of our minds, we desire to mirror that love and extend it to everyone but especially to our brothers and sisters in the faith.

How does your brotherly love fare when put to the test?

KV29 – BROTHERLY AFFECTION *Loving One Another*

| Consistently practice | Sometimes practice | Struggle | Mostly fail | Continually fail |

Kingdom Value #30: Serving *one another*

Service as a purpose of the Church has been mentioned above, under *Kingdom Value #22*, with an emphasis on reaching out to the needy in the community and abroad. Here, we will focus on how service relates to serving one another in the Body of Christ.

As I performed my youngest daughter's wedding, I told Melissa and her husband, Aaron, that service is a gauge for maturity. Perhaps as a typical dad, I was really thinking mostly about her husband on this one. Mostly because, over the years, I have seen and heard about husbands sitting back and making their wives do everything by themselves in the home, from buying the groceries, taking care of the babies, cleaning, and cooking to washing the dishes and paying the bills. And I have to admit that for several years in my own marriage, I did the same. But I began to notice that the men who are really emotionally well-balanced and mature are the ones who take the initiative to help around the house.

Serving others is being other-centered rather than self-centered.

You might have heard the illustration of the difference between heaven and hell. It goes like this:

> A man spoke with the Lord about heaven and hell. The Lord said to the man, "Come, I will show you hell."
>
> They entered a room where a group of people sat around a huge pot of stew. Everyone was famished, desperate and starving. Each held a spoon that reached the pot, but each spoon had a handle so much longer than their own arm that it could not be used to get the stew into their own mouths. The suffering was terrible.
>
> "Come, now I will show you heaven," the Lord said after a while. They entered another room, identical to the first — the pot of stew, the group of people, the same long-handled spoons. But there everyone was happy and well-nourished. "I don't understand," said the man. "Why are they happy here when they were miserable in the other room and everything was the same?"
>
> The Lord smiled, "Ah, it is simple," he said. "Here they have learned to feed each other."[9]

I believe one of the main lessons we are to learn on earth, before parting for eternity, is to look outside of ourselves, see others and serve them. Serve them by being kind, tenderhearted, generous and compassionate. Serve them by encouraging them, sharing their burden, helping them grow. Serve them by lending a helping hand, assisting with fixing, cleaning, and maintaining things. By offering refreshment or a glass of water on a hot day. Looking out for the weary and needy (as opposed to "looking out for number 1"). Yet the most important service we can offer others is to share the Good News of the Gospel of the Kingdom.

Perhaps because God knew we would be so self-conscious, He created us in such a way that we cannot physically see our own faces. We have seen images and reflections but not our own real, flesh and blood faces. We can – and do – see the faces of others all the time, however. This is not a design flaw but obviously intentional. Do you think God may be trying to tell us to stop worrying so much about ourselves and start caring about others around us? The more we care, the more we will serve. The more we serve, the more we will bless others and bring fruit to the Kingdom. This leads to a sense of fulfillment and a decrease in anxiety, boredom and depression.

Here is a *Kingdom Principle to keep in mind for serving others:* "whatever you do, do it enthusiastically, as something done for the Lord and not for men, knowing that you will receive the reward of an inheritance from the Lord. You serve the Lord Christ" (Colossians 3:23-24 - HCSB). We serve others even if we feel they don't deserve it because we understand we are ultimately serving the Lord, and He is worthy of our best.

Perhaps this principle is best seen in the eschatological passage of the return of King Jesus. He declares that the good done to others was, in essence, done to Him. And, He offers His Kingdom as "the reward of an inheritance."

> Then the King will say to those on His right, 'Come, you who are blessed of My Father, inherit the kingdom prepared for you from the foundation of the world. For I was hungry, and you gave Me something to eat; I was thirsty, and you gave Me something to drink; I was a stranger, and you invited Me in; naked, and you clothed Me; I was sick, and you visited Me; I was in prison, and you came to Me.' Then the righteous will answer Him, 'Lord, when did we see You hungry, and feed You, or thirsty, and give You something to drink? And when did we see You a stranger, and invite You in, or naked, and clothe You? When did we see You sick, or in prison, and come to You?' The King will answer and say to them, 'Truly I say to you, to the extent that you did it to one of these brothers of Mine, even the least of them, you did it to Me.' (Matthew 25:34-40 - NASB)

This general principle also applies to the workplace, where we are to "serve with a good attitude, as to the Lord and not to men, knowing that whatever good each one does, slave or free, he will receive this back from the Lord" (Ephesians 6:7-8 - HCSB; see *Work – Kingdom value #48*). When we serve others we are serving the Lord. He is ultimately our Boss.

When it comes to serving – especially the kind of service you don't get paid for – how are you doing on a scale of "continually fail" to "consistently practice"?

KV30 – **SERVING** *One Another*				
☐ **Consistently practice**	☐ **Sometimes practice**	☐ **Struggle**	☐ **Mostly fail**	☐ **Continually fail**

Kingdom Value #31: Tenderheartedness towards *one another*

Being tenderhearted means having a heart of compassion. What would life be like if we treated others like God treats us? How many times has God been patient and gentle with you? I sometimes wonder why God doesn't just zap me with a bolt of lightening after I've done something stupid. I wouldn't be here writing these lines if God had not been tenderhearted towards me. If He hadn't extended His mercy and compassion to me over and over again. Because we are loved by God, we should love each other. "So, as those who have been chosen of God, holy and beloved, put on a heart of compassion, kindness, humility, gentleness and patience" (Colossians 3:12 - NASB).

Being tenderhearted comes from a heart that is humble and willing to walk in the other person's shoes. "Finally, all of you should be of one mind. Sympathize with each other. Love each other as brothers and sisters. Be tenderhearted, and keep a humble attitude" (1 Peter 3:8 - NLT).

What we call "pastors" today are really called elders and bishops in the Bible. According to Scripture, "pastor" is a spiritual gift and literally means shepherd (see Ephesians 4:11). Shepherds in the Middle East, at least the good ones (see John 10), had a special relationship with their sheep and took good care of them, sometimes at great personal risk and sacrifice.

Listen to Nathan the prophet's description as he told a story to King David: "The poor man owned nothing but one little lamb he had bought. He raised that little lamb, and it grew up with his children. It ate from the man's own plate and drank from his cup. He cuddled it in his arms like a baby daughter" (2 Samuel 12: - NLT). That is a picture of tenderheartedness. That is what shepherds do: they nourish, protect, love on, encourage and help to carry their sheep through difficult terrain.

There is none as tenderhearted as our God. That is why David confessed: "The Lord is my shepherd," in the most quoted and cherished of psalms. See how he describes God's care. The Great Shepherd provides ("I shall not want"), refreshes ("He makes me lie down in green pastures"), and restores ("He leads me beside quiet waters. He restores my soul"). The Lord guides ("He guides me in the paths of righteousness"), protects (even when we must "walk through the valley of the shadow of death"), and dispels our fears ("I fear no evil, for You are with me"). He comforts ("Your rod and Your staff, they comfort me"), lavishes us with abundant blessings ("You prepare a table before me... My cup overflows"), has our best interest in mind ("surely goodness and lovingkindness will follow me all the days of my life"), and promises us an eternity by His side ("I will dwell in the house of the Lord forever") (Psalm 23 - NASB).

Being tenderhearted means being ready to receive God's forgiveness and willing to forgive others. "Be kind to one another, tender-hearted, forgiving each other, just as God in Christ also has forgiven you" (Ephesians 4:32 - NASB). While not condoning their sin, it's having a soft spot for other fellow strugglers, understanding their human condition, being patient, and extending God's grace to them.

The opposite of a tender heart is a calloused and closed heart. Jesus told His closest followers "you've been given insight into God's kingdom. You know how it works. Not everybody has this gift, this insight; it hasn't been given to them. Whenever someone has a ready heart for this, the insights and understandings flow freely. But if there is no readiness, any trace of receptivity soon disappears" (Matthew 13: 11-12 - MSG). Then Jesus described some of the other onlookers – and all of those who reject His message – by quoting Isaiah's prophecy: "for this people's heart has become calloused; they hardly hear with their ears, and they have closed their eyes" (Matthew 13:15a - NIV; Isaiah 6:9, 10).
Being repeatedly hurt by others and frustrated by the disappointments of life can convince us that being tenderhearted is counterintuitive and makes us vulnerable to more suffering. We sometimes become insensitive in order to not be overwhelmed. Still, we have in Jesus our great example and He was always tenderhearted, even though He was rejected by His own people (John 1:11). He cried out: "Jerusalem, Jerusalem! She who kills the prophets and stones those who are sent to her. How often I wanted to gather your children together, as a hen gathers

her chicks under her wings, but you were not willing!" (Luke 13:34 - HCSB).

Stop and ask yourself: How tenderhearted am I in my day-to-day life? Do I respect the feelings of those I claim to love and with those with whom I deal? Am I sensitive to their needs? Compassionate in view of their suffering? Or, have I become calloused by the way I myself have been treated by others? How do I fare on the Tenderhearted scale?

◀	KV31 – TENDERHEARTED TOWARDS *One Another*			▶
☐ Consistently practice	☐ Sometimes practice	☐ Struggle	■ Mostly fail	■ Continually fail

Kingdom Value #32: Encouraging *one another*

"Therefore encourage one another and build one another up, just as you are doing" (1 Thessalonians 5:11 - ESV). Great advice for the early believers; great advice for believers today. To encourage (*parakaleó*) carries the meaning of admonishing on the one hand, and comforting on the other. It is true that sometimes we need someone to encourage us by questioning our behavior and other times we just need someone to lift us up because we already know how much we have been failing. Either way, the goal is to strengthen the other person's faith and character. "Build up" or "edify" is the same verb used in Greek for constructing a building.

It is interesting that the etymology of the English word "encourage" comes from the idea of infusing the heart with courage.[10]

Many Kingdom Values will be used in the process of encouraging others, such as mercy, reconciliation, love, gentleness, forgiving, being tenderhearted, compassion, honesty, truth, and wisdom.

When Paul says to "encourage one another," the context of the passage is that of the second coming of the Lord (see also 1 Thessalonians 4:18). We are to encourage each other to remember who we are and how we should behave while we wait for the Lord's return. We are to stay "awake" and be sober – focused and ready.

Paul then mentions some specific ways we can encourage others in the church. We are to "build each other up," to "give recognition to those who labor among you and lead you" as well as "regard them very highly in love because of their work," to "comfort the discouraged, help the weak, be patient with everyone" and

130

to "always pursue what is good for one another and for all" (1 Thessalonians 5:11-15 - HCSB).

Barnabas to the rescue

Certainly Paul was one of the greatest encouragers of early believers and, through his writings, of Christians of all times. He wasn't content to plant a church, be on his way and never look back. He did all he could to keep young churches on the right path to maturity in Christ.

But even Paul needed an encourager. And if it were not for Barnabas, we may not have ever heard of Paul. There are no self-made men. There are only men and women who have been properly encouraged before and during their successful years of leadership. The Kingdom Principle of mutuality is that we cannot make it on our own. We need each other.

The persecution of believers that ensued due to Stephen's execution resulted in a diaspora, a scattering of Christians who spread the Good News wherever they went. While many were only sharing with Jews, some went to Antioch and proclaimed the message to non-Jews, and a great number believed. When the church in Jerusalem heard about this, they sent Barnabas, "for he was a good man, full of the Holy Spirit and of faith" (Acts 11: 24 - HCSB). "When he arrived and saw the grace of God, he was glad and encouraged all of them to remain true to the Lord with a firm resolve of the heart" (Acts 11: 23 - HCSB).

Following in his footsteps, that is what Paul would later do and that is what he meant when he wrote about encouragement. Barnabas would soon travel to "Tarsus to search for Saul, and when he found him he brought him to Antioch." Notice how they both invested in encouragement! "For a whole year they met with the church and taught large numbers." It was history in the making because "the disciples were first called Christians at Antioch" (Acts 11: 25, 26 - HCSB).

During their first missionary journey, Paul and Barnabas would preach the Gospel in different cities, then go back through, "strengthening the disciples and encouraging them to remain true to the faith." They explained that "we must go through many hardships to enter the kingdom of God" (Acts 14:22 - NIV; see *Enduring Suffering – Kingdom Value #57*). That may not seem like great consolation, but it explained what Jesus had already told His disciples: "In this godless world you will continue to experience difficulties. But take heart! I've conquered the world" (John 16:33 - MSG). Part of encouraging and strengthening is giving it to people straight and preparing them for difficult days ahead.

We are encouraged to encourage. Paul would tell the Roman believers about the importance of being "mutually encouraged by each other's faith, both yours and mine" (Romans 1:12 - ESV). A once in a lifetime bit of encouragement is not enough. We live under a lot of stress and pressure in this fallen world. We are tested daily, so we need encouragement daily. That is why we need to "encourage one another day after day, as long as it is still called 'Today,' so that none of you will be hardened by the deceitfulness of sin" (Hebrews 3:13 - NASB).

We need each other individually and we need each other corporately. We should "not neglect our meeting together, as some people do, but encourage one another, especially now that the day of his return is drawing near" (Hebrews 10:25 - NLT). Encouraging does not mean negatively provoking or shaming others into compliance. Instead, "Let us think of ways to motivate one another to acts of love and good works (Hebrews 10:24 - NLT).

Encouragement is also a spiritual gift, which means some are going to be better at it than others. "If your gift is to encourage others, be encouraging" (Romans 12:8 - NLT). But we all have a responsibility to encourage our loved ones, coworkers and neighbors. We can start by truly caring for them. "Your love has given me great joy and encouragement, because you, brother, have refreshed the hearts of the saints," Paul would tell a friend (Philemon 1:7 - NIV). On the other hand, nothing discourages leaders and turns seekers away like strife and disagreements in the church. "So then, let us aim for harmony in the church and try to build each other up" (Romans 14:19 - NLT).

There is nothing like encouragement that is capable of building people and churches up and motivating them to stay focused on the finish line while they await that special, final day. How are you doing as an encourager?

KV32 – **ENCOURAGING** *One Another*

Consistently practice | Sometimes practice | Struggle | Mostly fail | Continually fail

Kingdom Value #33: Celebrating with *one another*

I have always believed in celebrating victories – large and small. I once had a small ad agency which struggled from day one. When we finally landed our first account and things were looking up, I asked the gofer to purchase a gourmet pie and we all took a well-deserved break. We simply enjoyed the moment together.

Life can be tough. So when we hit a milestone, have a breakthrough, get a promotion, or simply survive another year (sometimes referred to as birthdays), it's time to stop and celebrate. We should join the people we care about on these special occasions because there's nothing that encourages and validates more than celebrating each other's victories!

Celebrating involves joy and rejoicing (see *Joy – Kingdom Value #10* and *Rejoicing in the Lord – Kingdom Value #44*). Joy and rejoicing can be based on past, present, or future realities. For instance, "we rejoice in hope of the glory of God" (Romans 5:2 - ESV; see also Romans 12:12). We can rejoice with something we are promised, even if it hasn't happened yet – especially when God is the One making the promise. That is the definition of hope. But celebrating, strictly speaking, is rejoicing with gratitude for something which has already happened – usually a victory of some sort. The greater the struggle, the greater the rejoicing, such as when our candidate wins a presidential election or our team wins a major tournament.

When Jesus spoke of the Father in the parable of the Prodigal Son, He described Him as being compelled to celebrate. The Father explains to the older son that "we **had** to celebrate... because this your brother was lost and now is found, dead but now alive" (Luke 15:32; "celebrate" also appears in verses 23, 24, and 29). The Father spoke as if celebrating were not an option: it was imperative! Jesus spoke of the same celebratory spirit in heaven when a lost sinner is found (Luke 5:7).

Some major victories in the Old Testament were celebrated by the whole nation. The Lord's seven festivals, enumerated in Leviticus 23, were not only to be observed, they were to be celebrated.

After the monumental task of building the walls around Jerusalem, Nehemiah and the people went all out in their celebration. "At the dedication of the wall of Jerusalem, they sent for the Levites wherever they lived and brought them to Jerusalem to celebrate the joyous dedication with thanksgiving and singing accompanied by cymbals, harps, and lyres" (Nehemiah 12:27 - HCSB).

When the lives of all the Jews in the Persian empire were spared because of Queen Esther's intervention, there was a Christmas-like celebration.

> Mordecai recorded these events, and he sent letters to all the Jews throughout the provinces of King Xerxes, near and far, to have them celebrate annually the fourteenth and fifteenth days of the month of Adar as the time when the Jews got relief from their enemies, and as the month when their sorrow was turned into joy and their mourning into a day of celebration.

133

He wrote them to observe the days as days of feasting and joy and giving presents of food to one another and gifts to the poor (Esther 9:20-22 - NIV).

And with that, the Jewish festival of Purim was established.

Christians celebrate the Lord's Supper, as a memorial, to express gratitude to the Savior for giving His life as a ransom for those who place their faith in Him. We are told Jesus "took bread and he gave thanks, he broke and he gave to them and he said, 'This is my body, which shall be given for the sake of your persons. You shall be doing this to commemorate me'" (Luke 22:19 - Aramaic Bible in Plain English).

The early Church believers "devoted themselves to the apostles' teaching, to the fellowship, to the breaking of bread, and to the prayers" (Acts 2:42 - HCSB). The "breaking of bread" can refer to having fellowship meals together or to celebrating the Lord's Supper (Matthew 26:26). It also served as a reminder of the time when Jesus was among them in Person (Luke 24:30). It was a "memorial" which called for reflection (1 Corinthians 11:23-34). All things considered, it was a celebration of the fellowship we have with the Lord because of His sacrifice on our behalf. A celebration of salvation and a celebration of His presence in our lives.

Jesus told the troubled church in Laodicea, "Behold, I stand at the door and knock; if anyone hears My voice and opens the door, I will come in to him and will dine with him, and he with Me" (Revelation 3:20 - NASB). If I were to paraphrase this verse, I would express it as: "Look! I'm right here in front of you, waiting for you to open up. If you welcome me, I will come into your life and we will celebrate!"

It is imperative to celebrate!

There is genuine cause for celebration for those who come to belong to the Lord and follow His ways. Being righteous is a great reason to celebrate: "But the righteous are glad; they rejoice before God and celebrate with joy" (Psalm 68:3 - HCSB). Having a Creator God and King like we do should make us *want* to celebrate! "Let Israel celebrate its Maker; let the children of Zion rejoice in their King" (Psalm 149:2 - HCSB). Cherishing the hope in such a glorious future which awaits the redeemed is a major cause for rejoicing: "Let the godly celebrate in triumphal glory; let them shout for joy on their beds" (Psalm 149:5 - HCSB). Witnessing God's wonders and work is enough to induce celebration: "And on that day you will say: 'Give thanks to Yahweh; proclaim His name! Celebrate His works among the peoples. Declare that His name is exalted'" (Isaiah 12:4 - HCSB).

134

But the ultimate celebration will be when we "receive a rich welcome into the eternal kingdom of our Lord and Savior Jesus Christ" (2 Peter 1:11; Luke 10:20). All our celebration on earth will pale in comparison to the one in heaven, "For the Lamb on the throne will be their Shepherd. He will lead them to springs of life-giving water. And God will wipe every tear from their eyes" (Revelation 7:17-NLT). Although this promise was given to the tribulation martyrs, we can know it also applies to all of those who have been saved by the blood of the Lamb (see Revelation 21:4).

The Eternal Kingdom of God will be a place of celebration because there will be no rebellion, sin, unrighteousness, or law-breaking. All that causes fear, pain, suffering, oppression, confusion, conflict, sadness, pessimism, depression, separation, prejudice and death will have been removed. Just think: no more bills to pay, doctors to visit, funerals to attend! There will only be life, peace, well-being, fellowship, tender loving care, security, understanding, acceptance, and a deep sense of belonging. It's what we were made for and what we have been waiting for. There will be no other alternative in heaven: we will just *have* to celebrate!

How has your spirit of celebration been doing lately? Do you encourage others by celebrating their special occasions or victories?

Kingdom Value #34: Speaking Scripturally to *one another*

I was walking out of the building where my wife Monica and I used to live, in Rio de Janeiro, Brazil, when I notice both doorkeepers speaking back and forth to each other in a very calm and respectful manner. One had a hard copy of the Bible, the other was reading from his cell phone. I asked them, "so, what does the Word have to say to us today?" Mr. José Carlos, the one with the printed Bible, said, "here, let me read it to you;" and proceeded to read part of a Psalm. We then exchanged some thoughts about the text and how important it is to stay on the narrow path. More times than not, when I go by the building's entrance, Mr. José Carlos is reading his Bible. This has become a daily practice for him.

135

There is a big difference between the righteous and the wicked. The wicked believe it is "useless to serve God" and they "consider the arrogant to be fortunate," since it seems like "those who commit wickedness prosper" (Malachi 3:14, 15 - HCSB). On the other hand, "those who feared the LORD spoke to one another. The LORD took notice and listened. So a book of remembrance was written before Him for those who feared Yahweh and had high regard for His name" (Malachi 3:16 - HCSB). God goes on to say He will claim them as His own and that "the difference between the righteous and the wicked" will become clear (v.v. 17, 18).

God enjoys hearing us speak about Him, His Kingdom, and the things from above (Colossians 3:2). Quoting Scripture, commenting on Bible lessons and reminding each other about truths discovered in God's Word all build us up in our faith and focus our attention in the right direction. Therefore, we are to "speak to one another with psalms, hymns and spiritual songs. Sing and make music in your heart to the Lord" (Ephesians 5:19).

We lend so much significance to the insignificant. We highly regard the opinion of celebrities, while glorifying superficial beauty. We value earthly riches and greatly acclaim worldly fame. And how much enthusiasm is expended on sports! Yet all of these are transitory values. Shouldn't our dearest passion, our deepest devotion, and our greatest interest be invested in that which has eternal value? Jesus said, "heaven and earth will pass away, but My words will not pass away"(Luke 21:33 - NASB).

Speaking Scripture to one another draws us closer to the Lord. Two disciples were walking home to Emmaus after Jesus had been crucified in Jerusalem. As they went on their way "they were discussing everything that had taken place." While they were doing so, "Jesus Himself came near and began to walk along with them," but kept His identity secret. He asked them what they were talking about. They were having a heated discussion about "things concerning Jesus the Nazarene," about His crucifixion and rumors that His body was missing from the tomb. They had been "hoping that He was the One who was about to redeem Israel." Jesus told them they were missing the point, and went on explain how these things had to happen. "Then beginning with Moses and all the Prophets, He interpreted for them the things concerning Himself in all the Scriptures."
When they reached their place they invited Jesus to stay for a meal. When He prayed and parted the bread, He opened their eyes and they recognized Who He was, but immediately disappeared from their sight. "So they said to each other, 'Weren't our hearts ablaze within us while He was talking with us on the road and explaining the Scriptures to us?'" (Luke 24:13-32 - HCSB).

What a privilege it was to "speak Scripturally" with the Son of God Himself! To have Him explain to His disciples the prophecy concerning His Person, His mission, and His Father's plans. No wonder their hearts were on fire! Speaking about God's Word – or meditating on it – will warm our hearts as well. And Jesus will come closer to us and reveal wonderful truths we would otherwise never learn. He will teach us directly, revealing insights concerning what the Scriptures mean and how they apply to our daily walk.

We talk about our interests. We share what is on our heart. We discuss what we have been wondering about. How important is God's Word to you? Important enough to *Speak Scripturally to One Another*?

KV34 – **SPEAKING SCRIPTURALLY TO** *One Another*

| Consistently practice | Sometimes practice | Struggle | Mostly fail | Continually fail |

Chapter

7

Kingdom Values
in Relation to God

*The sum of your word is truth, and every one of
your righteous rules endures forever.
Psalm 119:160 - ESV*

More Values of the Kingdom

God's standards still apply today. They've never changed. Some "sophisticated" people believe they have outgrown God's laws and can outwit or outrun God's judgment. How tragic. How destructive. Just as God does not change, neither do His standards. The Kingdom's standard of righteousness will stand forever.

Mike Huckabee clearly states that "our problems... result from the selfish decision to ignore God's standard of integrity. Standards based on anything else are relative, and relative standards are meaningless."[1]

The ultimate anti-Kingdom "value"

As we consider Kingdom Values that pertain to our relationship with God, let's first acknowledge His right to exercise authority over all His creation. Pride has led many to nourish an attitude of self-sufficiency and a refusal to acknowledge God's sovereignty over their life. In essence, they have decided to be their own god instead of answering to their Maker. This pride is the basis of atheism.

Ironically, atheists do not try to ignore God. In fact they cannot. Because most of their attention is focused on trying to deny His existence, they actually concentrate on the very Subject they are trying to negate. Why, even the name they go by contains a reference to God ("a-theist" or "a-theism"). Deep down it is not that they do not believe in the *existence* of God; they have for some reason come to doubt the *goodness* of God. And when they defend their position, many times they do so with a passion which betrays their anger and indignation against their Creator.

Atheists fancy themselves as a-theistic or God-less. But were their lives truly devoid of God in the absolute sense, they would be without His sustaining power or any of His benefits. Yet they still enjoy the air, water, food, and all He makes available, "For He causes His sun to rise on the evil and the good, and sends rain on the righteous and the unrighteous," as Jesus explained (Matthew 5:45 - HCSB).

Pride took Lucifer and made Satan out of him. He went from being "the shining one" to being God's "adversary." Pride is the desire to take God's place in one's own life. And that is why pride is the ultimate anti-Kingdom attitude.

Furthermore, Huckabee sees a direct link between believing in God and believing in immutable standards. "If I don't believe there is a God," he says, "then I don't believe character is fixed. I believe it moves as the culture moves. Therefore, what was wrong once is no longer wrong because the culture no longer considers it inappropriate; we are able to move the standards."[2]

The primary reason we were created is to establish and maintain a relationship with God. The Kingdom Values below reflect what God expects from us in this relationship, according to His own Word.

Kingdom Value #35: Glorifying God

There was a sense of wonder around the Billy Graham Crusade in Rio de Janeiro in 1974. Because I was studying at an American high school, I was invited, along with a few other students, to help the cameramen navigate the venue and the language. I remember being down on the field when time came for Billy Graham to take the stage. As the tall and slender evangelist walked passed me, I cannot express just how in awe I was of that man. As he preached to a crowd of over 150,000 at the *Maracaña* stadium, I was blown away with the way God powerfully used him to reach thousands of lives for Christ. We all have people we admire and wish to emulate. We were designed to highly esteem those who serve as heroes and models in our lives.

140

Our admiration for the King of kings leads naturally to giving Him glory. To glorify is to give credit where credit is due. When we glorify the Lord we acknowledge that God is the only Lord and King, the Sovereign over the universe. As such, only He is entitled to receive ultimate glory and recognition. Because He is the exclusive Creator-God and sustainer of all there is. His power far exceeds all we can appreciate and comprehend.

God is glorious. Only God is without beginning and without end, immutable, all-knowing, all-powerful, absolutely holy in His character and righteous in His actions; perfect in love and compassion. God is worthy. He deserves to be glorified by His people. Because God created and sustains them, loves and saves them, gives   them a purpose and wants them by His side for eternity. "He alone is immortal and dwells in unapproachable light. ... To Him be honor and eternal dominion! Amen" (1 Timothy 6:16 - BSB).

God is already the most glorious Being there could ever be. But He is honored when His creation willfully shows Him reverence. Somehow – lowly humans that we are – we can "magnify the LORD" (Psalm 34:3 - NASB).

While God remains the same, each person's perception of Who He is varies enormously. We bring glory to God when we expand our understanding of Him and, in this way, God is "magnified" – His importance *to us* increases dramatically. God begins to occupy more and more of our thoughts and receive more and more of our devotion.

Worshiping, glorifying and magnifying involve experiencing His greatness, connecting with Him in a deeper way, placing Him front and center on the stage of our lives, and turning the spotlights on *Him*.

It is through His Kingdom that God is exalted and glorified. The Kingdom's function is to be a vehicle for God's will. It is through His Kingdom that He accomplishes His plans and purposes. It's how He communicates with us. And it is in the context of the Kingdom that we now serve and worship Him and will one day reign with Him (Revelation 5:10). And the Kingdom has as its unchanging fundamental purpose to bring glory to God. This is the working definition for "The Secret of the Kingdom Series," as shown below:

> The Kingdom of God is God's rule over all creation through its universal, global, millennial and eternal aspects. Founded on righteousness and built on unchangeable values and principles, **it has the purpose of glorifying God**, conquering evil, redeeming sinners, testing faithfulness, and rewarding overcomers who will

serve and worship Christ, while reigning with Him forever. Only through Jesus does one inherit the Kingdom.[3]

The Scotch catechism declares that the purpose of humanity is "to glorify God and enjoy Him forever." C. S. Lewis sees these two truths to be the same: to enjoy God is to glorify Him. When ordering us to glorify Him, God is essentially inviting us to enjoy Him.[4]

We glorify God by:
1) Worshiping Him (*Kingdom Value #18*);
2) Enjoying Him (*Kingdom Value #44*);
3) Learning more about Him (*Kingdom Values #9, #41, #53, #60, #65, and #66*);
4) Seeking fellowship with Him (seeking ***Him*** – not just His blessings) (*Kingdom Value #19*);
5) Fully surrendering to Him and His will (*Kingdom Value #52 and #54*);
6) Obeying Him (*Kingdom Value #37*);
7) Fulfilling the mission He has given each one of us (*Kingdom Values #45-51*);
8) Serving Him and serving others (*Kingdom Values #22 and #30*).

God does not share His glory with anyone else. "My glory I give to no other" (Isaiah 42:8 - ESV; 48:11), God declares. Not so much as in splendor, bliss, blessings or heavenly wonders. But "glory" as in credit. If He created and sustains everything, if He is the Author of life itself, why should another receive the credit for what ***He*** does – even if He does it ***through*** them? If we accomplish any good in this life it is through the power of His Holy Spirit. So why should anyone else receive the praise and honor for what the Spirit has brought about? In a psalm which emphasizes the one true God contrasted with the "gods" of the surrounding nations, the psalmist confesses, "It does not belong to us, Lord. The glory belongs to you because of your love and loyalty" (Psalm 115 - NCV).

What is "Shekinah glory"? The term "Shekinah" does not appear in the Bible but is a transliteration from the Hebrew, meaning "dwelling."[5] While "glory" has been defined as the manifestation of God's majesty, His "Shekinah glory" is used in the sense of the glory of God's presence. The prophet Ezekiel saw God's glory depart from the Temple in Jerusalem (Ezekiel 10:18), then prophesied God's glory would return to His Millennial Temple (Ezekiel 43:1-7).

When Jesus was facing His final days and hours on earth, He spoke to the Father about glory. Jesus told the Father He had glorified Him and asked that the Father glorify Jesus (John 12:28; 17:1-5). Both the Son and the Father were glorified with

Jesus' earthly ministry because it cleared the way for people to enter the Kingdom and learn about Kingdom Values from Jesus' example. Jesus was eager to go back to the Father and to the glory He had enjoyed before His incarnation. From John's Gospel we learn that the Father glorifies Himself; the Son glorifies the Father; the Father glorifies the Son; and we ought to glorify God the Father, Son and Holy Spirit.

Jude, in his majestic doxology, proclaimed: "Now to Him who is able to keep you from stumbling, and to make you stand in the presence of His glory blameless with great joy, to the only God our Savior, through Jesus Christ our Lord, be glory, majesty, dominion and authority, before all time and now and forever. Amen" (Jude 1:24, 25 - NASB). (*All those excited about the King and the Kingdom, join in and say "Amen!"*). God's glory here refers to His exalted state as opposed to any toned-down manifestation to humans on earth (a theophany; see Exodus 33:20). Giving glory ("be glory") refers to giving God the credit He is due.

Do your actions and behavior glorify God? Do you give Him the credit when success comes your way?

Kingdom Value #36: Honoring God's Name

Today we usually choose names according to their sound. In the Bible, names are associated with a person's identity and even character. God speaks of His own name as virtually being His own Person. He declared to Solomon: "And I have now chosen and consecrated this temple so that My name may be there forever; My eyes and My heart will be there at all times" (2 Chronicles 7:16 - HCSB; see also 1 Chronicles 22:7, 19; Jeremiah 7:12; Malachi 1:11; and Revelation 2:13). We have just addressed the importance of glorifying God (above). Jesus prayed, "Father, glorify Your name.' Then a voice came out of heaven: 'I have both glorified it, and will glorify it again'" (John 12:28 - NASB). God takes His name as seriously as He takes His reputation, for it represents Who He is.

To show how His Father's name was dear to His heart, when Jesus provided a model prayer for His disciples, He began with "Our Father in heaven: May your holy name be honored" (Matthew 6:9 - GNT). That is, "may Your name be kept holy," or "sanctified." "Holy" implies set apart from common use. God is the King of the universe and is worthy of our utmost respect. When people offend the Father, the Son is saddened just as much or more. We learn in a Messianic psalm that "the insults of those who insult You have fallen on me" (Psalm 69:9 - HCSB; quoted as referring to Jesus in John 2:17 and Romans 15:3). What son does not suffer when he sees his father being insulted or criticized?

Unfortunately, we live in a society which no longer respects people in authority. We have confused freedom of press with freedom to destroy reputations, criticize celebrities' every move, and question every decision. No doubt many being attacked have brought some of the negative reactions upon themselves. But the attitude of disrespect is many times transferred to God and we see Youtube videos, movie characters and talk show hosts freely questioning God's existence and authority in the most derogatory ways imaginable.

If you take the King lightly you won't take His name seriously. Which is exactly what our culture has come to do. There was a time when there were civil laws against blasphemy in Western society. Not any more. You can use whatever curse word adjoined to the most holy and precious Name, and listeners will probably not even flinch. Use the "n" word and you will be in a heap of trouble! If there is no excuse for using derogatory name-calling applied to anyone created in God's image – and Kingdom Values prohibit such – how much more offensive is it to defame the very One Who created them?

There are those, of course, who don't associate God's name with a curse word. They "just" use His name as an expression. When my daughter Melissa was around 11 years old, I took her shopping with her friend Heather. Every time Heather saw something interesting, she would preface it with "God!" After hearing this "expression" in every other phrase I couldn't take it any longer. I began to say "Heather!" as an expression whenever I wanted to emphasize something. After calling out her name several times without actually addressing her, she looked at me quizzically and I asked her, "how do you think God feels every time you use *His* name for no reason at all?" She had never thought of it that way.

Refraining from taking God's name in vain is so important to God that He includes this prohibition in the Ten Commandments, coming in as number three. God warns us not to "misuse the name of the LORD your God. The LORD will not let you go unpunished if you misuse his name" (Exodus 20:7 - NLT). There are consequences for using God's name in a dishonoring manner. The Bible identifies those who do so as God's enemies. "They blaspheme you; your enemies misuse your name" (Psalm 139:20 - NLT).

144

Why is the promised punishment ("The LORD will not let you go unpunished") so severe and disproportional to that of the other commandments? Only one other command, the second one, mentions punishment, and that in a general sense. Perhaps because our tendency is to think this is not a big deal. This is God's way of emphasizing the severity of the offense. God does not take our disrespect, much less our blasphemy, lightly.

Or perhaps, as someone has suggested, the idea of misusing God's name would relate to those who "carry" God's name in a religious setting – pastors, priests, bishops, elders – abusing the confidence people place in them for personal gain. Those who claim to represent God in order to earn the trust of the unsuspecting and then manipulate them, cheating them out of their material resources, sexually abusing them or using them to gain power and prestige. They use God's name as an excuse to defraud and exploit the very people who are searching for the path to God. And that is inexcusable – the worst form of sin (Luke 17:2)!

Do you honor God's name by the way you "talk and walk"? Have you avoided misusing His holy name? Is there room for improvement?

Kingdom Value #37: Obedience

We were made to obey! Perhaps that doesn't sound as thrilling as stating that we were made to reign. But both are true. We see the Mirroring Principle at work in this truth. Because, just as Jesus rules over the whole universe while obeying the Father, we will rule with Jesus while carrying out His will. "You were chosen according to the purpose of God the Father ... to obey Jesus Christ" (1 Peter 1:2a - GNT). No other orders from any other source could bring as much good and blessing as following the Lord's lead.

Immediate and complete obedience separates the "heroes" from the "villains" in the Bible. Noah promptly obeyed and built the ark, even though constructing a ship in the middle of the desert probably drew some question marks. Abraham did not question and complain when the Lord commanded him to get his "only son" and head towards Moriah, where God told him to sacrifice Isaac. And, "Moses did exactly as the LORD had commanded," as he led the Israelites through the desert (Leviticus 16:34 - CEV).

The Lord rejected Saul as King because he didn't obey. Saul then tried to serve the Lord by sacrificing to Him, in order to compensate for his failure. "But Samuel replied, 'What is more pleasing to the LORD: your burnt offerings and sacrifices or your obedience to his voice? Listen! Obedience is better than sacrifice, and submission is better than offering the fat of rams'" (1 Samuel 15:22 - NLT).

Many of God's commands are counter-intuitive. They would make perfect sense if we could see the big picture and how everything will one day fall into place. But God doesn't always show us the end-game. He told Abraham to go to a land He would show him when he got there. Obedience takes faith and requires humility. We must be willing to keep our ego in check and our plans on the back burner – or, be ready to sacrifice them altogether. (You've heard the joke: "Want to make God laugh? Tell him your plans.")

We are not saved by obeying God's Law, but once saved by grace, obedience to God's will and His commands leads to righteousness. "Don't you know that if you offer yourselves to someone as obedient slaves, you are slaves of that one you obey —either of sin leading to death or of obedience leading to righteousness?" (Romans 6:16 - HCSB).

Everything we know about kings and kingdoms tells us that subjects obey their rulers. All the more so in the Kingdom of God. Obedience is key to our relationship with our Lord. Jesus made that abundantly clear. Jesus, now glorified, tells the church in Sardis to "remember, therefore, what you have received and heard; **obey** it, and repent" (Revelation 3:3a - NIV). He told His closest disciples: "If you love Me, you will keep My commands" (John 14:15; 23 - HCSB). Obedience acts as a gauge for our love for the Lord: the more we love Him, the more we will obey Him.

One of my Dad's favorite hymns was "Trust and Obey," which the little country church in Brazil he pastored seemed to sing every other Sunday. Growing up the words impacted me both in English and Portuguese. Here is a portion:

> When we walk with the Lord in the light of His Word,
> What a glory He sheds on our way!
> While we do His good will, He abides with us still,
> And with all who will trust and obey.
> Trust and obey, for there's no other way

To be happy in Jesus, but to trust and obey.
(...)
What He says we will do, where He sends we will go;
Never fear, only trust and obey.

(*Words by John H. Sammis, 1887*)

A simple truth we do well to treasure.

There are many Kingdom Values and all are important. But in certain situations some may trump others. That is the case with obedience and service (*Kingdom value #22*). Service is the *modus operandi* of the Kingdom and one of the five purposes of the Church. But when Jesus went to visit Martha, her sister Mary chose to sit at Jesus' feet, listening to His word, while Martha was agitated and busy trying to serve Jesus and the other guests (Luke 10:38-42).

Serving is good, but she should have asked Jesus what **He** wanted her to be doing. When she complained with the Lord and demanded He tell her sister to come and help her, Jesus gently reminded her that only one thing is necessary, that Mary had chosen correctly and that would not be taken from her. Listening to the Lord in an attitude of obedience trumps serving, especially when our service is not what or where the Lord wants it to be, or done according to His timing. Again, "obedience is better than sacrifice."

No army can succeed if its soldiers decide to go off and do their own thing instead of following orders from the command center. In the Kingdom the same principle applies. Nothing substitutes obedience. Obedience is proof positive of our faithfulness to, and love for, the Lord. God wants us to live by faith (*Kingdom Value #39*), but faith must lead to obedience.

God is love and Jesus is meek (*Kingdom Values #3 and #16*). So, even though obeying God may not be easy at times, we know His character, which makes all the difference. After the fall of Jerusalem to the Babylonian forces, a group of people who were left behind and did not know what to do, asked the prophet Jeremiah to pray for them. "Ask the LORD to tell us where he wants us to go and what he wants us to do" (Jeremiah 42:3 - CEV). Then they committed themselves to obey God no matter the cost. "Whether it is pleasant or unpleasant, we will obey the voice of the LORD our God ... so that it may go well with us. We will certainly obey the voice of the LORD our God!" (Jeremiah 42:6 - HCSB).

One area of obedience which is extremely difficult to deal with is when God's will conflicts with that of the authorities over us. This is becoming more and more a reality in the society we live in today. But we have a "Peter Principle" to guide us. "Peter and the apostles replied, 'We must obey God rather than people'" (Acts 5:29 - CSB). For us, this may mean being shunned by society or fined by the government. For our brothers and sisters in turbulent parts of the world this can mean imprisonment and execution. As I write these lines, I am looking at a letter from "The Voice of the Martyrs" I received today, with a headline that reads, "China – New Law Leads to Crackdown on Christians." Christians there are being harassed, house churches raided, Bible sales prohibited, and pastors cuffed in front of their congregations.

Obedience is also a struggle for those who deal with bad habits and addictions. Obedience, under these circumstances, is easier said than done. Yet, obedience is still required and has the power to restore our life and wellbeing before the Lord (Deuteronomy 30:2-3). Obedience is the acid test of faithfulness. In fact, obedience is precisely what we are tested for (*Kingdom Value #15*).

How faithful have you been in obeying the Lord?

Kingdom Value #38: Rest

There is a time for everything. Well, there ***should*** be. We tend to clutter our lives with too many responsibilities, pass-times, hobbies, special interests, sports, work, bills, church activities, chores, errands, projects, ministries, and goals. Our time is filled with distractions, urgent matters and a few essential items.

When Melissa, my youngest daughter, was a little girl she never wanted to go to bed. She was too busy living. Sleeping would just be "a waste of time." Besides, there was always something else to do, somewhere else to go, or something else to watch on TV. She played like there was not tomorrow.

When I was about seven, everyday after lunch my mother would tell me to rest in bed for one full hour. That was one of the worst parts of my day. One day, when we were up at the Baptist camp my father directed, I had a brilliant idea. I would take the initiative and inform my mother I was going to go lay down "for a little

148

while" after lunch. That way I would be free to get up and play with my friends after just a few minutes (remember, I had said "for a little while"). Besides, there were trees to climb, pools to swim, fish to catch, fruit to pick! Getting out of the house without being seen was the easiest part, since the bed was right next to window. That was the first and last time I got away with that scheme.

After God created the heavens and the earth in six days, "On the seventh day God completed the work he had been doing; he rested on the seventh day from all the work he had undertaken. God blessed the seventh day and made it holy, because on it he rested from all the work he had done in creation" (Genesis 2:2, 3 - NABRE). God's creation gave us the seven-day week, while God's example gave us the six-day work week, the extra day being set apart for Sabbath rest. We were made for work and we were made for rest. We cannot work effectively if we do not adequately rest and sleep.

Both work and rest were examples set and activities prescribed before the fall. Perhaps because He knew there would be workaholics, procrastinators, and un-disciplined and unorganized people, God made the Sabbath holy. By doing so He made resting imperative, not optional. Some will argue that we now live in a peri-od of grace and the "Law" of the Sabbath no longer applies. But we are still made of flesh and blood and if we are going to "glorify God in your body" (1 Corinthi-ans 6:20 - NASB), we need to be as fresh and ready for action as possible.

Jesus was concerned for His own wellbeing and that of His disciples. After a full day of activity, when "they did not even have a chance to eat," Jesus told them, "Come with me by yourselves to a quiet place and get some rest" (Mark 6:31 - NIV). On another occasion, "as he and his disciples were out in a boat," Jesus "lay down for a nap." While He was asleep a storm suddenly engulfed them and they had to wake Jesus from His slumber so He could save them (Luke 8:22-25 -TLB). Jesus was clearly exhausted and needed this rest.

There is physical rest and there is spiritual rest. Elijah needed both. He was drained. Think about what he had just gone through on Mount Carmel: he preached a revival service, demonstrated the power of God, had the prophets of Baal put away (to put it mildly), prayed for a three-year drought to end, and ran ahead of the king's chariot on foot for what was a distance of roughly 19 miles. All in a day's work! At the end of it all, he had to be exhausted (1 Kings 18). So when news reached him that the queen wanted him dead for getting rid of her proph-ets, "Elijah was afraid and ran for his life" (1 Kings 19:3 - NIV). He fled to the desert, "sat down under a broom tree and prayed that he might die" (1 Kings 19:4 -HCSB).

149

Elijah's reaction may surprise us because, judging by any standard, God just had granted him phenomenal success and used him to bring a tremendous victory to His Kingdom. He had brought the people back to their roots, to their faith in God. He had just defeated 950 false prophets in a momentous showdown (1 Kings 18:19). But when we are mentally and physically exhausted and emotionally drained, we tend to see things in a negative light. The prophet was experiencing the normal symptoms of fatigue.

And there was one more thing Elijah had to be experiencing: post-traumatic stress disorder (PTSD). Let's not sanitize what the Bible states very clearly: "Then Elijah commanded them, 'Seize the prophets of Baal. Don't let anyone get away!' They seized them, and Elijah had them brought down to the Kishon Valley and slaughtered there" (1 Kings 18:40 - NIV). He had just witnessed close to 1,000 false prophets being put to death – at his command! That had to have affected his emotions, even if it was the right thing to do in the context of a theocratic kingdom.

So, thankfully, in the next scene we see: "Then he lay down and slept under the broom tree" (1 Kings 19:5 -HCSB). He was then treated to an angelic rest and food therapy. Elijah was woken up by an angel who had prepared food and water for him. He ate, drank, and went back to sleep. Then the angel woke him up for a second round. After that, he regained his physical strength. But there was still his emotional stress to deal with, which God did 40 days later, when he reached the cave on mount Horeb. Part of his recovery process was achieved by hearing God's voice and being commissioned to go and do the work the Lord had for him (1 Kings 19:6-18).

The author of Hebrews speaks of rest in a spiritual sense. He addresses "entering God's rest" (Hebrews 4:3) much like "entering the Promised Land," and says this can only be done by faith. Faith opens the door to salvation and fellowship with God, and faith sustains the believer as he or she trusts Him as a Father Who cares, protects, and provides. Only those who place their faith in God can find true rest.

Are you getting enough rest? Do you recharge your emotional and spiritual life through daily quiet times and other positive means?

KV38 – REST

| Consistently practice | Sometimes practice | Struggle | Mostly fail | Continually fail |

Kingdom Value #39: Faith

The Global Kingdom – God's Kingdom on earth – runs on faith. For some reason God decided that this is how we are to relate to Him on this side of eternity. There are many possible reasons for this, not the least being the fact that having to deal with a fallen race is a very delicate matter. Our real motivation can be ambivalent, as it is easy to seek God for all the wrong reasons – selfish ones, that is. People only tend to seek God if they believe He will make them happier, healthier, wealthier or more powerful. God wants us to seek Him for Himself, not for what we can get out of Him. I believe this is why He put up some barriers, allowed for some suffering, and normally doesn't make millionaires or celebrities out of His followers (1 Corinthians 1:26).

There is the story of a father who always brought a surprise gift to his child whenever he returned from a business trip. He soon noticed his child was excitedly anticipating the gift, not his return. The child began to focus on the father's presents instead of the father's presence. This led the father to withhold his gifts for awhile and focus on spending more quality time with his child when he returned from his travels. Likewise, our Heavenly Father sometimes withholds His material blessings to help us better appreciate His Person and Presence.

In the great Biblical chapter on this Kingdom Value, the author of Hebrews says "it is impossible to please God without faith." That makes sense, because "anyone who wants to come to him must believe that God exists and that he rewards those who sincerely seek him" (Hebrews 11:6 - HCSB; see Matthew 7:7; Jeremiah 29:13; and 1 Chronicles 22:19). Those who do not have faith complain, saying that if God exists He should reveal Himself more clearly. Apparently they do not wish to "sincerely seek him." Perhaps they want to remain in the dark about God because they "loved the darkness rather than the light because their works were evil" (John 3:19 - ESV).

But those who do seek God by faith have found it to be true that "he rewards" them for their research. The Bible contains story after story about those who found this to be true, as the faith chapter reminds us.

Here are highlights from Hebrews chapter 11. By Faith:
- We have the assurance about things we cannot see (11:1);
- We understand the universe was made by God's command (11:2);
- We see that Abel brought a more acceptable offering to God than Cain and showed he was a righteous person (11:4);
- Enoch was taken to heaven without dying (11:5);
- Noah obeyed God, built an ark to save his family from the flood, and received

151

the righteousness that comes only by faith (11:7);
- Abraham obeyed God's call, left his home and went to another land (11:8-9).
- Abraham offered Isaac as a sacrifice when God tested him (11:17).
- Sarah, though barren and old, was able to have a child (11:11).
- All of these heroes of the faith were anticipating a better place, a home in heaven (11:16).
- Isaac blessed his sons with promises for the future; Jacob blessed Joseph's sons; and Joseph foretold that the Israelites would leave Egypt (11:20-22).
- Moses' parents hid him for three months when he was born (11:23).
- Moses refused to be considered the son of Pharaoh's daughter. He chose, instead, to share in the oppression of the people of God (11:24, 25).
- Moses led the people out of Egypt, instituted the Passover, and showed them the way right through the Red Sea (11:27-29).
- The people of Israel marched around Jericho for seven days, "and the walls came tumbling down" (11:30); and Rahab and family were spared (11:31).
- Other heroes of faith are Gideon, Barak, Samson, Jephthah, David, Samuel, and all of the prophets (11:31). Some performed great feats by faith and had their weakness turned into strength (11:32-34). But many were tortured and refused to turn away from God in order to be spared (11:35). They suffered great cruelty and showed they were too good for this world (11:38; see v.v. 36, 37). By faith, all of them looked to the future for their great reward (11:26).

There are many factors involved in the process of salvation, but the two "keys" which are absolutely essential are faith and repentance.[6] We have already considered the issue of repentance (*Kingdom Value #2*). Faith, the other key, is the starting point in a relationship with God. Faith is also the essential Kingdom Value which sustains a Christian's daily walk, enables a Christ-follower to endure trials and temptations and to remain strong in fellowship with the Master.

God's advice for hard times is to "be careful, keep calm and don't be afraid. Do not lose heart" because "if you do not stand firm in your faith, you will not stand at all" (Isaiah 7:4a, 9b - NIV). If Christians weaken in their faith, they are left with nothing to stand on and nothing to work with.

Faith is so important because:
- Salvation depends on God's grace and our faith. "For by grace you have been saved through faith; and that not of yourselves, it is the gift of God" (Ephesians 2:8 - NASB).
- "We walk by faith, not by sight" (2 Corinthians 5:7 - ESV).
- "So faith comes from hearing, that is, hearing the Good News about Christ" (Romans 10:17 - NLT).

- Faith leads to being declared righteous: "God presented Him to demonstrate His righteousness at the present time, so that He would be righteous and declare righteous the one who has faith in Jesus" (Romans 3:26 - HCSB). God is both just and justifier.

Faith includes an attitude of surrender, a desire to fellowship with God and willfully coming under His control. Nothing does more damage to the Kingdom than a person who boldly claims to be a Christian but who has an utterly broken relationship with the Lord. Mike was arguing with our neighbor, who gently defended himself by explaining he was being falsely accused and that he was trying to do the right thing because he was a Christian. Mike told him he too was a Christian. He even had a tattoo on his arm to prove it, with the words "Nothing but the Blood." He had made "a decision" some time back but is now living with his girlfriend, drinking so heavily the ambulance had to come and take him to the emergency room, and freely uses profanity to express himself. Instead of proudly identifying themselves as Christians, people living in obvious disregard of Kingdom Values should first evaluate if their decision to follow Christ is real, repent, believe, and be healed. Only then proclaim they are sinners saved by grace (see *Kingdom Values #21 and #49* on Proclamation and Witnessing)!

Faith looks back and learns to trust God today because of all He has done in the past. Hope looks forwards and continues to trust in God's character, knowing He can be counted on to keep His promises.

How is your faith? Do you seek the Lord with an attitude of surrender and the desire for a deeper fellowship with God? Do you identify more with one of the heroes of the faith in Hebrews 11 or with "doubting Thomas"?

Kingdom Value #40: Hope

"Da-da's coming home! He's coming from the sky!" My granddaughter Heidi Joy would burst out with excitement every time she heard a helicopter fly over the house. She was only two years old and her father was deployed to Afghanistan as an Apache pilot at the time. She didn't know how or when, but she knew that sooner or later her father would come home. Hope keeps us going when the going gets tough.

Brazilians have a popular saying: "hope is the last thing to die." Because if hope is gone there is nothing left to fight for. While we still have hope we hang on for dear life in the midst of the worse of crises. The Body of Christ, the universal Church, constitutes a community of hope! The members of this community should be encouraging each other, lifting each other up. But ultimately, each of us has to "run the race that we have to run with patience, our eyes fixed on Jesus the source and the goal of our faith" (Hebrews 12:1, 2 - PHILLIPS).

We are creatures of hope. We are "prisoners of hope" (Zechariah 9:12 - ESV). We must envision tomorrow in order to live out our lives today. We need that context. For instance, say you were kidnapped by a terrorist group and were told that tomorrow you would be executed. Just knowing there was no chance of survival tomorrow would radically modify your outlook, thought process, dreams, routine – everything – today. We need to believe in the future, otherwise we will lack the needed perspective and motivation to go on with the present.

Knowing that heaven awaits us in our future allows us to endure the suffering we are subjected to in our present daily lives. That is why Paul could say, "For our present troubles are small and won't last very long. Yet they produce for us a glory that vastly outweighs them and will last forever!" (2 Corinthians 4:17 - NLT).

The quality of the Christian's hope is entirely different from that expressed in phrases like, "I hope that will work out for me;" or, "I really hope things will get better tomorrow." Biblical hope is based on a sure thing which has not yet taken place – but is just as certain as though it had – because it rests on the promises of God, Who always keeps His word. That's why we can count on "the hope of eternal life that God, who cannot lie, promised before time began" (Titus 1:2 - HCSB). And because "it is impossible for God to lie, we who have fled for refuge might have strong encouragement to hold fast to the hope set before us" (Hebrews 6:18 - ESV). All the same, hope remains future-based, because "hope that is seen is not hope, because who hopes for what he sees?" (Romans 8:24 - NET Bible).

We can have real, solid hope because of God's promises which are registered in His Word. Remember: "Everything that was written in the past was written to teach us, so that through endurance and the encouragement of the Scriptures we might have hope" (Romans 15:4 - NIV).

Hope is a guarantee that acts like a "predated check." We have God's guarantee that one day we will be able to go to Him and cash our check. And we know it won't bounce because God has deposited into our "account" everything we will need for eternity (Matthew 6:20). Scripture both warns and encourages us when

154

it says, "And do not make God's Holy Spirit sad; for the Spirit is God's mark of ownership on you, a guarantee that the Day will come when God will set you free" (Ephesians 4:30 - GNT).

Those who do not believe in God and His promises have no hope (1 Thessalonians 4:13). Those who die without hope will remain without hope forever (Isaiah 38:18). But for those who do believe, faith and hope work together to bring about a new relationship with God "as we look forward to sharing in the glory of God" which gives us "a hope that will never disappoint us" (Romans 5:1-5 - CEV). Through His prophet God declared, "Blessed is the man who trusts in the LORD and whose trust is the LORD" (Jeremiah 17:7 - NASB).

What is it we hope for?
- We hope for a better place, where there is no suffering;
- We hope to see our departed loved ones again;
- We hope expectantly for the day we will meet our Creator and Savior;
- We long for the Messianic Age, the Millennial Kingdom, as it ushers in justice, health, and prosperity. And as it leads to the deep and meaningful worship of our Lord and Savior;[7]
- We eagerly await the Eternal Kingdom, where righteousness dwells.[8]

Hope leads to joy and peace (see *Kingdom Values #10 and #11*), as expressed in this encouraging prayer: "I pray that God, the source of hope, will fill you completely with joy and peace because you trust in him. Then you will overflow with confident hope through the power of the Holy Spirit" (Romans 15:13 - NLT).

What do you hope for? Is hope helping you to keep the Kingdom in focus? Is hope an encouraging factor which makes you stronger in your daily battles? Does hope help you persist in your faith and obedience to the Lord?

KV40 - **HOPE**

| Consistently practice | Sometimes practice | Struggle | Mostly fail | Continually fail |

Kingdom Value #41: Grace

We just looked at hope. There would be no grounds for hope if it were not for God's grace. The legal system can be harsh and the workplace unforgiving, but God is "full of compassion, and gracious, longsuffering, and abundant in mercy

155

and truth" (Psalm 86:15 - King James 2000 Bible).

God is the King of the universe. But He is also a Father to those who come into His Kingdom. He is perfect. His standards are high. His discipline is strict. But then, there is a side to God's character which is mind-boggling: He is a God of forgiveness, of second chances, of mercy and grace. He is a God of love. And His love compels Him to be full of grace towards us.

Grace is God's way of maintaining the just demands of the law while providing a way of escape from its penalties to those who ask for His forgiveness. Grace is a Kingdom Value. Without it, there would be no inclusion of humans in the Kingdom. With it, God has made it possible for us to inherit and thrive in His domain.

There are so many aspects to God's grace! At its core it means an unmerited favor received from God. That favor can mean anything from God calling us to Himself, to providing our salvation and spiritual growth, to endowing us with special abilities to serve.

God is a God of grace (1 Peter 5:10). God's throne is a throne of grace which we can approach with confidence (Hebrews 4:16). It follows that the Gospel – the Good News of the Kingdom – is a message of God's grace (Acts 14:3). For this reason, we can set our hope completely on the grace we will receive when Jesus comes back (1 Peter 1:13).

The Bible speaks of "the manifold grace of God" (1 Peter 4:10 - NASB), which literally means the multicolored grace of God. God's grace is pervasive in the Kingdom, with many dimensions and multiple applications. God's grace can color and brighten that which would otherwise be a grayish existence. Because of God's grace we can be saved, forgiven (repeatedly), restored, and transformed. God then expects us to extend this grace to others.

Below are five dimensions and applications of God's grace in our lives.

1. Saving grace
The two essential steps everyone must take to enter the Kingdom are to "repent and believe in the Good News" (Mark 1:15). That is the necessary human response to God's free offer of salvation. "For the grace of God has appeared that offers salvation to all people" (Titus 2:11 - NIV). This is the Good News: "for you are saved by grace through faith, and this is not from yourselves; it is God's gift" (Ephesians 2:8 - HCSB). We don't have to deserve it, work for it, pay for it. In fact, we cannot. We have nothing to pay with, since we are spiritually bankrupt. And the debt we have accumulated with God because of our sin is of such magnitude

that even multiple lifetimes would not be enough to liquidate it (Matthew 18:23-35).

Fortunately, God's grace has led Him to plan a way out for us, not as an afterthought, but even before we were created and the problem existed. Because God loves us, He chose to show us His favor, even though that meant sacrificing His own Son.

2. Forgiving grace

After being saved, we still fall and need God's forgiveness for our failures, character flaws, shortcomings, and sins. Though redeemed, we still have a fallen human nature to contend with. Each day is a test of our loyalty (see *Faithfulness – Kingdom Value #15*), and many times we d o not pass the test: we choose to please self instead of pleasing God. Confession and repentance are then necessary to restore our fellowship with the Lord. Otherwise, we risk cheapening grace (as Bonhoeffer warns us in *The Cost of Discipleship*), or abuse "God's marvelous grace" entirely (Jude 1:4).

On the contrary, "because of God's exceptional grace" (2 Corinthians 9:14 - ISV) we tend to want to stay close to the Lord, to love and obey Him even more: those who are forgiven much, love much (Luke 7:47). "Christ's love compels us" (2 Corinthians 5:14) to desire to get it right, to please our Master and King. God's "abundance of grace" and His "gift of righteousness" go hand-in-hand (Romans 5:17 - NASB). This is how Nehemiah described the Lord: "But you are a God of forgiveness, gracious and merciful, slow to become angry, and rich in unfailing love" (Nehemiah 9:17b - NLT). "You are a God of grace and you are merciful" (Nehemiah 9:31b - ISV), he said.

3. Restoring grace

Sometimes the fall is severe, for long periods of time, and traumatic. We need to be restored from past hurts and failures. After denying Jesus three times (John 18:15-27), Peter might have seen himself as a failure and may have imagined it was all over for him. We may deduce that from the fact that he went back to his old profession as a fisherman. But even in his comfort zone he found himself failing, as he and the other disciples who went with him couldn't catch any fish that night (see John 21:1-17).

Jesus tells them what to do and they come back with a boatload of fish. Jesus was waiting for them with a hot breakfast. Jesus asked Peter if he loved Him "more than these." Peter simply answers, "yes, Lord, you know that I love you." He is in no mood for bragging. While Jesus asks Peter three times if he loved Him, the first two times He uses the Greek *agapaó (or agape)*, signifying unconditional love. Peter answers with *phileó*, indicating fraternal or brotherly love (the PHILLIPS version has "you know that I am your friend"). Finally, Jesus asks Peter if he *phileó* loves Him, to which Peter responds, "You know all things, You know that I *phileó* love you." While Scripture says Peter was hurt because Jesus asked him the third time, Jesus was giving Peter the opportunity to confess his love the same number of times he had denied knowing his Lord.

After each time Peter confessed his love, Jesus said "feed my lambs," then "take care of my sheep" and, finally, "feed my sheep." Not only was Jesus extending forgiving grace, He was extending restorative grace. And more: Jesus was offering Peter a position of honor and authority; a ministry which involved leadership over the other disciples.

This process is to be followed by the church. Once the church has disciplined the sinner, he or she should be forgiven and encouraged. Paul told the Corinthians "so you should rather turn to forgive and comfort him, or he may be overwhelmed by excessive sorrow" (2 Corinthians 2:7 - ESV). The word translated as "forgive" comes from the Greek *charisasthai* (notice *charis* or grace is at the root of the word) and means "to show favor to."

It is Peter who comforts his readers by telling them that, "Now the God of all grace, who called you to His eternal glory in Christ Jesus, will personally restore, establish, strengthen, and support you after you have suffered a little" (1 Peter 5:10 - HCSB). What happened in Peter's experience can happen to us as well. After we have slipped or fallen, Jesus can *personally* restore us back to fellowship with Himself.

4. Transforming grace

God's grace includes His unmerited power which He places at our disposal to fight temptation and live a life of sanctification. He gave Himself not only for our redemption but to purify us for Himself.

Grace is what God freely *gives* and *does* for us without the precondition of merit. God does not duplicate: He does for us what we cannot do for ourselves. Those who lack the humility to accept this, struggle on their own with frustrating results. Yet, God "gives grace to the humble" (Proverbs 3:34 - HCSB).
Because of our lower nature, this is one of the most difficult lessons a disciple will ever have to learn (see *Self-denial – Kingdom Value #54*). The concept has been popularized as "let go and let God." And if we will, "the grace of God" can teach "us to say 'No' to ungodliness and worldly passions, and to live self-controlled, up-

right and godly lives in this present age, while we wait for the blessed hope—the appearing of the glory of our great God and Savior, Jesus Christ, who gave himself for us to redeem us from all wickedness and to purify for himself a people that are his very own, eager to do what is good" (Titus 2:11-14 - NIV).

It is in the context of transforming grace that we are told both to grow and to be strengthened in grace. Peter said we must "grow in the grace and knowledge of our Lord and Savior Jesus Christ" (2 Peter 3:18 - ESV). At first, I struggled to understand what growing in grace could mean. It became clear that growing in grace is learning to rely more and more on God's strength and less and less on our own. We learn to step aside and let God fight our battles as we move forward in the area of sanctification.

The concept is the same as that announced by "little David" as he faced the giant Goliath. David had been anointed king not long before that confrontation. On that occasion "the Spirit of the LORD came mightily upon David from that day forward" (1 Samuel 16:13b - NASB). As David faced the giant he declared "that it is not by sword or spear that the LORD saves! For the battle is the LORD's, and he will deliver you into our hand" (1 Samuel 17:47 - NET Bible). David's faith, boldness and power to defeat such a formidable enemy came from God's Spirit. David recognized this battle was the Lord's to win.

Grace in the form of salvation, forgiveness, restoration and transformation is a precious gift from God. Now, we know that God blesses us so we can also be a blessing in the lives of others. How can we pass the blessing of grace on to others?

5. Transferring received grace

Those who have received God's grace are to mirror God's action and offer this gift to others. Grace (Greek *charis*) is not only God's unmerited *favor*, as in His forgiveness and salvation. It is also His unmerited gift of the Holy Spirit residing in us and the gifts (*charismatōn*) of the Spirit, given so we may serve and bless others (see 1 Peter 4:10). As God, by His grace, forgives and restores us, He wants us to be a channel of His grace to others. We receive grace to extend grace. We are forgiven and must forgive. We are treated with respect and honor and we are to treat others in the same way. Jesus states this concept as **the *freely you have received freely give* Kingdom Principle** (Matthew 10:8b - NIV).

Where are you on the grace scale? Have you received God's offer of salvation? Have you learned to accept His forgiveness when you fail? Have you been or do you need to be restored? Are you growing in God's grace?

◀	KV41 – GRACE				▶
TYPE OF GRACE	**Consistently practice**	**Sometimes practice**	**Struggle**	**Mostly fail**	**Continually fail**
SAVING	☐ YES (received)		☐ NO (not received)		
FORGIVING	☐	☐	☐	☐	☐
RESTORING	☐	☐	☐	☐	☐
TRANSFORMING	☐	☐	☐	☐	☐

Kingdom Value #42: Thanksgiving

I was eating strawberries when Heidi Joy, my granddaughter who was two at the time, asked me for some. When she finished eating what I had given her, Monique, her mother, reminded her: "What do we say, Heidi?" –"More," she answered casually. We both burst out laughing. She was *supposed* to say "thank you."

Even older kids tend to take the blessings they receive from their parents for granted. Many parents sacrifice and go to great lengths to provide the best education and the basics of food, clothing and lodging yet receive little or no gratitude. "Thank you" is such a powerful expression. It has the power to encourage and to bless. To cheer and to make people smile. It takes little effort to write or pronounce. So simple and easy to say, yet so frequently withheld for no apparent reason.

I believe the Lord gives us children to show us how we often treat Him. God gives us so much! Yet we seem to think that is His job. And, when we don't get everything on our wish list, we are quick to complain. The Bible calls this murmuring or grumbling (Numbers 14:26-27). We take the blessings of life, health, water, air, food, safety, family, friends and so much more for granted. Yet, if we stop and take note of all the details God takes care of and provides each day, we will marvel at His tender loving care for us. Jesus taught that "He causes His sun to rise on the evil and the good, and sends rain on the righteous and the unrighteous" (Matthew 5:45 - NASB). Every day. Whether we deserve it or not.

Recent studies have shown that an attitude of gratitude does wonders for one's health. Just in case we need a little push, we are commanded: "in everything give thanks; for this is the will of God in Christ Jesus for you" (1 Thessalonians 5:18 - NKJV).

160

Jesus revealed the Kingdom Principle that those who are forgiven much, love much, while those who are forgiven little, love little (Luke 7:47). It seems that Jesus was speaking about people's perception, because there really is no human being who has been "forgiven little." Any sin is a terrible offense against God. But some sins are so serious and destructive that even the offender can scarcely believe he or she could be forgiven.

Jesus told a parable of a servant whose debt (compare to the accumulation of sins in need of forgiveness) was so huge, he would never be able to repay it – not even during multiple lifetimes. When the king sentenced him he pleaded for forgiveness and the king decided to cancel his debt in full. But this same servant went out and found a colleague who owed him infinitely less, yet didn't forgive his debt, even though he pleaded with him. Word got back to the king, who called him in and said: "you should have given that other man who serves with you the same mercy I gave you" (Matthew 18:33 - ERV). The King called him a "wicked servant" because his lack of gratitude kept him from extending forgiveness to his colleague.

Grateful people extend the blessings they have received to others. They ask, "How can I repay the LORD for all the good He has done for me?" (Psalm 116:12 - HCSB). At least part of the answer is passing along those benefits to others. And it works both ways. For example, "Blessed are the merciful, for they will be shown mercy" (Matthew 5:7 - NIV). Receiving mercy and then offering mercy to others is proof of true gratitude and confirms the mercy received. "What comes around goes around" also applies to the good we do.

The importance of expressing your gratitude in thanksgiving

Remember the story of the 10 lepers who where healed? They kept their distance as the Law required and cried out to Jesus, begging Him to have mercy on them. Jesus gave them an order with no further details: "Go, show yourselves to the priests." They were not healed immediately. They had to first demonstrate their faith by obeying Jesus' command. "And so it was that as they went, they were cleansed." They had done everything right up to that point: they called out to the one and true Savior Who could help them. They obeyed without questioning His command. And one could argue that not turning back to thank Jesus meant they were focused on obeying His command to first go and show themselves to the priests who could clear them, allowing them back into the community.

But Jesus didn't see it that way. When only one of them went back to thank Him, Jesus asked, "Were there not ten cleansed? But where are the nine? Were there not any found who returned to give glory to God except this foreigner?" They knew how to be very vocal about asking for a favor. But when their wish was granted, they just as quickly forgot about the frightful predicament they had endured and what God had graciously done for them. They moved on with life and to "business as usual."

However, "one of them, when he saw that he was healed, returned, and with a loud voice glorified God, and fell down on his face at His feet, giving Him thanks." This man, a Samaritan, transcended the cold letter of the Law, was moved by Jesus' compassion, and knew this was more than a physical healing – it was a life-changing experience. Jesus confirmed this fact when He told him, "Arise, go your way. Your faith has made you well" (Luke 17:11-19 - NKJV). The verb for "made well" (cured, healed) can also mean to save or rescue.

Showing gratitude and expressing it in thanksgiving is like telling the Lord, "I know I don't deserve this and I know You owe me nothing, so I thank You for going beyond justice and showing me mercy." That is a healthy spiritual perspective. Contrast that with those who, "though they knew God, they did not glorify Him as God or show gratitude. Instead, their thinking became nonsense, and their senseless minds were darkened" (Romans 1:21 - HCSB).

The notion of being grateful has been popularized today and you can see celebrities thanking "the universe" or some other "force" as they believe this will have a positive impact on their well-being and generate more happiness. It's Positive Psychology 101. But when we are thankful to the *Creator* of the universe, then gratitude is a Kingdom attitude. C. S. Lewis observed the difference in the attitude of those who are grateful and express it in praise and those who do not. He noticed that the malcontents praise least while those who enjoy life and beauty, those who find life to be magnificent, are the ones who praise most and more often.[9]

There is so much to be grateful for! Knowing that God has invited us to participate in His Kingdom forever is cause for great jubilation and praise, which results in "giving thanks to the Father who has qualified us to be partakers of the inheritance of the saints in the light. He has delivered us from the power of darkness and conveyed us into the kingdom of the Son of His love, in whom we have redemption through His blood, the forgiveness of sins" (Colossians 1:12-14 - NKJV).

Thanksgiving goes on all the time in heaven's courtroom. The "twenty-four elders who are seated on their thrones before God threw themselves down with their faces to the ground and worshiped God," by declaring, "We give you thanks, Lord God, the All-Powerful, the one who is and who was, because you have taken your great power and begun to reign" (Revelation 11:16-17 - NET Bible).

The Psalms are full of expressions of thanksgiving and praise. "Praise the Lord! O give thanks to the Lord for He is good. His loving-kindness lasts forever. Who can put into words the great works of the Lord? Who can make known all His praise?" (Psalm 106:1-2 - NLV). And, when just saying it is not quite enough, "Sing praises to God, sing praises! Sing praises to our King, sing praises!" (Psalm 47:6 - ESV).

How thankful have you been for all God has done for you? Have you forgotten any of His benefits (Psalm 103:2)? Do you cultivate an attitude of gratitude?

Kingdom Value #43: Prayer

"And, finally, take the microphone of prayer in the Spirit and always call out to God with every form of prayer and requests." I am convinced that if Paul were alive today he would add a mic and radio equipment to his description of the armor of God in order to represent prayer (Ephesians 6:10-18). Prayer is our lifeline to God. Through prayer we have instantaneous access to the Lord. We should constantly live and move about in God's presence, hearing His voice, following His Spirit's prompting, doing His will. That is what is implied by the command to "pray without ceasing" (1 Thessalonians 5:17 - ESV).

If you grew up going to Sunday School then you might remember being taught that the four main components of prayer are confession, adoration, petition, and intercession (or a similar list). It is a good idea to begin with confession, so that our prayers will not be hindered or go unanswered. To confess is to recount to the Lord what happened. He already knows, but we must verbally acknowledge our sin to Him. After confession comes adoration. Before requesting anything, we honor the Lord by confessing our love for Him and thanking Him (thanksgiving) for Who He is (worship) and what He has done (praise). We then present our requests to the Lord and ask for His provision ("give us this day our daily bread") and protection ("and deliver us from the evil one"). And we intercede for the needs of others: their health, salvation, and other concerns.

If you have ever wondered how you should pray and what you should be praying for, the Bible says we are to pray with our spirit and understanding (1 Corinthians 14:15). We are to pray: without calling attention to ourselves (Matthew 6:5); privately (Matthew 6:6); corporately with holy hands and without anger or quarreling (1 Timothy 2:8); for one another (James 5:16); and for those who are sick (James 5:14). God expects "that petitions, prayers, intercession and thanksgiving be made for all people" (1 Timothy 2:1). We should pray for kings and all those in authority (1 Timothy 2:2). We are told to "ask the Lord of the harvest to send out workers into his harvest field" (Luke 10:2). We may pray for boldness to witness and proclaim (Acts 4:29-31); for success and favor before authorities (Nehemiah 1:11); for forgiveness (1 Kings 8:30); for God's mercy (Daniel 2:18); for comfort in affliction (Psalm 119:76); and for compassion (Psalm 119:77). And, Jesus told us to pray for God's Kingdom to come (Luke 11:2).

The Bible teaches us the secret to answered prayer. We are promised an answer when we pray according to God's will (1 John 5:14), in Jesus' name (John 14:13), with faith (Matthew 21:22; James 1:6), in private (Matthew 6:6), and with persistence (Matthew 7:7-11; Luke 11:5-8).

Prayer is a powerful connection to the King. Corporate prayer, when there is agreement, can be even more powerful (Matthew 18:20). Because He wants our participation, we are invited to ask God to fulfill His plans on earth (see Daniel 9:1-4). Tom Elliff, former president of the International Mission Board (IMB), for years a prayer advocate, believes "God has given us prayer, not primarily as a method for getting things or changing circumstances, but as a means of cooperating with Him in His great plan for the redemption of the lost and other great spiritual exploits."[10]

Jesus gave His followers special Kingdom authority through prayer. He assured them, "I will give you the keys of the kingdom of heaven, and whatever you bind on earth is already bound in heaven, and whatever you loose on earth is already loosed in heaven." He also told them, "Again, I assure you: If two of you on earth agree about any matter that you pray for, it will be done for you by My Father in heaven" (Matthew 16:19; 20:19 - HCSB).

Jerry Rankin, also a former president of the IMB, reminds us of the need to expand our prayer circle and to have a Kingdom-minded prayer life. "Isn't Satan clever! He gets us to limit our praying to personal matters – our personal needs and concerns, our families, our communities, and our churches – and it never occurs to us to intercede for the nations. His strongholds remain secure against the kingdom of God when we never pray for the nations and intercede for the peoples of the world." Rankin, who led one of the largest mission organizations in the world, speaks from personal experience when he says "prayer is not peripheral to missions strategy. It is not to undergird and support mission strategy. It is the heart of our strategy to reach the nations and fulfill the Great Commission."[11]

The Lord shared some Kingdom Principles related to the importance of persistence in prayer. He taught His disciples to "keep asking, and it will be given to you. Keep searching, and you will find. Keep knocking, and the door will be opened to you." Jesus then makes a comparison between earthly fathers and the heavenly Father. When a son asks for bread will he get a stone? Or for fish, will he be given a snake? Then, if earthly fathers know how to give good presents, so much more our Father in heaven to those who pray to Him (Matthew 7:7-11 - HCSB). As a loving and righteous Father, God enjoys answering our prayers and giving us good things.

The Lord's Model Prayer (Matthew 6:9-13) is a Kingdom prayer, since all four aspects of the Kingdom are referred to there: Heaven refers to the Universal Kingdom, the coming Kingdom refers to the Millennial Kingdom, the daily provisions and relationship needs refer to our life in the Global Kingdom, and the recognition that God's Kingdom, power and glory are forever refers to the Eternal Kingdom. All four aspects impact our lives now, albeit in different ways. We pray to a God Who we understand retains complete control over all creation – and will continue to do so forever and ever. We pray that His Millennial Kingdom be set up on earth, in accordance with His will and His timing. Yet, most of our prayer life will center on God's will being done on earth and in our lives, by requesting His provision, forgiveness and deliverance on a daily basis.

The Lord's Priestly prayer, found in John 17, is a privileged conversation between the Son and His Father which His disciples were allowed to listen in on. In His prayer Jesus reports to the Father on His "mission accomplished" and intercedes for His present and future disciples. Jesus' love for the Father and for His followers is very evident in everything He says. As is His focus on the mission He received and the one He gave the Church: "As you sent me into the world, I have sent them into the world" (John 17:18 - NIV). One day, Jesus wants those the Father has given Him to be with Him and to see His glory (v. 24). Those no longer living in the Global Kingdom, but who have died and are in the Eternal Kingdom, in all its majesty.

There is another tool the Lord has given believers which helps them in their spiritual battles and as they seek answers for their prayers. Fasting is not a magic formula for success. It is a cry of the heart, a sacrifice, a willingness to abstain from food in order to seek the Lord with more intensity in prayer. Fasting is our way of showing the Lord we mean business, that our cry for help is a desperate plea from the heart for divine intervention.

Fasting can be planned and part of a spiritual discipline routine, or it can happen spontaneously, given the seriousness or urgency of a matter. The felt need is so great that the believer scarcely thinks of food or temporarily loses his or her appetite.

Fasting is a private thing. It is between the believer and the Lord. It is not for gaining "spiritual points" or proving to others how mature we are as Christians. Jesus warned His disciples that, "Whenever you fast, do not put on a gloomy face as the hypocrites do, for they neglect their appearance so that they will be noticed by men when they are fasting. Truly I say to you, they have their reward in full" (Matthew 6:16 - NASB).

How would you rate your prayer life? Is there a good balance between personal petitions, intercession for the needs of others and worship with thanksgiving? Do you pray without ceasing and as well as intensely in a disciplined manner?

Kingdom Value #44: Rejoicing in the Lord

When we first approach God there is usually a chain reaction which takes place. We feel attracted to the Good News and to God's claim on our life. The Holy Spirit shows us how far we've have fallen from His standards and love. We recognize our guilt, understand we stand condemned, and feel the weight of our sin. We then repent for all we've done and cry for forgiveness. We accept God's pardon while placing our faith in Him. A tremendous weight is lifted. We feel lighter than ever before. A wonderful feeling of acceptance, peace, wellbeing and love sweep over us and we begin to rejoice!

Rejoicing is a sign that the Kingdom – God's reign in your life – has arrived. It's time to stop feeling guilty and beating ourselves up. It's time to rejoice. After the population of Jerusalem had listened to the reading of the Scriptures for several hours, they began to weep. But then Nehemiah told them, "Go and celebrate with a feast of rich foods and sweet drinks, and share gifts of food with people who have nothing prepared. This is a sacred day before our Lord. Don't be dejected and sad, for the joy of the LORD is your strength!" (Nehemiah 8:10 - NLT).

Rejoicing involves Joy (*Kingdom Value #10*). According to the dictionary, to rejoice is to "feel or show great joy or delight." And it may lead to Celebrating Together (*Kingdom Value #33*). The main difference is that celebrating is an outward expression which includes some form of demonstration, such as singing, dancing, hugging, eating, and throwing a party.

In the Bible, rejoicing is specifically related to our relationship with God. Rejoicing in the Lord is a direct consequence of our walking righteously before the God, when He has His way in us and we feel connected to the purposes of the our King. "But may the righteous be glad and rejoice before God; may they be happy and joyful" (Psalm 68:3 - NIV). This state should not be the exception in the Christian's life, but an ongoing experience. "Keep on rejoicing in the Lord at all times. I will say it again: Keep on rejoicing!" (Philippians 4:4 - ISV).

There are many reasons why we can rejoice in the Lord: He loves us, He will never leave us, He has prepared a place for us to spend eternity by His side. We should rejoice over what we are able to accomplish for the Lord during our ministry here on earth, but this does not compare with the joy that awaits us in Heaven. Jesus told His disciples: "Nevertheless, do not rejoice in this, that the spirits are subject to you, but rejoice that your names are written in heaven" (Luke 10:20 - ESV).

We can rejoice now even through suffering, because we know our experience is preparing us to meet the King, when all our pain will be a thing of the past. "But rejoice, since you are partakers of Christ's sufferings; that, when his glory shall be revealed, you may be glad also with exceeding joy" (KJV 2000 Bible).

While rejoicing should be the rule, not the exception, it is true that we are greatly influenced by our physical bodies (pain and aches, sickness, hormones, fatigue), our psyche (feelings, mood, psychological stress), and spirit (being in step with God's will, filled with the Spirit – or not). Sometimes everything is fine, but because we are tired or there is some concern that is nagging us, we just don't feel exuberant joy or the desire to rejoice.

But one day our joy and desire to rejoice will not be limited by the suffering we see all around us or bound by our unredeemed bodies. In the eternal state, rejoicing will be unrestrained! One event which will be great cause for rejoicing will be when the Lord Jesus takes the Church as His bride. The call will go out: "Let us rejoice and exult and give him glory, because the wedding celebration of the Lamb has come, and his bride has made herself ready" (Revelation 19:7 - NET Bible).

Rejoicing, therefore, is an act of faith. It is based on the belief that God is in control of our lives as well as everything around us and that He can be trusted to deliver on all of His promises.

Is rejoicing a reoccurring theme in your life? Do you daily bring to mind the awesome things the Lord is doing in the world? Do you express your joy in the Lord on a constant basis?

KV44 – REJOICING IN THE LORD

| Consistently practice | Sometimes practice | Struggle | Mostly fail | Continually fail |

Chapter
8

Life Mission Kingdom Values

Jesus answered, "Let the dead bury their own dead.
You go and proclaim the Kingdom of God."
Luke 9:60 - GNT

Kingdom Value #45: Fruitfulness

Producing much fruit, Jesus said, glorifies the Father and proves we are His disciples (John 15:8). "Fruit," in Scripture, refers to the results brought about when we do what is right. Paul speaks of the fruit of the Spirit which describes what He produces in and through us. But when he refers to what the flesh produces, he uses the term "works" (Galatians 5:19-23). And, after providing another list of deeds which stand in opposition to Kingdom Values, Paul refers to them as "fruitless deeds of darkness," contrasting them with "the fruit of the light" which "results in all goodness, righteousness, and truth" (Ephesians 5:9, 11 - HCSB).

Fruitfulness means being productive for the Kingdom (Titus 3:14 - ESV). On the flip side, the dictionary defines fruitlessness as "failing to achieve the desired results; unproductive or useless," and, of course, as "not producing fruit."

To say Jesus led a very fruitful life would be an understatement. But it was His death that was to be His most fruitful deed. "Truly, truly, I say to you, unless a grain of wheat falls into the earth and dies, it remains alone; but if it dies, it bears much fruit" (John 12:24 - NASB). By becoming "the author of their salvation" through His death and resurrection, Jesus was able to bring "many sons to glory" (Hebrews 2:10).

As a general rule, our spiritual gifts are to be used for the benefit of the Church (in and outside of its walls) and our natural talents for the benefit of society (see *Work, Kingdom Value #48*). Of course, everything we do should be for God's glory and the benefit His Kingdom. For instance, my main spiritual gift is teaching while illustrating is one of my main natural talents. Whenever possible, I have tried to enhance my teaching and Bible studies with illustrations and graphics.

Wherever God has placed us, He expects us to be fruitful. And He will call us to account for what we have done with the resources He has provided. Someone has categorized these resources under Time, Talents and Treasures. We will be evaluated and rewarded according to the fruit we produce when we use our time wisely, our gifts and talents to bless and build up, and our financial resources to contribute to the good of others. Jeremiah acknowledged that God is "great in counsel and mighty in deed, whose eyes are open to all the ways of the sons of men, giving to everyone according to his ways and according to the fruit of his deeds" (Jeremiah 32:19 - NASB).

> Jesus "told this parable: 'A man had a fig tree that was planted in his vineyard. He came looking for fruit on it and found none. He told the vineyard worker, 'Listen, for three years I have come looking for fruit on this fig tree and haven't found any. Cut it down! Why should it even waste the soil?' But he replied to him, 'Sir, leave it this year also, until I dig around it and fertilize it. Perhaps it will bear fruit next year, but if not, you can cut it down'" (Luke 13:6-9 - HCSB).

It isn't called a *fig* tree for a reason. Producing figs is its primary function.

Then there was the time Jesus pronounced a curse on a fig tree because, even though it wasn't the season for figs, He was hungry and the fig tree was all leaves and no fruit (Mark 11:12-14; 20-21). As far as we know, this is the only miracle Jesus performed where He brought death to a living organism. To understand this prophetic act we must remember Jesus was on His way to the Temple area where He would aggressively confront those who had turned it into a street market. There He would once more be rejected by the Jewish leadership. The fig tree was symbolic of Israel. God was "hungry" to see His chosen nation bearing fruit. It had the leaves which promised much, but offered no fruit. So it would fall under God's judgment like a withering fig tree.

Fruit is also equated with leading others to salvation. Remember that the only way to expand God's Kingdom – on earth and for eternity – is by adding new citizens to it (see *Witnessing, Kingdom Value #49* and *Missions, Kingdom Value #50*).

Our main purpose is to glorify God and one of the main ways we can do so is by living a fruitful life. If we are self-centered and self-serving, we are not just being immature and missing the point, we are denying God the glory He deserves and frustrating the purpose for which we exist.

How fruitful has your life been lately? Have you been using your time, talents and treasures, for God's glory? Have you helped others find their way to the Lord?

Kingdom Value #46: Compassion

Teaching on the miracles of Jesus at church showed me just how much He was motivated by compassion. Many verses state this clearly (Matthew 9:36; 14:14; 20:34; Mark 5:19; 6:34; 8:2). But it was only after rereading Mark 1 that this truth began to sink in. There we find the story of a man who had leprosy and came to Jesus on his knees, begging for healing. "If You are willing, You can make me clean," he cried out to Jesus. Jesus, "moved with compassion," said He was willing, touched the man and healed him immediately. Jesus then "sternly warned him and sent him away at once, telling him, 'See that you say nothing to anyone; but go and show yourself to the priest.'" But the man, instead, went and told everyone what had happened to him, "with the result that Jesus could no longer enter a town openly. But He was out in deserted places, and they would come to Him from everywhere" (Mark 1:40-45 - HCSB).

The point is this: Jesus had so much compassion for this man that He was willing to heal him even though He knew he would disobey His strict orders and force Jesus to change His proclamation strategy. Now, instead of being able to enter towns openly, He had to remain in deserted areas waiting for the needy to come and find Him. As I asked my class why they thought Jesus would be willing to do this, it occurred to me that this is what He does for all of us: He loves, heals, and saves us even though He knows we will fail Him over and over again.

Justice seeks fairness and win-win situations (see *Justice, Kingdom Value #65*). Compassion goes a step further in favor of the other party. It does not mind, sometimes, being on the loosing side of a win-lose situation. It considers the Law and regards justice in high esteem, yet seeks to give the other party the benefit of the doubt, offer a second chance, or extend forgiveness for the other person's misgivings. Compassion is feeling and acting on the basis of grace and mercy.

God is a God of justice. But woe to us if He were not also a God of compassion! If God were a "bean counter" Who kept up with our every misstep, failure and sin – little and big, there would be no hope for us to escape His just judgment and wrath. Yet, surprisingly, God is able to be both just *and* compassionate. The Lord both loves justice and longs to show us His favor in difficult circumstances.

Isaiah wrote: "Therefore the LORD is waiting to show you mercy, and is rising up to show you compassion, for the LORD is a just God. All who wait patiently for Him are happy." The prophet declared that "He will show favor to you at the sound of your cry; when He hears, He will answer you" (Isaiah 30:18-19b - HCSB). In His justice, God shows us mercy. He doesn't compromise His standards and values, yet manages to be compassionate in the process.

When God revealed Himself in a very deep and personal way to Moses, He did so in the context of giving him the stone tablets with the Ten Commandments a second time. Yet, God revealed His heart of hearts as "the LORD, the LORD, the compassionate and gracious God, slow to anger, abounding in love and faithfulness" (Exodus 34:6 - NIV). This is a fact usually overlooked when considering "the God of the Old Testament." One would think that when giving the Law, especially for a second time, due to the infidelity of the people after the first time, that God would emphasize His justice. But punishment and consequences for sin was the last thing He mentioned. His main focus was His compassionate, loving and forgiving character. And it was with that tone that God established His covenant with Moses and His people (Exodus 34:1-10).

There are many lessons to be extracted from the two times Jesus performed the miracle of multiplying bread and fish. He wanted to show He could be trusted to provide. He wanted to strengthen the disciple's faith – especially when there were 12 baskets left over the first time and seven the second (both very important and symbolic numbers).

But the main reason – the reason Jesus gave His disciples – was compassion, pure and simple. Jesus said "I feel compassion for the people because they have remained with Me now three days and have nothing to eat" (Mark 8:2 - NASB). He was concerned and moved by their need and condition because "if I send them away hungry to their homes, they will faint on the way; and some of them have come from a great distance" (Mark 8:3 - NASB). Jesus was aware of their effort and moved by their sacrifice. So He honored them by supplying a meal before they went back to their homes. His compassion led Him to care for them.

"The LORD is good to all, and has compassion on all he has made" (Psalm 145:9 - NET Bible). "As a father shows compassion to his children, so the LORD shows compassion to those who fear him" (Psalm 103:13 - ESV). Compassion is a Kingdom Value because it is something near to our King's heart. We must follow the King's lead and offer compassion to those around us.

When it comes to giving people a second chance, caring for their needs, being sympathetic concerning their troubles, where to you see yourself on the compassion scale?

Kingdom Value #47: Stewardship

"Then God said, 'Let us make human beings in our image, to be like us. They will reign over the fish in the sea, the birds in the sky, the livestock, all the wild animals on the earth, and the small animals that scurry along the ground'" (Genesis 1:26 - NLT). Later, "the Lord God took the man and put him into the garden of Eden to cultivate it and keep it" (Genesis 2:15 - NASB).

Neither Judaism nor Christianity subscribe to deism. God is not distant from or disinterested in His creation. He is heavily and intimately involved. He cares, He loves, and He wants people – and plans – to turn our right. He doesn't turn people loose and forget about them. He has a specific plan for each individual and delegates a customized mission to each person. He expects the plan to be fulfilled and the mission to be accomplished.

Some God will call "wicked servants" (Luke 19:22). But look what Jesus says about those who fulfill the mission they received: "'Well done!' the king exclaimed. 'You are a good servant. You have been faithful with the little I entrusted to you, so you will be governor of ten cities as your reward'" (Luke 19:17 - NLT).

The Bible calls this arrangement stewardship (as in Luke 16:3 - KJV). Nowadays, instead of steward, we use terms like administrator or manager, personal attendant or overseer. But these terms don't take into account the twenty four-seven involvement stewards had in Bible times (see the example of Joseph at Potiphar's house in Genesis 39:1-6).

While humans were given authority to reign on earth, they do so under God's final authority because, "The earth and everything in it, the world and its inhabitants, belong to the Lord" (Psalm 24:1 - HCSB). This leaves nothing out. Everything and everybody belong to the Lord. Consider the implications of this. All we *think* we own really does not belong to us at all. The Lord has simply loaned it to us. And if it's all on loan, then we need to take even better care of everything, because one day we will have to give an account concerning how we managed *His* resources which He entrusted to us for a season.

While everyone gets the same amount of time (24 hours a day), some receive more financial resources, natural talents, or spiritual gifts than others. Did we waste our time (Ephesians 5:16)? Squander our treasures? Fail to develop our talents? Did we use our resources to bless others or only for selfish gain? If God has shown you the mission He has for you, are you using all you've got to pursue it? In the parable of the talents, the master did not *give* the talents to his servants; he entrusted *his* property to them *to be invested*. To multiply what they received (Matthew 25:14-30). It's the same concept as being fruitful (see *Kingdom Value #45*).

The implications of God's ownership are even more far-reaching than most dare to contemplate. Saying that everyone on planet earth belongs to the Lord is the same as saying He owns us – and that includes our bodies. Stating that a woman owns her body is only half true. She owns her body in the general, human sense. But technically her body is a resource God has given her on loan to take care of, to use properly and for which she will have to give an account. When contemplating an abortion, a woman should begin by asking: is this *God's* will?

If we – men and women – owned our bodies we would not have to answer to God for using them for immorality, for abusing them with drugs, seeking to change their original gender, overeating, and not getting enough sleep and exercise. If we owned our life and our body we could justify committing suicide. If God had *given* us our bodies (as opposed to lending them to us), He would have given up His authority over us; He would not have the right to call us into account. But as it is, we are surely answerable to Him.

Christians and non-Christians alike will have to give an account of their time on earth to their Creator, Who retains the authority to judge them accordingly. "But they will have to give account to him who is ready to judge the living and the dead" (1 Peter 4:5 - NIV). No one gets a free pass. "Yes, each of us will give a personal account to God" (Romans 14:12 - NLT). We will have to give an account for wasting resources (Luke 16:1), for every careless word spoken (Matthew 12:36), for those under our leadership (Hebrews 13:17), for the way we celebrated in our youth (Ecclesiastes 11:9). In fact, "Nothing in all creation is hidden from God's sight; everything is uncovered and exposed before the eyes of Him to whom we must give account" (Hebrews 4:13 - BSB).

While all will answer for their actions, their eternal fate will already have been sealed, so that the lost will be judged for condemnation and the saved will be judged as an evaluation to determine rewards. "For we must all appear before the tribunal of Christ, so that each may be repaid for what he has done in the body, whether good or worthless" (2 Corinthians 5: 10- HCSB).

What kind of "steward" have you been? How have you managed the time and resources God has given you? Have you acknowledged God's authority over your body and life? Have you dedicated yourself to the mission He gave you?

Kingdom Value #48: Work

In some people, working is not a virtue, but a necessary evil. You only work if you absolutely have to. If you are one of the few lucky Lotto winners or receive a huge inheritance, you've got it made. You can then "retire," and go on a perpetual vacation. This may be the seen as ideal even for those in a work oriented culture, but this is not Biblical. Work is a Kingdom Value. Work was assigned at the very beginning of the Global Kingdom – not as an afterthought.

As soon as God created the first human being, He put him to work. God "caused to grow every tree pleasing in appearance and good for food" (Genesis 2:9 - CJB), planted a garden, called it Eden and placed the person He had created there "to cultivate and care for it" (Genesis 2:15 - CJB). God also gave this person another assignment. He brought the animals to him "to see what he would call them. Whatever the person would call each living creature, that was to be its name. So the person gave names to all the livestock, to the birds in the air and to every wild animal (Genesis 2:18-20 - CJB). We must remember these assignments came before the fall, still under the "God saw that everything was good" environment.

There are some things only God can provide and only He should decide. There are other things for which He expects us to take initiative and accomplish. Together, God and humans can create synergy. "For we are God's fellow workers; you are God's field, God's building" (1 Corinthians 3:9 - NASB). The word translated as "fellow workers" is the Greek *sunergos (sun* meaning together, and *ergon* work*)*, from which we get the term synergy. You may have heard the story of the pastor who visited one of his members and, noticing the nice landscaping, exclaimed: "Isn't God's creation beautiful!" To which the member answered: "Yes, but you should have seen it when only God was taking care of it."

With the fall came the curse, and with the curse work would become difficult, tiresome and frustrating, because nature would no longer cooperate (Genesis 3:17-19).

Working is a spiritual matter. Having a family and working to provide for its needs is a Kingdom Value (see *Family, Kingdom Value #66*). I knew a young woman who had grown up in a very poor community in the northeast of Brazil. Her father abandoned the family and her mother spent her days praying at church while the children were left to fend for themselves. While the mother did well to seek God's counsel and blessing, she ought to have gotten up and looked for ways to feed her children. Here is a Kingdom Principle: "but if anyone does not provide for his own, and especially for those of his household, he has denied the faith and is worse than an unbeliever" (1 Timothy 5:8 - NASB).

Contrast this with the description of the "capable wife" in Proverbs 31:10-31 who is energetic, proactive, creative, industrious, socially well-connected, and productive. She "works with willing hands" (Proverbs 31:13 - HCSB). Consistently. Daily. She provides abundantly as a dynamic companion to her husband. The comparison between these two wives may be unfair, but the point is we need to work in cooperation with God, doing our part and allowing Him to do His part.

King Solomon spoke of the value of being active. He warned: "a little extra sleep, a little more slumber, a little folding of the hands to rest—then poverty will pounce on you like a bandit; scarcity will attack you like an armed robber" (Proverbs 6:10-11 - NLT). Sometimes we must be self-starters, learning to get things done even when there is no supervisor breathing down our necks. Solomon told the work-shy to "take a lesson from the ants, you lazybones. Learn from their ways and become wise! Though they have no prince or governor or ruler to make them work, they labor hard all summer, gathering food for the winter" (Proverbs 6:6-8 - NLT).

We get our work ethics from God Himself. "But Jesus responded to them, 'My Father is still working, and I am working also'" (John 5:17 - HCSB). God sets the example He wants us to follow. He creates, is productive and always active. He wants us to do the same. He expects us to be productive citizens who provide for their families and make a difference in society.

Scripture sets the standard for the Kingdom work ethics. It boils down to this: "those unwilling to work will not get to eat" (2 Thessalonians 3:10b - NLT). Paul insists his example must be followed: "you ought to imitate us," he told his readers, because when he was with them "we wanted to give you an example to follow" (v.v 7, 9). While with the Thessalonian believers, this is what he modeled: "we were not idle" and "never accepted food from anyone without paying for it. We worked hard day and night so we would not be a burden to any of you (2 Thessalonians 3:7-8 - NLT).

Word had reached Paul that "some of you are living idle lives, refusing to work and meddling in other people's business." He commanded them in the strongest terms "to settle down and work to earn their own living" (2 Thessalonians 3:11-12b - NLT). Notice the Mirroring Principle at work here: God is still working and Jesus is too. The Son reflects the Father. The apostle Paul reflects the Son and we are to reflect Paul's example of working hard.

Where do you see yourself on the work scale? Are you working in cooperation with God? Are you being productive and providing for yourself, family or those in need?

Kingdom Value #49: Witnessing

We enjoy sharing the good things that happen in our lives with those we care about. When God touches our heart and transforms our life we naturally want to tell others what He's done. Witnessing should be our natural response to God's activity in us.

Communicating to others what we have learned from God is a Kingdom Value. Telling them about the need and availability of salvation through Jesus is our privilege and duty as Kingdom citizens. We must not be content to go to heaven alone. This is so critical to Kingdom living because leading others into the Kingdom is the only way we can truly participate in the Kingdom's expansion.

Aside from direct divine intervention, witnessing is the only way people are exposed to the Gospel and have the opportunity to enter the Kingdom. Sure, we can help build hospitals, church buildings and community centers, and that is all valid and good (see *Serving One Another, Kingdom Value #30*). But the Kingdom only "expands" when new citizens are added to it. "'I, even I, am the Lord, and apart from me there is no savior. I have revealed and saved and proclaimed— I, and not some foreign god among you. You are my witnesses,' declares the Lord, 'that I am God'" (Isaiah 43:11-12 NIV).

A Christian author set out to write a book concerning how the unchurched view evangelicals in their attempt to witness. The responses he posted were disturbing. There were scores of "testimonies" of a negative kind. His interviewees felt they had been bullied by Christians and were begging the over zealous to back off. Permanently. They had been hurt and were not going to take it any longer.

That got me thinking. There is no excuse for verbal abuse of any kind. Especially because the Bible specifically instructs us to "be prepared to give an answer to everyone who asks you to give the reason for the hope that you have. ***But do this with gentleness and respect***, keeping a clear conscience, so that those who speak maliciously against your good behavior in Christ may be ashamed of their slander" (1 Peter 3:15, 16 - NIV).

Let's look at what Peter says. First, be prepared. Christians should know their Bible and understand the basics of their faith. They should especially know how to explain salvation by grace and the non-negotiable need for repentance and faith.

Second, Christians should be able to "give the reason for the hope that you have," which may require answering questions about faith and science (as in creationism vs. evolution), or explaining why Biblical faith is not a clueless leap in the dark, but is based on fulfilled prophecy, verifiable archaeological finds, and historical records.

Third, notice we are told to *answer* (the initiative here is taken by the non-Christian inquirer) with "gentleness and respect." It is usually the unprepared who feel threatened and may think the only way to defend their faith is to attack the one who questions it. Yet there is no excuse for arrogance and bullying when defending the faith.

178

And, finally, we are to have a good conscience and demonstrate good behavior, so that those who may wish to slander us or our faith will have no ammunition, and no smoking gun, because there will be nothing bad to point at. Remember that Jesus was aggressively confronted, lied about, falsely accused, and dishonored by some of His critics. He answered gently then pronounced a stern warning when needed. Even when accused of being demon-possessed – a serious form of blasphemy and the gravest of offenses, "Jesus answered, 'I don't have a demon. On the contrary, I honor my Father, and you dishonor me'" (John 8:49 - ISV).

But having said all of the above (and back to the book on reactions to being on the receiving end of witnessing), many of the criticism we are hearing today are exaggerated and malicious. Some are outraged that Christians dare to share their faith at all in the public square.

I feel like writing a book too. A book that shares the motivation behind our attempts to witness to those around us. Non-Christians have no idea what goes on in our minds and hearts when we try to approach them and share. They do not know that for us it would be more comfortable and easy *not* to share, not to risk upsetting them or being rejected and misunderstood. We share because we care. Otherwise we would keep silent, content to keep this treasure to ourselves.

It is also doubtful they have any clue just how much we would love to be able to transfer the conviction and knowledge we have to them in a nonthreatening way. We would be thrilled if they could only see what we see and feel what we feel before they decide to accept or reject our attempts to share the message.

The "problem" with the Good News is that it implies there is bad news. And people do not like being confronted with reality when all is not rosy. To say that Christians are unloving because they speak Biblical truth about sin and judgment is like saying the doctor is mean because he warns a patient of a blocked artery and potential heart attack.

While we may be surprised with the growing opposition to the Gospel message, this is nothing new. Jeremiah complained: "to whom can I give warning? Who will listen when I speak? Their ears are closed, and they cannot hear. They scorn the word of the Lord. They don't want to listen at all" (Jeremiah 6:10 - NLT).

Witnessing is sharing your story. Peter said "we did not follow cleverly devised stories when we told you about the coming of our Lord Jesus Christ in power, but we were eyewitnesses of his majesty" (2 Peter 1: 16 - NIV). John shared "that which was from the beginning, which we have heard, which we have seen with our eyes, which we have looked at and our hands have touched—this we proclaim concerning the Word of life" (1 John 1:1 - NIV). Both had been with Jesus for three years. They had authority because they were eyewitnesses. Jesus' story became *their* story.

You don't have to be an apostle to witness. After freeing a man from a legion of demons that had torn his life apart, Jesus restored the man's sanity and told him to "go home to your own [family and relatives and friends] and bring back word to them of how much the Lord has done for you, and [how He has] had sympathy for you and mercy on you." Although his preference would have been to leave the area and accompany Jesus, he obeyed. "And he departed and began to publicly proclaim in Decapolis [the region of the ten cities] how much Jesus had done for him, and all the people were astonished and marveled" (Mark 5:19-20 - AMP).

Although this anonymous man did not have the training, knowledge or experience the apostles had, when it came to his story, he was the expert. And he was under orders to go and share.

All of us are wired to share. So here is the irony: When non-Christians complain about Christians sharing that which is the most important aspect of their lives, do they not realize they do the same? Non-Christians are very insistent and aggressive in their own form of "evangelizing." Sometimes it comes through peer pressure. Sometimes through advertising. Or it can take the form of suing and boycotting. It involves "selling" their "product" by enticing, pressuring, intimidating, insisting, and ridiculing others who do not conform. Then they turn around and cry foul when Christians witness to them, accusing them of pushing their ideas down their throat. How dare they! Of course, just as not all Christians are bullies, not all non-Christians are like the description above. Yet, sometimes the simple presence of a Christian in the workplace or at school is enough to set some on edge.

They tried to shut Paul up. They threw him in prison and sent him off because he was preaching something they didn't agree with. Those who were about to stone Stephen covered their ears so they couldn't hear him (Acts 7:57). But Paul said, "Proclaim the message; persist in it whether convenient or not; rebuke, correct, and encourage with great patience and teaching" (2 Timothy 4:2 - HCSB).

No matter how people react, we should be wise, loving, compassionate, truthful and bathe all witnessing effort in prayer. People can see right through hypocrisy, a patronizing attitude, a judgmental superiority complex, and legalism. May the Lord use us to "rescue those being taken off to death, and save those stumbling toward slaughter. If you say, 'But we didn't know about this,' won't He who weighs hearts consider it? Won't He who protects your life know? Won't He repay a person according to his work?" (Proverbs 24:1-12 - HCSB).

How have your witnessing efforts been coming along?

Kingdom Value #50: Missions

David Livingstone, the great missionary to Africa, once said, "God had an only Son, and He made Him a missionary." And His Son came to make us missionaries as well. "Again Jesus said, 'Peace be with you! As the Father has sent me, I am sending you.' And with that he breathed on them and said, 'Receive the Holy Spirit'" (John 20:21, 22 - NIV).

"Missions" is not a Biblical term, but it is definitely a Biblical concept. Shortly before returning to the Father, Jesus gave His Church this command: "Go, therefore, and make disciples of all nations, baptizing them in the name of the Father and of the Son and of the Holy Spirit, teaching them to observe everything I have commanded you. And remember, I am with you always, to the end of the age" (Matthew 28:19-20 - HCSB).

Not only did Jesus give His disciples the Great Commission, He "appeared to them repeatedly over a period of *forty days talking with them about the affairs of the kingdom of God*" (Acts 1:3 - PHILLIPS). The following verses and the content of the book of Acts clearly indicate that "the affairs of the kingdom of God" of which Jesus spoke were the coming outpouring of the Holy Spirit which would give the disciples the power needed to be His witnesses around the globe. It would also be through the Holy Spirit that the Church would be inaugurated. The Holy Spirit, the disciples' mission, and the Church were intimately intertwined. They still are.

Notice the parallels between the Great Commission in Matthew 28 and what Jesus told His disciples right before His ascension. He said: "But you are to be given power when the Holy Spirit has come to you. You will be witnesses to me, not only in Jerusalem, not only throughout Judea, not only in Samaria, but to the very ends of the earth!" (Acts 1:8 - PHILLIPS). From its inception the Church has had a clearly defined mission – in short, to be on mission. To go to all the nations, make disciples, baptize them, and teach them.

To make disciples presupposes the Good News has been proclaimed and accepted. Discipleship essentially means the apprentice imitates the master. We are to teach followers of Christ to walk like He walked, by observing how we do the same. They should imitate us as we imitate Christ.[1] Paul told believers from the church at Thessalonica, "You became imitators of us and of the Lord" (1 Thessalonians 1:6 - ISV).

By baptizing disciples, a symbolic statement is made: buried to the old self and life; resurrected to the new life brought about by Jesus. A public statement is also made, as the believer declares his or her allegiance to the new Lord and Savior of his or her life. The believer has been indwelt by God the Father, Son and Holy Spirit and is therefore baptized in the name of each Person of the Trinity.

Teaching the disciples to "observe everything I have commanded you" is an ongoing effort which aims to equip disciples in the process of sanctification. To observe, of course, means to obey; to take to heart, and to put into practice.

To "make disciples of all nations" is the scope of the mission. That is, the whole world with all its ethnicities or people groups (the Greek here for "nations" is *ethnē* or *ethnos* which refers to people groups instead of geopolitical nations). According to the Joshua Project, there are a total of 17,014 people groups in the world, made up of 7.60 Billion individuals (the total world population). Of these, a total of 7,063 people groups or 3.14 Billion individuals are still unreached.[2] A people group is considered "unreached" when they "lack enough followers of Christ and resources to evangelize their own people."[3] Besides whole people groups which remain unreached, many individuals living among reached people groups do not know the Lord and are still lost in their sins.

Ken Sorrell reminds volunteers who wish to go on short-term mission trips that "of all the people who have been born since the beginning of the world, more than half are alive today" and that "nine out of 10" of them "are lost, living without hope and a Savior."[4]

Implicit in the command to make disciples is planting churches. Many mission organizations understand their task as making disciples in an effort that leads to planting churches. It is important to understand there is, therefore, a fundamental difference between missions and simply doing ministry abroad. The work of the

182

missionary is the modern equivalent of the work of an apostle (*apostolos* means "one commissioned" and "sent on a mission").[5] Missionaries take the Good News to areas where there are unreached peoples, disciple new believers, and plant new churches. Some missionaries are pioneers. Others must stay behind to train trainers. The emphasis now is less on buildings and more on a sense of urgency to plant churches which can easily multiply themselves via local leadership.

Has God called you to the mission field? Are you willing to pray, give or go?

Kingdom Value #51: Benevolence

Mathematicians would say it doesn't add up. Human logic would explain why it couldn't make sense. Pragmatists would warn it just won't work. And yet many have discovered this ageless Kingdom Principle to be true: "give, and it will be given to you: good measure, pressed down, shaken together, and running over, will be given to you. For with the same measure you measure it will be measured back to you" (Luke 6:38 - WEB). In the mysterious ways of the Kingdom we can observe that, "One gives freely, yet grows all the richer; another withholds what he should give, and only suffers want" (Proverbs 11:2 - ESV).

If that doesn't sound counterintuitive, consider this: "remember the words that the Lord Jesus himself said, 'It is more blessed to give than to receive'" (Acts 20:35 - ISV). Benevolence, in the Bible, means being generous with your resources. *It is a Principle of the Kingdom of God that we are blessed to be a blessing.* We receive so we can share. We are given so we can give. The more you give, the more you receive. You just can't outgive God.

Paul set up a collection for Christians in Jerusalem, as the "mother church" had fallen on hard times (read 2 Corinthians 9 for the whole story). He encouraged the believers at Corinth to be ready when he came by to pick up their offering to take it to Jerusalem. He told them he had been bragging about them to the Macedonian believers, who had taken their cue and decided to pitch in and contribute as well.

Paul then states some *Kingdom Principles related to giving* that are important to keep in mind: First, *"The person who sows generously will also reap generously,"* just as "a farmer who plants only a few seeds will get a small crop" (v. 6 - HCSB). Second, *"You must each decide in your heart how much to give"* (v. 7a - NLT).

Pastor Jerry Key challenged the Brazilian congregation to pray and determine how much God wanted them to give to the upcoming missions offering. Monica, my wife, was a new Christian and in her teens at the time. She asked the Lord how much He wanted her to give. An amount "came to her," she wrote it down on a piece of paper and placed it in the offering plate. The value would be close $50. But she had no money, no allowance and could hardly ask her parents for help, as they were not happy she was frequenting a Baptist church. She needed a miracle. She had to trust the Lord to provide.

A few days later she received a letter from her grandmother who lived about six hours away. This was odd, because her grandmother had never written her before. It wasn't Christmas and it wasn't her birthday. She opened the letter and there was some cash inside (you just don't send cash through the mail in Brazil). Stranger still: it was the exact amount she had committed to give for missions! Once Monica had "decided in her heart how much to give" she saw God's provision and faithfulness at work, and it greatly impacted her life. And so, Monica gave her offering with a most cheerful heart (2 Corinthians 9:7)!

Third, *"Don't give reluctantly or in response to pressure"* (v. 7b - NLT). Fourth, *"God loves a person who gives cheerfully"* (v. 7c - NLT). Fifth, *The giving cycle works like this: "God will generously provide all you need. Then you will always have everything you need and plenty left over to share with others"* (v. 8 - NLT). To be clear, *"You will be enriched in every way to be generous on every occasion"* (v. 11a - BSB). And to be abundantly clear, God *"will provide and increase your resources and then produce a great harvest of generosity in you"* (v. 10 - NLT).

And sixth, when our offering reaches those in need (v. 11), this will happen: a. *"They will thank God"* (v. 11b - NLT). "They will joyfully express their thanks to God" (v.12b - NLT). b. *"The needs of the believers ... will be met"* (v.12a - NLT). c. *"As a result of your ministry, they will give glory to God"* (v. 13a - NLT). d. *"And they will pray for you with deep affection because of the overflowing grace God has given to you"* (v. 14 - NLT).

There are givers and there are takers in this life. Kingdom citizens are called to be givers. The difference between these two mindsets and lifestyles can be illustrated by contrasting the Sea of Galilee and the Dead Sea. The snow on Mount Hermon melts, forms a stream and flows into Lake Tiberius, as it is known today. There it

184

provides abundant fish and fresh water for the surrounding communities. But not only that. It shares its water by forming the Jordan river, providing for irrigating fields, thereby making fruitful what otherwise would be dry, desert land. We are to be channels of blessing, like the Sea of Galilee.

The Dead Sea, on the other hand, receives the Jordan River's water but does not "pass it on." The water sits there. Stagnant. And since it is the lowest body of water on earth, its waters quickly evaporate. It's called the Dead Sea for a reason: no fish can survive in its extremely salty and bitter water.

A giving mentality is the exact opposite of greediness. It always seeks a win-win situation, while greed is self-serving and doesn't care about others, as long as it gets what it wants. It grabs all it can and asks: "what can I get out of this?" It's life question is, "What's in it for *me*?"

Service is the modus-operandi of the Kingdom, yet there is no service without giving. When we serve we give either of our time, of our talents or of our treasures. If there was no giving in the process, there was no real service rendered. Yes, there is much service that is paid for but even paying for service is a "giving matter" in which one party agrees to give its goods or services and the other agrees to give of its financial resources for the service. But here we are concerned about the selfless giving which demands nothing in return. This is Kingdom giving.

James urges his readers to do more than just say nice things to others in need, but to act, serve, contribute, give, and make a difference (James 2:14-17). Christians are charged to be benevolent as an ongoing lifestyle, being a blessing to all they can, but giving priority to those of the faith family (Galatians 6:10; see *Goodness, Kingdom Value #14*).

"But since you excel in everything–in faith, in speech, in knowledge, in complete earnestness and in the love we have kindled in you –see that you also excel in this grace of giving" (2 Corinthians 8:7 - NIV).

Are you excelling in the area of benevolence? Grade yourself:

KV51 – BENEVOLENCE

| Consistently practice | Sometimes practice | Struggle | Mostly fail | Continually fail |

Chapter

9

Character Kingdom Values

But now you must be holy in everything you do,
just as God who chose you is holy. For the Scriptures say,
"You must be holy because I am holy."
1 Peter 1:15, 16 - NLT

Kingdom Value #52: Being Spirit-Controlled

The promised Holy Spirit

Jesus was only with His disciples for some three years. Yet, when He came to the end of that time, He was ready to go back to His Father and leave His Church in the hands of the Apostles. They had learned so much by being in His company (Acts 4:13)! But how could they be ready for such an undertaking? The secret was the Holy Spirit.

Jesus said He would ask the Father to send "another Helper" to "abide with you forever" (John 14:16, 17 - NKJV). Jesus was **with** them, but the Holy Spirit would be **in** them. The Holy Spirit was to only begin His ministry and forever indwell believers after Jesus returned to the Father. Because of this, we see in the book of Acts that at first this was a slow process since there were believers who had placed their faith in Messiah Jesus before His ascension who now needed to know about the Holy Spirit and His indwelling (Acts 19:2). Soon, receiving the Holy Spirit at the time of conversion became standard procedure (Ephesians 1:13).

Jesus told His disciples He must go before He could send the promised Holy Spirit to them, Whom He called "the Advocate" (John 16:7 - NABRE). He described the Holy Spirit's ministry to them as convicting "the world in regard to sin and righteousness and condemnation" (John 16:8 - NABRE).

The Holy Spirit will convict of sin "because they do not believe in me" (John 16:9 - NABRE). Jesus had already taught that, "The one who does not believe has been condemned already, because he has not believed in the name of the one and only Son of God" (John 3:18b - NET Bible). The Holy Spirit will convince people of the sin of unbelief. We may try but only the Spirit can convince the spiritually blind and show them the Light.

The Holy Spirit will convict of "righteousness, because I am going to the Father and you will no longer see me" (John 16:10 - NABRE). Jesus, "The Righteous One," preached the Kingdom and righteousness during His earthly ministry. But now He was leaving and convincing people of the need for right standing with God (through justification by faith and repentance) would fall to the Holy Spirit.

The Holy Spirit will convict of condemnation "because the ruler of this world has been condemned" (John 16:11 - NABRE). Either the Holy Spirit convinces people of the coming judgment of God and the certainty that those who oppose the Lord already stand condemned and defeated, or they will continue to be oblivious and deceived. They argue that "God doesn't judge anybody and neither should you." They do not wish to accept the fact that God **will** judge and condemn them if they do not repent and believe. This is a promise.

As Jesus further instructed His closest disciples concerning the ministry of the Holy Spirit it became clear the Holy Spirit relates to Jesus as Jesus to the Father. Jesus had just claimed to be the truth (John 14:6). Then He declared that, "When the Spirit of truth comes, he will guide you into all the truth" (John 16:13a - ESV; see John 14:17). The Holy Spirit, Jesus continued, "will not speak on his own authority, but whatever he hears he will speak" (John 16:13b - ESV). Just as Jesus claimed not to speak on His own but according to what He received from the Father (John 5:19, 30; 14:10), the Spirit speaks what He hears from the Son.

When He performed miracles or proclaimed the Good News of the Kingdom, the reaction of the people was to glorify the Father. In the same way, when the Holy Spirit is at work or manifesting His power, we will know it because people will be inclined to glorify Jesus. He will not draw attention to Himself but will direct the focus on the Son. "He will bring me glory by telling you whatever he receives from me" (John 16:14 - NLT).

188

Controlled by the Spirit versus controlled by the flesh

There is a battle raging inside of every Christian. It is the war between the lower, fallen nature and the new nature – the nature of Christ, brought about by the presence of the Holy Spirit in the Christian's life. The problem is "the flesh **desires** what is against the Spirit, and the Spirit desires what is against the flesh" (Galatians 5:17a- HCSB). The secret to success is "escaping the corruption that is in the world because of **evil desires**" (2 Peter 1:4b - HCSB). And the way to do that is to "walk by the Spirit and you will not carry out the **desire** of the flesh" (Galatians 5:16 - HCSB).

The key word here is "desire." There are two wills, two strong desires, pulling in opposite directions. Which of these two desires will we allow to control us? We must realize that "the mind-set of the flesh is death, but the mind-set of the Spirit is life and peace" (Romans 8:6 - HCSB).

Fleshly desires are futile and deceitful; they darken our understanding and harden our hearts. They can never be fulfilled. They just want more and more (Ephesians 4:17-22), "and their desire for sin is never satisfied" (2 Peter 2:14a - NLT). Following our evil desires results in "fruitless works of darkness" (Ephesians 5:11 - HCSB) and a whole list of sinful activities, practiced and valued by those who will not inherit the Kingdom (Galatians 5:19-21).

But when we are *under the influence* of the Holy Spirit and controlled by Him, we will produce a precious cluster of fruit (Galatians 5:22, 23; see the *Fruit of the Spirit Kingdom Values #s 9* through *17*).

The sun was shining directly on my laptop in the front seat of the car on a very hot summer day. Concerned, I reached over to feel just how hot it might be. To my surprise, the laptop was cool to the touch. I realized the air-conditioner was blowing directly on its surface, counteracting the sun's heat. I had this insight: The flesh acts like the sun, heating up evil desires and trying to lure us into "the works of the flesh." But the Spirit also works in our lives, blowing refreshing, spiritual winds of renewal which keep us cool. The cool air cancels out the effects of the hot sun. It doesn't make the sun go away or be any less hot (temptations will always be with us and they will always be appealing in and of themselves). But we must be careful to always allow the cool wind of the Spirit to blow on our lives – constantly. As soon as we don't, the hot sun rays will heat things up again. That's why Paul said to "stop getting drunk with wine, which leads to wild living, but keep on being filled with the Spirit" (Ephesians 5:18 - ISV).

If we are going to take Kingdom Values seriously, we must be filled with and walk in the Holy Spirit. Either He controls our lives, or the flesh does. There's no middle ground, no third option (Galatians 5:17).

Without the ministry of the Holy Spirit in the world and in the life of the believer, it would be impossible for the Global Kingdom of God to advance and achieve all the Lord desires to accomplish. We should never underestimate the importance of the ministry of the Holy Spirit, understanding that without Him there would be no conviction of sin, righteousness, or judgment. There would be no One to guide us to all truth. There would be no way to battle our flesh and we would not be sealed for the day of redemption (Ephesians 4:30).

Controlled by the Spirit Kingdom Principles:
• When we control our own lives, we will inevitably lead a fruitless life, controlled by the flesh, with dire consequences. "Whoever sows to please their flesh, from the flesh will reap destruction; whoever sows to please the Spirit, from the Spirit will reap eternal life" (Galatians 6:8 - NIV). "Beloved, I urge you, as foreigners and exiles, to abstain from the desires of the flesh, which war against your soul" (1 Peter 2:11 - BSB).

• When we allow the Holy Spirit to control our lives we will naturally live out Kingdom Values and produce much fruit.

• Living under the Spirit's influences brings life and peace, resulting in close fellowship with God and a well-balanced life.

• He who tries to please both the flesh and the Spirit, or keeps going back and forth in his devotion, "is a double-minded man, unstable in all he does" (James 1:8; 4:8; Psalm 119:113).

Are you Spirit-filled and controlled? Do you and others see the fruit of the Holy Spirit in your daily life? Are you using your Spirit-given gifts in God's service?

KV52 – BEING SPIRIT CONTROLLED

| Consistently practice | Sometimes practice | Struggle | Mostly fail | Continually fail |

Kingdom Value #53: Holiness

God is holy. God is different and separated: untouched and untouchable by sin, anything unclean or impure. God is perfect. God never thought, said or did anything He shouldn't have, even though He has existed forever. All God does is flawless. He is the model of integrity. No wonder the seraphim could not help but cry out "Holy, holy, holy is the LORD of Heaven's Armies! The whole earth is filled with his glory!" (Isaiah 6:3 - NLT). Nor could the living beings keep from repeating, "Holy, holy, holy is the Lord God, the Almighty— the one who always was, who is, and who is still to come" (Revelation 4:8 - NLT).

Because God *is* holy, He *does* what is righteous. His righteousness is the direct result and the practical application of His holiness. If righteousness is central to the Kingdom, then holiness is as well. We were created in the image of our holy God. It was His will that we be similar to Him, including in terms of His character. That His chosen would be holy was predetermined even before human beings existed. "For He chose us in Him before the foundation of the world to be holy and blameless in His presence" (Ephesians 1:4 - BSB). We were destined for holiness. Since His will doe not change, that is still God's desire for our lives. "God's will is for you to be holy" (1 Thessalonians 4:3a - NLT).

Holiness is so fundamental to our identity in Christ that the Biblical term for Christians is "saints" (Colossians 1:12). The *Kingdom Core Values* chart on page 10 shows that the purpose of the Kingdom is our holiness, for God's glory. Living up to this ideal presents a tremendous challenge because while we are ***positionally*** holy in Christ, He expects us to ***actually*** lead holy lives on a daily basis. "But now you must be holy in everything you do, just as God who chose you is holy. For the Scriptures say, 'You must be holy because I am holy'" (1 Peter 1:15, 16 - NLT).

We are positionally holy in Christ because it is "the blood of the covenant, which made us holy" (Hebrews 10:29 - NLT). And the process of living holy lives during our earthly pilgrimage is called sanctification, which is carried out by the ministry of the Holy Spirit in each believer. This too was predetermined, "because from the beginning God has chosen you for salvation through sanctification by the Spirit and through belief in the truth" (2 Thessalonians 2:13 - HCSB).

We all come from a background of sin. "But you were cleansed; you were made holy; you were made right with God by calling on the name of the Lord Jesus Christ and by the Spirit of our God" (1 Corinthians 6:11b - NLT; see 1 Peter 1:14). Living holy lives is the challenge and the goal for every Christian.

Yet we are fallen creatures, living in a fallen world, and still possessing a fallen nature. This fallen nature, "the flesh," continues to feel fallen tendencies. Were that not problematic enough, we also have an archenemy who desires nothing more than to see our defeat and destruction. Which is why he concentrates a large portion of his ammunition by targeting Christians precisely in the area of holiness.

Since God designed us to be holy, what could frustrate God's plans more than leading His people to fall into sin? By tempting them to live immoral, unethical, and generally wicked lives?

God has allowed Satan to temp His saints for reasons known and unknown. We do know that every day we are being tested for our loyalty (see *Overcoming, Kingdom value #62*). Although the odds seem to be against us, "if God is for us, who can be against us?" (Romans 8:31b - ISV). We have received God's grace and have His calling on our lives; we have His Spirit living in us; and we have the nature of Christ. "By his divine power, God has given us everything we need for living a godly life" and what is needed to "enable you to share his divine nature and escape the world's corruption caused by human desires" (2 Peter 1:3a - NLT).

Still, the battle within and without for sanctification will continue as long as we are alive. As we try to live out Kingdom Values, we may find ourselves scratching our heads like the Apostle Paul. He confessed:

> But I need something *more*! For if I know the law but still can't keep it, and if the power of sin within me keeps sabotaging my best intentions, I obviously need help! I realize that I don't have what it takes. I can will it, but I can't *do* it. I decide to do good, but I don't *really* do it; I decide not to do bad, but then I do it anyway. My decisions, such as they are, don't result in actions. Something has gone wrong deep within me and gets the better of me every time.
>
> It happens so regularly that it's predictable. The moment I decide to do good, sin is there to trip me up. I truly delight in God's commands, but it's pretty obvious that not all of me joins in that delight. Parts of me covertly rebel, and just when I least expect it, they take charge.
>
> I've tried everything and nothing helps. I'm at the end of my rope. Is there no one who can do anything for me? Isn't that the real question?
>
> The answer, thank God, is that Jesus Christ can and does. He acted to set things right in this life of contradictions where I want to serve God with all my heart and mind, but am pulled by the influence of sin to do something totally different (Romans 7:17-25 - MSG).

Whatever theological inclinations we may have, or however we may feel about the issue, the direct command still stands: "for I am the LORD your God. Consecrate yourselves therefore, and be holy, for I am holy" (Leviticus 11:44a - NASB).

Do you take to heart the fact you are positionally holy in Christ? Are you allowing the Holy Spirit to lead you to holy living each day?

Kingdom Value #54: Self-Denial

Kingdom Values are **Christian** values and therefore address many of the same issues related to discipleship. This is one of them.

Denying self may be the hardest lesson we have to learn – a lesson which usually takes a whole lifetime! Self-denial is a paradoxical value, "because whoever wants to save his life will lose it, but whoever loses his life for my sake and for the Gospel will save it" (Mark 8:35 - ISV). Our basic instinct is to save our own life. Feed our own flesh. Look out for "number one."

Studying about self-denial is absolutely no guarantee we will practice it. Our ego gets in the way. Our pride demands revenge. Our flesh craves comfort and pleasure. And our feelings often differ from our knowledge: the problem is not **knowing** what we should do (or refrain from doing), but the toxic emotions and selfish feelings that clamor for control.

A former colleague, with whom I worked in a Christian organization years ago, recently left his wife of 30 plus years. He told her, "I just want to be happy." He abandoned her for a young lady who is about his daughter's age. Ironically, he was the one who introduced me to the works of Victor Frankl, whose person and work I came to admire. While reading through an article on Frankl, these words of his stood out: "Being human always points ... to something or someone, other than oneself. ... The more one forgets himself – by giving himself to a cause to serve or another person to love – the more human he is."[1] Frankl, the bestselling author of **Man's Search for Meaning**, also concluded that, "It is the very pursuit of happiness that thwarts happiness."[2]

Daniel Goleman believes that "those who are at the mercy of impulse–who lack self-control–suffer a moral deficiency: The ability to control impulse is the base of will and character."[3] Goleman sees the great need in our days for self-restraint, which he calls a moral stance. For the Christian, self-denial is a question of self-control, and self-control is misnomer: the One doing the controlling is the Holy Spirit.

Jesus was clear about the cost of following Him: "If anyone wants to come with Me, he must deny himself, take up his cross daily, and follow Me" (Luke 9:23 - HCSB).

John the Baptist was doing his job faithfully when Jesus came on the scene and "stole the spotlight." John's disciples expressed their concern to John but he told them his mission was to point people to His Lord. John said, "He must become greater and greater, and I must become less and less" (John 3:30 - NLT). John's attitude is an example we all should follow.

Aside from Jesus' humbling (Philippians 2:5-11), and the sacrifice of His own life (Matthew 26:36-46), one of the greatest examples of self-denial is found in Acts 16:22-34. You will recall that Paul and Silas were unjustly beaten in the public square and then thrown in prison. Their "crime"? They had cast out a demon from a slave girl.

If there is something that sets my ire on fire, it's being falsely accused. But Paul and Silas were not only accused, they were physically and psychologically abused. Instead of sitting in prison licking their wounds, "at midnight Paul and Silas were praying and singing hymns to God, and the prisoners were listening to them" (Acts 16:25 - NKJV). Because they were able to deny their own desire for comfort – and justice – and were able to concentrate instead on God's plan and glory, they impacted the whole prison population in a mighty way.

God sent a powerful earthquake that shook the foundations of the building, opened the prison doors, and loosened the prisoner's chains. The prison keeper woke up and saw what had happened and thought everyone had escaped. He was about to take his life when Paul told him not to harm himself. He came over to Paul and Silas and asked, "Sirs, what must I do to be saved?" (Acts 16:29 - NKJV). They told him about Jesus and were invited to his home, where the jailer's whole family heard the Good News and was baptized.

Things could have turned out very differently if Paul and Silas had felt sorry for themselves and their undeserved treatment.

On the other end of the scale, Samson is one of the most notorious examples of a Bible hero who allowed himself to be entangled and brought down by his own fleshly desires. Physically he was one of the strongest men who ever was, and yet he was a weakling when it came to self-control. "Self-denial" was simply not in his vocabulary. Not, at least, until the end of his life.

Samson was a judge, a protector of Israel for 20 years. According to the message of an angel who visited his parents, Samson's mission was to begin the process of setting Israel free from the Philistines, who had been oppressing its people for 40 years. At a certain point in his life, "the Spirit of the Lord took control of him" (Judges 13:25 - CEV), a statement that is repeated at critical times in his story, when he was attacked by a lion or when in battle with the Philistines.

But Samson had a weakness for beautiful women. One day he saw a Philistine woman and told his parents he wanted to marry her. When they asked why, his answer was, "She looks good to me" (Judges 14:3 - CEV). The seven-day wedding feast did not go well and, eventually, things ended in tragedy for the bride and her family (Judges 14:10-15:7). Samson stoops to a new low and visits a prostitute (Judges 16:1), and later falls in love for the infamous Delilah (Judges 16:4).

Part of Samson's weakness involved allowing himself to be worn down and giving up vital secrets. He gave Delilah false answers and observed how she would betray his confidence by calling the Philistine guards three separate times. But then she used the "if you really love me" argument and, sadly, Samson fell for it (Judges 16:15. This argument is used to this day, with great success). She kept nagging him until he finally gave up his secret. When the soldiers came, he did not realize his strength – and the Lord – had left him. The first thing the Philistines did was to gouge out his eyes.

Samson was so obsessed and out of control that he placed pleasure above mission, sex before safety, and the thrill of risking it all over common sense and restraint. Being dominated by evil desires has led many Christians down a slippery slope, destroyed ministries and families, and kept many believers in the chains of bad habits and addiction. This is a matter we all should take very seriously. "So, if you think you are standing firm, be careful that you don't fall!" (1 Corinthians 10:12 - NIV).

This is why there can be no discipleship without self-denial. To follow Jesus means picking up the cross and dying to self (Luke 9:23-27; 14:26-32). Paul declared, "My old self has been crucified with Christ. It is no longer I who live, but Christ lives in me. So I live in this earthly body by trusting in the Son of God, who loved me and gave himself for me" (Galatians 2:20 - NLT).

Rate your self-denial on the scale below. When temptation comes in your area of weakness, do you deny those evil desires and submit to God's will instead?

Kingdom Value #55: Integrity

"Integrity," according to the dictionary, is "the quality of being honest and having strong moral principles; moral uprightness." More literally it means "the state of being whole and undivided."[4] It's where we get the word "integral" from.

When I worked at the Baptist Spanish Publishing House in El Paso, Texas, one of the senior manager's sons came to offer a seminar. He worked at a multinational corporation and spoke about the fundamental importance of trust and integrity. He said that at his company they had a working definition of integrity, and what he said so many years ago remains with me to this day. It's simple and easy to remember: "Say what you do, and do what you say."

The implications of this definition are more profound than one might suspect at first glance. In order to better take in the fuller meaning, let us divide the statement into two parts and examine them separately.

Say what you do (preach what you practice)

People have a right to know about decisions that will affect their lives. Corporations (churches, organizations and companies) do well to communicate to their members and employees what is happening, what has been accomplished and what future plans are being made. To hide this information or fail to adequately communicate it creates confusion and suspicion. The informal network within rushes to fill the void, eagerly supplying unverified "news" which is usually inaccurate and negatively slanted. Sharing what the leadership is doing is not only an act of integrity, it's a smart move.

At work, the "say what you do" principle may involve supervisors, team members, workers, board members, investors, customers, the general public, and suppliers. At home it includes parents, spouse and kids. And at church it involves the staff, leaders, volunteers, members and regular attendants.
We all have different ways of acting and interacting with those around us. But when there is a disconnect between our public persona and our inner self – the person we really are when alone – then the problem is one of integrity. If we say in

public that we believe in a certain set of values and then in private we intentionally disregard those values, we lack integrity. We are saying one thing and doing another and hiding behind a mask. We are being hypocrites.

Nobody's perfect and all Christians have their struggles. But the very notion of struggling means there is an ideal the Christian believes in, strives for, yet has a hard time consistently achieving. We should readily admit we have shortcomings (Romans 7) and that we have not yet reached our Christian ideals (Philippians 3:12-13). Unfortunately, Christian circles are such that believers many times feel they must "fake it till they make it."

It was a Wednesday night Bible study and our group of Brazilians in South Florida was small. We were sharing prayer requests and mentioning our personal struggles. When it was one of our leader's turn, he said something that caught me by surprise. Everyone loved him. He was selfless, always ready to help and cheerful in his Christian walk. He said, "Well, I don't know why, but I have no personal struggle; nothing bad to speak of. It's all good." Since there was no reason to doubt his sincerity, I remember envying him when he shared this testimony.

Fast-forward a couple of years. A member of our group calls me for an urgent meeting at a coffee shop. He was in shock. He told me he was trying out a new app when this same leader asked him to clear his computer from a vicious virus. He decided to install this stealth application on the leader's computer to try it out but later forgot to deinstall it before returning the machine. The app registers everything that is typed on the computer, no matter what program is being used. He knew he had violated this leader's privacy and for this he was sorry. But what he found was mind-boggling: this leader was consorting with virtual prostitutes, saying the most ignoble and immoral things imaginable, and worse: his chat was full of blasphemous references to the Lord, mixing Christianity and paganism as though they were one and the same.

This was the epitome of hypocrisy with an extremely evil twist.

King David warned, "And Solomon, my son, learn to know the God of your ancestors intimately. Worship and serve him with your whole heart and a willing mind. For the LORD sees every heart and knows every plan and thought. If you seek him, you will find him. But if you forsake him, he will reject you forever" (1 Chronicles 28:9 - NLT). There are numerous passages that admonish us to seek the Lord with our whole heart or to render to Him wholehearted devotion. That is integrity, the opposite of which leads to a fractured personality that attempts to serve two masters – both, necessarily, with halfhearted devotion (Matthew 6:24).

There really is no place for pride as we seek to be people of integrity. The following question should help keep any arrogance in check: "Who can say, 'I have kept my heart pure; I am cleansed from my sin'?" (Proverbs 20:9 - CSB). Yet, we should not be discouraged or give up on pursuing a life of integrity. As King David once prayed, "I know, my God, that you test the heart and are pleased with integrity" (1 Chronicles 29:17a - NIV).

Do what you say (practice what you preach)
Keep your promises! Have you ever tried to work with someone who suffers from "selective amnesia"? They can make impressive promises to gain time or favor but they don't really mean a thing they say. If you later try to collect on their offer, they take offense, deny everything, and accuse you of fabricating lies. To state there are people who relate to others in this manner may seem exaggerated but I have had to deal with a few leaders who behaved precisely in this manner.

Do these people understand just how much harm they cause and how detrimental they are to the cause of Christ? Their word is worthless. You cannot count on them, because when the time comes to fulfill their promises, they'll only do it if they *feel* like it. They'll even tell you as much, as though that were a valid excuse.

Bosses, spouses and parents who act in this manner destroy trust and create instability and uncertainty in the lives of those they lead. Political candidates are notorious for offering false hope with their extravagant promises before elected, only to ignore or dismiss many of them as unattainable after taking office. "The integrity of the upright guides them, but the unfaithful are destroyed by their duplicity" (Proverbs 11:3).

If you are a leader you cannot effectively lead when people don't trust you. If your word is worthless there is nothing to build on. David, a man of his word, described the person who enjoys close fellowship with God, as, among other things, "the one who lives honestly, practices righteousness, and acknowledges the truth in his heart" and "who keeps his word whatever the cost" (Psalm 15:2, 4b - HCSB). That is being a person of integrity. Such a person understands that his or her word is worth more than money, even if it means personal sacrifice.

There is no one who has more integrity than the Lord Himself. Throughout the book of Isaiah God explains how He foretells what will happen in the future so people understand He knows and controls everything. "Behold, the former things have come to pass, Now I declare new things; Before they spring forth I proclaim them to you" (Isaiah 42:9 - NASB). It's God both saying what He will do and then doing what He said He would. He claims, "I, the Lord, speak the truth; I declare what is right" (Isaiah 45:19b - NIV). Can you imagine what would happen if the Lord did not take Holy Spirit-inspired prophecies seriously or changed His mind and decided not to fulfill them after all? God also swears by Himself (there is no higher authority) and utters promises "in all integrity" (Isaiah 45:23a). Fulfilled prophecy has proven this to be true, over and over again.

Are you a person of integrity? Do you keep your promises? Are you the same in public as you are in private?

Kingdom Value #56: Contentment

We could say that contentment is the perfect balance between stagnant passiveness and unbridled ambition. It's not so passive that it sits and watches the world go by, nor so aggressive that it obsesses with having, doing or controlling everything. It feels the normal stresses of life, but has learned to be patient – yet persistent – as goals are pursued.

Contentment does not come by seeking to please ourselves, but from serving God and others. Paul told Timothy that "godliness with contentment is a great gain" (1 Timothy 6:6 - HCSB). Not just contentment, but **godliness** with contentment. Then he gives Timothy some healthy perspective when he reminds him that "we brought nothing into the world, and we can take nothing out," so that we should be content if we have the basics, and that "those who want to be rich fall into temptation, a trap" because "the love of money is a root of all kinds of evil" (1 Timothy 6:7-10 - HCSB).

There is a similar warning that comes with a profound explanation: "Keep your life free from love of money, and be content with what you have, for he has said, 'I will never leave you nor forsake you'" (Hebrews 13:5 - ESV). We can be content with what we have because we understand God is always with us, supplying our every need, seeing our problems and struggles. He is always there. And we can always count on Him.

The lack of contentment can lead people to overindulge, overspend, and develop harmful habits in an attempt to soothe their boredom and fill an existential void. There are many ways people try to fill their lives with meaning and reach a state of contentment. Unfortunately the route taken by those who do not trust in the Lord leads to frustration and emptiness, as seen below.

The 4 P's of worldly values
Power, pleasure, possessions, popularity. These are some of the main values people pursue. But they are transitory and overrated. Instead of being obsessed with having more of these, we should be thankful for what we have been allotted. Gratitude leads to contentment. Contentment leads to more gratitude.

Power
When Philip, the evangelist, and the Apostles went to Samaria to proclaim the Good News of the Kingdom, they met Simon, a man who had previously practiced sorcery there. He claimed to be great and the people went along with that, saying "This man is called the Great Power of God!" He heard the Gospel message, accepted it and was baptized. But when he "saw that the Holy Spirit was given through the laying on of the apostles' hands," he offered money in order to have that same power. That did not go over well with the Apostles. Peter rebuked him and told him he needed to repent (Acts 8:9-10, 18-19 - HCSB).

Power is something God gives His own so they can better serve in the Kingdom (see *Authority and Power – Kingdom Value #66*). Power is never given so we can be self-serving. Although we may desire a certain degree of control over our problems and circumstances, we should not crave power over others or become overly impressed with the power God has allowed us to possess.

Pleasure
Solomon was a great administrator who enjoyed an era of peace during his reign. Although he led many building projects, he must have had lots of spare time on his hands because Ecclesiastes is filled with notes pertaining to his experimentation with different aspects of life. He wanted to understand the meaning of life and what made people truly happy. He was an expert in pleasure. "King Solomon loved many foreign women. (...) He had seven hundred wives, princesses, and three hundred concubines." He allowed pleasure to become more important than guarding his heart against idolatry, and "his wives turned his heart away" (1 Kings 11:1, 3 - NASB).

If pleasure were equal to meaning and happiness, Solomon of all people would have known. Yet when he experimented with pleasure it left him feeling empty. "I thought to myself, 'Come now, I will try self-indulgent pleasure to see if it is
200

worthwhile.' But I found that it also is futile" (Ecclesiastes 2:1 - NET Bible). He knew that pleasure couldn't last forever (Ecclesiastes 12:1).

Possessions

We are needy creatures who cannot survive without external resources: we need clothing, food, water, air, medical help, tools, shelter, furniture, and so much more, just to get along. Jesus taught us it's okay to ask the Father for our needs: "Give us today our daily bread" (Matthew 6:11 - HCSB). He also said not to worry about where our food, water, and clothing will be coming from, because while "the idolaters eagerly seek all these things" the fact is "your heavenly Father knows that you need them" (Matthew 6:31-34 - HCSB).

In order to find true contentment in our lives, instead of accumulating *stuff* we are to "seek first the kingdom of God and His righteousness, and all these things will be provided for you" (Matthew 6:33 - HCSB). Jesus also taught: "be careful to guard yourselves against every kind of greed, because a person's life doesn't consist of the amount of possessions he has" (Luke 12:15 - ISV).

As important as possessions may be, they too cannot bring contentment to the human soul. Neither do they create meaning or bring fulfillment. The truth about material possessions is that "in the blink of an eye wealth disappears, for it will sprout wings and fly away like an eagle" (Proverbs 23:5 - NLT).

The Tenth Commandment requires: "Don't covet your neighbor's house. Don't covet your neighbor's wife, or his male or female workers, his car, or anything else that belongs to your neighbor" (Exodus 20:17. Oops! Slightly adapted for today's reality). The antidote to covetousness is contentment. We can be content even if we are financially poor. In fact, some of the happiest people I have met are simple people with very few worldly possessions. Paul wrote, "I am not saying this because I am in need, for I have learned to be content whatever the circumstances" (Philippians 4:11 - NIV). Being content is a state of mind, a lifestyle, a very healthy way of looking at life.

Popularity

Popularity that comes from true talent and service, that is not sought but is given in recognition of some good deed, product, or service is not what we are talking about here. There will always be those who are more popular than others. The problem is believing that popularity can bring true inclusion and joy, when it usually isolates on the one hand and creates a false sense of superiority on the other.

The bottom line is, who are we living for? Who is our audience? We can't please everybody, so who is it we choose to please? Unfortunately many "loved the praise of men more than the praise of God" (John 12:43 - KJV). Why fight for a place in the spotlight when you are accepted and loved unconditionally by God – right now and as you are? Knowing we don't have to earn God's love should calm our fears and anxiety and foster a sense of well-being and contentment.

Do you lead a life of contentment? Are you grateful for the way you are and what you have? Do you crave the 4 P's or are you good with your identity in Christ?

KV56 – **CONTENTMENT**

| | Consistently practice | | Sometimes practice | | Struggle | | Mostly fail | | Continually fail |

Kingdom Value #57: Enduring Suffering

Right now our brothers and sisters in Africa and the Middle East are enduring horrible atrocities at the hands of those who feel it is their duty to persecute, torture, maim, and kill Christians. To tear down their church buildings and destroy their houses. For most of us living in the western hemisphere, suffering this intense is hard to fathom.

But just because we do not suffer this sort of onslaught (yet) does not mean we do not suffer. Suffering is a universal problem which is not limited to religiously motivated attacks, but to all areas of life – from flat tires to cancer. Try as we may, there is no way to continuously avoid suffering in its many forms. Which easily leads us to conclude: suffering was built into the fabric of life when the first couple fell (Genesis 3:14-19).

First century believers had their share of intense suffering as well. Not long after being stoned and left for dead, Paul and his fellow apostle Barnabas went back through the cities where they had planted churches "strengthening the disciples by encouraging them to continue in the faith and by telling them, 'It is necessary to pass through many troubles on our way into the kingdom of God'" (Acts 14:22 - HCSB; see v. 14). This Kingdom Principle could be expressed as "no pain, no gain."

Peter wrote about suffering for doing wrong, for which "you get no credit;" and suffering for doing what is right. Patiently enduring the latter is pleasing to God and means we are being guided by the example of our Lord and following in His steps. Jesus' reaction to unfair treatment was exemplary. "He did not retaliate when he was insulted, nor threaten revenge when he suffered. He left his case in the hands of God, who always judges fairly" (1 Peter 2:19-23 - NLT; see also 1 Peter 3:13-14).

Suffering is a stumbling block for many people. They begin to doubt God's goodness when suffering comes to them or to others – especially to good people and little children. Admittedly, this is a difficult matter to understand. The argument heard from God's critics is that either God is incapable or unwilling to do away with pain. If He is incapable, they say, then what kind of God is He? And if He is unwilling, then, that is even worse.

But there are several issues we must consider when looking at this problem. First, we live in a fallen world which is in rebellion against God, and for this it is under His wrath (Ephesians 2:1-3). Living in this fallen world means our life here will be affected by sickness, weakness, brokenness, pain, accidents, and death.

Second, we all have fallen human natures and we tend to hurt each other – willingly or not. Because of our egocentrism, we have to go out of our way to learn to put other people's needs first – a process usually accomplished through suffering.

God also uses suffering to get our attention, to help us learn to look to Him for answers, and to purify our motives. Otherwise, if those who follow God were immune to suffering, everyone would want to serve God for the wrong reason. We must learn to love God for God's sake and not because of blessings He showers on us.

Everything on planet Earth – including suffering – is temporary.

And, we must remember that God loves His Son more than anyone could ever know, and yet He allowed *Him* to suffer the agony of the cross. This should be proof enough that in God's economy and Kingdom, allowing someone to suffer is not a sign of lack of love. "In bringing many sons to glory, it was fitting that God, for whom and through whom everything exists, should make the author of their salvation perfect through suffering" (Hebrews 2:10 - NIV). "Make perfect" (Greek *teleioó*), literally means "to carry through completely; to accomplish, finish, bring to an end."[5]

Can there be joy in the midst of suffering? Ask Paul and Silas, who were attacked, "stripped and beaten with rods" and then "thrown into prison" in Philippi, after they had been "severely flogged." The jailer then "put them in the inner cell and fastened their feet in the stocks." But "about midnight Paul and Silas were praying and singing hymns to God, and the other prisoners were listening to them" (Acts 16:22-31 - NIV). The joy of the Lord can trump even the worst circumstances, when we know we are doing what God wants us to do. For this reason Paul could say that "we glory in our sufferings, because we know that suffering produces perseverance; perseverance, character; and character, hope" (Romans 5:3-4 - NIV). Paul knew he could trust God and that He had a reason for this suffering.

Jesus warned His disciples that "in the world you'll have trouble." He had no hidden agenda and was very sincere with them. They should not expect an easy road ahead. Yet, despite the suffering, there was plenty to be positive about. So, Jesus added, "But cheer up! I have overcome the world" (John 16:33 - GOD'S WORD).

There is a Bible passage that speaks directly to the issue of suffering for the Kingdom. Paul tells the Thessalonians that as a result of the persecutions and trials they were enduring, their faith was growing more and more and their love for one another was increasing. That was proof that God's judgment is right and would result in them being counted worthy of the Kingdom of God, for which they were suffering. And it would lead to the name of our Lord Jesus being glorified in them (2 Thessalonians 1:3-12).

How well do you endure suffering? What is your attitude when faced with pain or persecution? Is your first reaction to complain and question God? Does suffering create distrust in the way God is handling your situation? Are you able to quickly or eventually move to the point of giving thanks in all things?

KV57 – ENDURING SUFFERING

| Consistently practice | Sometimes practice | Struggle | Mostly fail | Continually fail |

Kingdom Value #58: Perseverance

When I was eight years old I gave my life to the Lord, in response to a message at a Baptist camp in Arkansas. I don't remember the theme of the message, but I clearly remember that, although I was so young, I felt a deep sense of guilt and the need for forgiveness. I felt joy when going forward with the decision of surrendering my life to Christ, especially because my father was assigned to be my counselor after the service. I recall that the invitation hymn we sang was "No Turning Back." The lyrics include statements like "I have decided to follow Jesus;" "The

204

world behind me, the cross before me;" and "No turning back, no turning back."[6]

No turning back. Jesus said that "No one who puts his hand to the plow and looks back is fit for the kingdom of God" (Luke 9:62 - HCSB). As important as the decision to receive God's offer of salvation may be, it must be followed by a lifelong commitment. There must be perseverance. Receiving salvation is a one-time occurrence (like *getting* married) but living each day for the Lord is a process (like *being* married). This process demands patience (see *Kingdom Value #12*), endurance, and requires that we never give in and never give up.

We have in Jesus, again, our supreme example. We are given the challenge, "Let us run with endurance the race that lies before us" and to keep our eyes on Jesus as our model, "who for the joy that lay before Him endured a cross and despised the shame and has sat down at the right hand of God's throne" (Hebrews 12:1-2 - HCSB). Jesus had a plan, the fulfillment of which would bring Him great joy. He kept His focus on what He was accomplishing and this allowed Him to endure the most painful of executions and arguably the worst experience of His entire existence: being separated from the Father as He took on our sins and God's wrath in our place.

Our Lord expects us to persevere, just as He did. "But my righteous one will live by faith, and if he shrinks back, I take no pleasure in him" (Hebrews 10:38 - NET Bible). This becomes very clear when the Lord addresses the seven Revelation churches in Asia Minor. They were told to be overcomers (see *Kingdom Value #62*) and to "be faithful until death, and I will give you the crown of life" (Revelation 2:10 - NKJV; see chapters 2 and 3).

Why do some persevere and overcome while others give up and succumb on their spiritual journey? Life is a faithfulness test (see *Kingdom Value #15*). We will constantly be under spiritual attack and exposed to carnal temptations while being challenged to choose the narrow gate to life, even when it would be easier to give in to the pressure of traveling the broad highway to destruction (Matthew 7:13).

Each person must decide: "Am I ready to pay the price and remain faithful for life? Am I willing to stick to it and persevere to the end?" It's pay now or pay later. Either way we will pay a price for the decisions we make. If it is the right decision, we will pay the price of going up against the enemy of our souls – but the rewards will be more than worth it. If we make the wrong decision and give in to worldly pressure, we may have it easy now, but will pay a hefty price up ahead.
It's like the boat heading down the stream, being carried by the waters without any counter currents or resistance. The problem is, the stream is headed for a massive

waterfall. Everything seems to be fine, until you see the end result. Escaping destruction requires turning around and heading upstream, in the opposite direction. Now, all of the sudden, the force of the current can be felt like never before. Going upstream is difficult and may seem counterintuitive, but it will save you from death and destruction.

For the Apostle Paul, paying the price of persevering to the end was more than worth it. "I have fought the good fight. I have completed the race. I have kept the faith. The victor's crown of righteousness is now waiting for me, which the Lord, the righteous Judge, will give to me on the day that he comes, and not only to me but also to all who eagerly wait for his appearing" (2 Timothy 4:7-8 - ISV).

The Church in Smyrna was told not to fear the suffering that would be coming their way, as soon they would be severely tested. Jesus challenged them: "Be faithful, even to the point of death, and I will give you life as your victor's crown" (Revelation 2:10 - NIV). Nothing could be better than to pass the faithfulness test of life by persevering to the very end, and to be rewarded by our Savior with His approval and the crown of victory.

As we go through the most difficult of days and the most trying experiences, we should do the same as our Lord: focus on the end result of what God has challenged us to achieve; concentrate on our final destination and the rewards that it will bring. "For our present troubles are small and won't last very long. Yet they produce for us a glory that vastly outweighs them and will last forever!" (2 Corinthians 4:17 - NLT).

Have you been persevering in your faithfulness to the Lord? Have trials or temptations dampened your resolve? Do you need to recommit your decision to follow through and stand firm to the end?

Kingdom Value #59: Honesty

Honesty is the application of truth (see *Kingdom Value #60*, below) in our daily life – especially where finances and relationships are concerned. As for finances, "The Lord abhors dishonest scales, but accurate weights are his delight" (Proverbs 11:1 - NIV). When it comes to relationships, "These are the things you are to do: Speak the truth to each other, and render true and sound judgment in your courts" (Zechariah 8:16 - NIV).

Unfortunately, today honesty is in short supply. This Kingdom Value makes life simpler. If everyone were honest, there would be no need for locks, surveillance cameras, lie detectors, multiple checks and balances, gatekeepers, and security personnel. Life would also be a lot less expensive and stressful. If only people could be trusted! There is a cable news anchorman who has a segment called "Keeping them Honest." The question is, who's keeping *him* honest?

Being honest with those we relate to or deal with is something that delights the Lord. Family relationships and the global economy have this in common: they both need honesty in order to work properly. Dishonesty creates an atmosphere of mistrust and generates corruption. And state-sponsored corruption leads to poverty and chaos.

In the time of the prophet Jeremiah, things were so bad that no one would stand up for the truth. Even brothers were taking advantage of each other and everyone would "fool and defraud each other" with lies they were good at telling (Jeremiah 9:3-5 - NLT).

Honesty is the antidote for corruption. The basic motivation for financial dishonesty – such as the misappropriation of funds (embezzlement), robbery and cheating – is covetousness. The Tenth Commandment says: "You shall not covet ... anything that belongs to your neighbor" (Exodus 20:17 - NIV). When it is more desirable to take what does not belong to us than to be content with what we have gained through honest work, then we are in great need of a Kingdom wake up call.

In case we lack common sense or a basic notion of right and wrong, the Lord spells it out directly: "do not use dishonest standards when measuring length, weight, or volume" (Leviticus 19:35 - NLT). We can know honesty is a big deal to the Lord because He added "you shall not steal" (Exodus 20:15 - NIV) to the Ten Commandments. The Bible uses that terrible word "abomination" when dealing with dishonesty: "Unequal weights are an abomination to the LORD, and false scales are not good" (Proverbs 20:23 - ESV).

Honesty is a question of character. Jesus said that "one who is faithful in a very little is also faithful in much, and one who is dishonest in a very little is also dishonest in much" (Luke 16:10 - ESV). Those who go for "ill-gotten gain" will "ambush only themselves" and "it takes away the life of those who get it" (Proverbs 1:18-19 - NIV). While honesty is a Kingdom Value we should gladly embrace, "ill-gotten treasures have no lasting value" (Proverbs 10:2a - NIV). Another Kingdom financial principle is that "wealth from get-rich-quick schemes quickly disappears; wealth from hard work grows over time" (Proverbs 13:11 - NLT).

Corruption in religious circles

Honesty is especially expected from those who represent God and His Kingdom on earth. Therefore, dishonesty in Christian circles is especially disappointing –and serious. A disturbing example of corrupt religious leaders comes from the sons of one of Israel's greatest spiritual guides. "As Samuel grew old, he appointed his sons to be judges over Israel. Joel and Abijah, his oldest sons, held court in Beersheba. But they were not like their father, for they were greedy for money. They accepted bribes and perverted justice" (1 Samuel 8:1-3 - NLT).

How sad! An institution which was to serve as a model of integrity, now led by people who didn't even try to hide their corruption. It was common knowledge. A full-blown scandal. Before them, the sons of Eli served as utterly corrupt priests, going as far as blaspheming God, eating meat set aside for sacrifices and "seducing the young women who assisted at the entrance of the Tabernacle," for which the Lord punished them with death and brought a curse on their family line (1 Samuel 2:22; see verses 12-36).

The solution to the problem of corruption in religious circles had been given years earlier to Moses by his father-in-law. He advised him "to look for capable men among the people, men who fear God, men of integrity who hate dishonest gain" (Exodus 18:21a - ISV). The solution is finding men and women of character who will become honest leaders.

Corruption left unchecked

Corruption is a way of life for some politicians and whole governments throughout the world. When dishonesty gets out of hand, people will stop at nothing to make a quick buck. That includes using violence and destroying lives. "But your eyes and your heart are intent only upon your own dishonest gain, and on shedding innocent blood and on practicing oppression and extortion" (Jeremiah 22:17 - NASB).

Corruption reaches such levels that perpetrators come to the point of deriving pleasure from deceiving and taking advantage of others. It's a sick world out there! Taking what belongs to others is financial bullying. "A merchant, in whose hands are false balances, he loves to oppress" (Hosea 12:7 - ESV). When the dishonest wealthy are powerful and have the means to oppress, they may create specific problems, then turn around and charge for a solution only they can offer. It's an oversized money-making scheme.

Honesty in relationships

Honesty is the character trait of people of integrity (see *Kingdom Value #55*). They have no hidden agendas and are usually not good at playing politics. But honesty runs even deeper in the family, where hiding your true self is next to impossible, because you can't fool your children or your spouse – at least not for long. The opposite of honesty in relationships is hypocrisy, which is sometimes compared to wearing a mask, and can include creating a "persona" in order to project an image of how we would like to be perceived.

Honesty taken to the next level is called intimacy, which someone defined as "in-to-me-see." It means laying yourself bare – to your spouse or your closest friends and family members. It involves confessing your struggles and weaknesses, sharing your deepest feelings and aspirations. This process comes more naturally to women and can be quite painful to men (comparable to extracting a tooth!). And yet it is a necessary step for those who wish to grow closer to others and to the Lord.

It is actually easier to be totally transparent with the Lord, because He already knows all about us. There is no hiding or withholding of information from Him. King David knew that and prayed, "O Lord, You have searched me and known me. (...) You understand my thought afar off (...) And are acquainted with all my ways" (Psalm 139:1-3 - NKJV). But David also knew his own heart and how deceitful it could be if left unchecked. So he also prayed, "Search me, O God, and know my heart; Try me, and know my anxieties; And see if *there is* any wicked way in me, And lead me in the way everlasting" (Psalm 139:23-24 - NKJV).

Find yourself on the honesty scale below: how consistently honest are you with God, your loved ones, friends, boss, co-workers, the IRS...?

Kingdom Value #60: Truth

What is truth?

"Are you a king?," Pilate inquired. Jesus declared that He was and had come into the world to bear witness to the truth. His next statement defined how to discern which people are on the side of the truth. He said, "Everyone who is of the truth listens to my voice." Pilate pressed Him: "What is truth?" To that, Jesus did not answer (John 18:37, 38 - ESV).

But Jesus had already told His disciples a good deal about the truth and what it is. He claimed "I am the truth" (John 14:6). And when He prayed to His Father, He asked for His followers, that God would "sanctify them in the truth; Your word is truth" (John 17:17 - NASB). We see that: a) King Jesus came to bear witness to the truth; b) He Himself is truth; and c) God's word is truth. If we want to know the truth about God and His Son, we must understand His word. And when we do, "you will know the truth, and the truth will set you free" (John 8:32 - ISV). Free from darkness, ignorance, and condemnation. Free from the punishment, the power, and eventually the presence of sin.

The Gospel truth

Whatever God says is true and the essence of truth, for God "cannot lie" (Titus 1:2). No matter how clever the arguments of those who oppose God and His truth, we would do well to remember this basic rule: "let God be true but every man a liar" (Romans 3:4 - NKJV). God's worldview is the correct, ultimate and only reliable worldview. It is untainted by culture, personal experience, human limitations, and psychological filters.

The Kingdom is based on truth and the trustworthiness of the King. God promises: "I, the LORD, speak only what is true and declare only what is right" (Isaiah 45:19b). The Holy Spirit is "the Spirit of truth" (John 15:26). Jesus always told the truth (John 8:45, 46). Likewise, those who stand with Jesus "cannot oppose the truth, but must always stand for the truth" (2 Corinthians 13:8 - NLT). In relation to the Father, Jesus declared that "those who worship Him must worship in spirit and truth" (John 4:24 - HCSB). The Apostle John wrote, "For I was very glad when some brothers came and testified to your faithfulness to the truth--how you are walking in the truth" (3 John 1:3 - HCSB). On the other hand, "all will be condemned who have not believed the truth but have delighted in wickedness" (2 Thessalonians 2:12 - NIV).

It is repentance that leads a person to the knowledge of truth. It is the knowledge of truth that brings people to their senses and allows them to escape the devil's trap (2 Timothy 2:25, 26). Accepting the truth is a life choice. Some people "are forever inquiring and getting information, but are never able to arrive at a recognition and knowledge of the Truth" (2 Timothy 3:7 - AMP). They have enough evidence, they just don't want to believe and commit to it. They prefer to lie to themselves and live in darkness. But choosing to ignore the truth will have devastating consequences.

Truth as light

As one of God's first acts of creation, He said, "'Let there be light,' and there was light" (Genesis 1:3). The Word, the Lord Jesus Christ, was there in the beginning with the Father (John 1:1-2). He is the Author of life, "and that life was the light of men. That light shines in the darkness, yet the darkness did not overcome it" (John 1:4-5 - HCSB). Light represents the knowledge of God. Jesus is the light of the world (John 8:12). Because the light came and was rejected, the world is under God's judgment. Although sinners wish to avoid being exposed by the light, "anyone who lives by the truth comes to the light, so that his works may be shown to be accomplished by God" (John 3:19-21 - HCSB).

Light is equated with truth, darkness with ignorance, lies, and evil. If you are in the dark, you are clueless as to the reality that surrounds you. You don't know where to go or how to get there. Jesus said that "if one blind person guides another, they will both fall into a ditch" (Matthew 15:14 - NLT).

When people reject the truth of the knowledge of God and close their hearts to Him, they open themselves right up to spiritual deception. I have seen people who demand proof from the Bible and the Christian faith – and continually refute it when it is given – turn around and accept some of the weirdest religious ideas with open arms. While they refuse to believe God's truth, they are more than happy to entrust their lives to unfounded and irrational philosophies and religions.

The Bible says some people, "by their unrighteousness suppress the truth," that by refusing to acknowledge God "their thinking became nonsense, and their senseless minds were darkened" and that they have "exchanged the truth of God for a lie." Because "they did not think it worthwhile to acknowledge God" their minds became worthless, which led them on a downward spiral of unrighteousness. Ironically some who claim not to believe in the existence of God, when under fire, confess to be "God-haters." Although their minds are now mush, they claim "to be wise," when in truth "they became fools." (Romans 1:18, 21, 25, 28, 30 - HCSB). Though written two thousand years ago, this description seems even more relevant today.

Accepting the truth results in a paradigm shift of major proportions. Once you see the light, *everything* changes. "For you were once darkness, but now you are light in the Lord. Walk as children of light — for the fruit of the light results in all goodness, righteousness, and truth" (Ephesians 5:8-9 - HCSB). Just as those who were healed of their blindness by Jesus leaped for joy, when we make our transition to the truth we become overjoyed and thankful (see Colossians 1:12-13).

211

Truth versus lies

Sarah Sumner, in her thought-provoking article "The Seven Levels of Lying," argues that in level four "you now believe the lies that you are telling others. We can lie so effectively that we even lie to ourselves. We self-deceive." And it just gets worse. By level six you've come up with a technique for lying and by level seven you see it as your duty to lie![7] Just as the Pharisees reacted with hatred and intolerance when confronted with the truth of Jesus, our culture today believes it is its duty to continue promoting lies when confronted with Kingdom Values.

Satan invented lying. By all indications, he was the first to ever sin and tell a lie in all of God's creation (Ezekiel 28:15, 18). Uttering false statements, half truths, and outright lies – this all originated with him. We see him in the Garden of Eden doing precisely that (Genesis 3:1-5).

If there were ever a kingdom of darkness "value," it would be lying. Because the prince of darkness "has nothing to do with the truth, because there is no truth in him. When he lies, he speaks out of his own character, for he is a liar and the father of lies" (John 8:44b - ESV). And those who lie and reject the truth act like him. They become his children and lose the ability to believe (John 8:42-45).

One of the 10 Commandments is "you shall not give false testimony against your neighbor" (Exodus 20:16 - NIV). That's how important telling the truth is to God. He takes this so seriously we are warned that "everyone who loves and practices lying" is kept "outside" of God's glorious presence (Revelation 22:15b - NASB).

Proverbs repeatedly makes the point that you can't achieve lasting value if what you do is based on wickedness, ill-gotten gain, or lies. "Truthful words stand the test of time, but lies are soon exposed. The Lord detests lying lips, but he delights in those who tell the truth" (Proverbs 12:19, 22 - NLT). Want to make God smile? Speak the truth. God hates lies and liars (Proverbs 6:16, 19).

Most of us have a hard time facing the truth about our own shortcomings. We'd rather live in denial. The truth about our sinful tendencies, failures, character flaws and outright sins is hard to face. Living in the light and relating to others in truth is the ideal we should always pursue. That means speaking the truth about ourselves. "So stop telling lies. Let us tell our neighbors the truth" (Ephesians 4:25a - NLT).

How truthful are you in your dealings and relationships? Do you always "tell the truth, the whole truth, and nothing but the truth?"

212

Kingdom Value #61: Wisdom

Wisdom is the practical side of knowledge. It teaches us what to do with what we know. How to apply theoretical knowledge to the circumstances and crises of life. Wisdom means knowing how to live.

"The fear of the LORD is the beginning of wisdom, and the knowledge of the Holy One is understanding" (Proverbs 9:10 - HCSB). If we fear the Lord we will honor Him and hold His standards in high regard. This should lead us to be loyal and obedient to Him. Conclusion: Wisdom is knowing how to obey God.

There are intellectuals who have a vast internal database of knowledge but are socially clumsy or don't know what to do with their feelings. Others may have a clear understanding of right and wrong but lack the willpower to make the correct choices in life. They are carried away by their emotions and seduced by worldly desires. It is obvious that knowledge is not enough. We must have wisdom: the power to do what we know is right. The power to be free from our destructive desires brought on by negative emotions. That is why "wisdom is better than strength" (Ecclesiastes 9:16 - NASB). Samson had strength in abundance, but very little wisdom. He allowed himself to be carried away and destroyed by his evil desires (see the second half of *Self denial – Kingdom Value #54*).

Solomon loved the Lord and God appeared to him in a dream and told him to request something for himself. Solomon was in the process of taking over the kingdom, was young and painfully aware of his inexperience. He felt overwhelmed with the daunting task of leading a whole nation. So Solomon asked for "an understanding heart to judge Your people, that I may discern between good and evil" (1 Kings 3:9a - NKJV). This request pleased the Lord and He made Solomon the wisest man there ever was (1 Kings 3:11, 12; 4:30). But he too allowed his desires and emotions to get the best of him and began to disobey the Lord and contradict what he had taught others.

Still, Proverbs is proof of Solomon's great wisdom. This is the stated goal of that book:

To know wisdom and instruction,
To discern the sayings of understanding,
To receive instruction in wise behavior,
Righteousness, justice and equity;
To give prudence to the naive,
To the youth knowledge and discretion.
– Proverbs 1:2-4 - NASB

The Message interprets "wisdom" in this passage to mean to "know how to live well and right" (Proverbs 1:2 - MSG). "A wise man will hear, and will increase learning" while "fools despise wisdom and instruction" (Proverbs 1:1-7 - BRG). The contrast between the wise and the fool is a reoccurring theme in the book.

Wisdom is personified and cries out in the streets warning fools and mockers to change before calamity overtakes them (see Proverbs also 8:1-20).

If we "seek it like silver and search for it like hidden treasure" we will find wisdom in the form of "the fear of the Lord" and "the knowledge of God" because the Lord will give it to us. "Then you will understand righteousness, justice, and integrity— every good path" (Proverbs 2:1-10 - HCSB). Notice again how Kingdom Values are related to each other and flow from righteousness.

"Happy is a man who finds wisdom and who acquires understanding" (Proverbs 3:13 - HCSB), because wisdom is more profitable than silver and jewels, she brings long life, peace, discretion, safety and protection, eliminating the sense of fear.

"Wisdom is supreme" and should be cherished and embraced (Proverbs 4:5-9 - HCSB). Wisdom will help us to maintain discretion and keep us safe from "the forbidden woman" whose "feet go down to death" (Proverbs 5:1-6 - HCSB; see also Proverbs 6:20-35 and chapter 7).

Proverbs 8:22-31 speaks of wisdom in such a personal way that some have wondered if it does not refer to Jesus. The argument is compelling, but a closer examination shows "Wisdom" claiming to have been created (see John 1:3; Colossians 1:16, 17).

Proverbs 9 contrasts wisdom and foolishness. Proverbs 13 mentions that the wise respond to discipline (as in a son to a father), that "wisdom is gained by those who take advice" and that wise instruction "is a fountain of life" (Proverbs 13:1, 10, 14 - HCSB).

We learn that "every wise woman builds her house, but a foolish one tears it down with her own hands" (Proverbs 14:1 - HCSB). We are informed that "a wise heart instructs its mouth and increases learning with its speech" (Proverbs 16:23 - HCSB). You can't out-wit the Lord or use wisdom against Him. "No wisdom, no understanding, and no counsel will prevail against the Lord" (Proverbs 21:30 - HCSB).

We are told to "listen closely, pay attention to the words of the wise, and apply your mind to my knowledge" (Proverbs 22:17 - HCSB). Solomon observed that "a house is built by wisdom, and it is established by understanding" and that "Wisdom is inaccessible to a fool" (Proverbs 24:3, 7a - HCSB).

"A fool gives full vent to his anger, but a wise man holds it in check" (Proverbs 29:11 - HCSB). This and other similar warnings are given in the latter chapters.

Brother Andrew ("God's Smuggler") once asked his audience what we would do if we were stranded on an island and God told us He would provide us with one thing of our choosing. "What would you request?," Brother Andrew asked. Many answered "a Bible." "Oh, you all are just too spiritual," Brother Andrew said. Then he shouted enthusiastically: "Why not a boat? Then you could get off of the island and have all the Bibles you want!" Wisdom is logical and practical. The fact that Solomon requested wisdom was, in itself, a very wise choice. Because with wisdom he could gain riches, a long life, and so much more. Riches, on the other hand, cannot bring about a wise mind.

Solomon had said that "the fear of the LORD is the beginning of wisdom" and yet he had come to the point where he showed no respect for the Lord and His commands. "So the Lord became angry with Solomon, because his heart had turned from the Lord God of Israel" and informed him that "I will surely tear the kingdom away from you," which resulted in a split kingdom and the dire consequences which followed (1 Kings 11:1-13 - NKJV; see also Nehemiah 13:26).

Two better examples of Old Testament heroes whose lives exemplify true wisdom during their whole lives would be Joseph and his leadership in Egypt, and Daniel and his leadership in Babylon.

God's wisdom and the world's "wisdom"
James says there are two kinds of wisdom. God's wisdom leads to humility, purity, peace, gentleness, mercy, good deeds, impartiality, sincerity, peace-making, and righteousness. The world's "wisdom" leads to bitter jealousy, selfish ambition, boasting, lying, selfishness, leading to disorder and all kinds of evil (James 3:13-18).

Paul also saw a difference in the "wisdom" from this world and the true wisdom from above. He shares about the overall and supreme wisdom of God as he writes to the Christians in Corinth. He tells them:

> ... I do speak with words of wisdom, but not the kind of wisdom that belongs to this world or to the rulers of this world, who are soon forgotten. No, the wisdom we speak of is the mystery of God--his plan that was previously hidden, even though he made it for our ultimate glory before the world began.
> 1 Corinthians 2:6-7 - NLT

True wisdom comes from God, while those who think they are too smart for God come up with their own set of rules and values. It's kind of like processed food. We discovered how to make all things artificial and began to substitute chemicals for natural ingredients. Several years down the road we are seeing just how harmful this move was, and now there is an attempt to return to natural foods. It turns out that God knew what He was doing after all. And He still knows what is best for us in all areas of life. That is why if we diligently follow His Kingdom Values our lives will be more meaningful and fruitful, blessing others and pleasing the Lord.

God's wisdom is His profound and limitless knowledge put into action in an infinite variety of ways and which are motivated by His love for all He has created. It was because of and through this wisdom that God planned and executed our creation. And through His wisdom that He sent His Son to die in our place and to give us the hope of eternal life along side Him.

Are you wise when it comes to knowing how to obey God and practice Kingdom Values? Do you need more wisdom (James 1:5)? How would you rate yourself?

KV61 – **WISDOM**

Consistently practice | Sometimes practice | Struggle | Mostly fail | Continually fail

Kingdom Value #62: Overcoming

Jesus wants us to win, just like He did! Winning over the obstacles in life, staying focused on His Kingdom and righteousness, being loyal and faithful during one's whole life. That is what the Bible calls an overcomer: one who obeys Jesus to the very end (Revelation 2:26).

216

In his "Be Series," Wiersbe sees Revelation's central message as "Be Victorious." He writes, "The overriding theme of the Book of Revelation is the return of Jesus Christ to defeat all evil and to establish His reign. It is definitely a book of victory and His people are seen as 'overcomers'. In his first epistle, John also called God's people 'overcomers.'"[8]

In the risen Lord's evaluation of each of the seven churches in the book of Revelation, there is an emphasis on being an overcomer or victor. That is the goal for every church and believer. Those who fail are sternly warned, while overcomers are promised extraordinary rewards. The stakes could not be higher, because "if we endure, we will also reign with him; if we deny him, he also will deny us" (2 Timothy 2:12 - ESV).

Overcomers will "eat from the tree of life" (Revelation 2:7 - HCSB); "will never be harmed by the second death" (2:11 - HCSB); will eat hidden manna and receive a white stone with their new name inscribed on it (2:17 - HCSB). They will be given "authority over the nations" just as Jesus received this authority from His Father; they will also receive "the morning star" (2:27-28 - HCSB); they will be "dressed in white clothes," will never have their names erased from the Book of Life, and Jesus will "acknowledge his name before My Father and before His angels" (3:5 - HCSB). Winners will be permanent pillars in God's sanctuary and will be inscribed with God's name, the New Jerusalem's name and Jesus' new name (3:12 - HCSB). And, Jesus promises that "he who overcomes, I will grant to him to sit down with Me on My throne, as I also overcame and sat down with My Father on His throne" (Revelation 3:21 - NASB).

We have in Jesus the perfect example of an overcomer. He told His disciples to "take heart! I have overcome the world" (John 16:33b - NIV). Mirroring Jesus, "everyone born of God overcomes the world. This is the victory that has overcome the world, even our faith" (1 John 5:4 - NIV; see also 1 John 4:4).

Yet, so many Christians do *not* overcome – they are not faithful to the end. Why? The reasons are many, but lie in the fact that we live in a fallen world, are under attack by a fallen enemy, and have to contend with a fallen nature. Jesus told His disciples: "The spirit is willing, but the flesh is weak" (Matthew 26:41b - HCSB). Overcomers would see this as a warning; those who fail would use it as an excuse.

In order to understand what it is we are expected to overcome, we must first ask, "what is life?" Life on earth has been compared to a journey, a school, and so much else. But the Apostle Paul shared the following, as he approached the end of his life: "I have fought the good fight, I have finished the race, I have kept the faith" (2 Timothy 4:7 - HCSB). Paul compared life to three things:

a) A battle – "I have fought the good fight." Life on earth is a constant battle between good and evil, between our new and our old nature, between those who love God and those who loathe God. It is a constant battlefield where "the cosmic powers of this darkness" try to deceive, as well as to "steal and kill and destroy" those who wish to follow the Lord (Ephesians 6:12 - BLB; John 10:10).

b) A race – "I have finished the race." The human race is a marathon. It is an endurance test. "Therefore, since we also have such a large cloud of witnesses surrounding us, let us lay aside every weight and the sin that so easily ensnares us. Let us run with endurance the race that lies before us, keeping our eyes on Jesus" (Hebrews 12:1, 2a - HCSB). It is a race *for* accomplishing the mission we were given. And it is a race *against* time, which is limited and running out.

c) A test – "I have kept the faith." Keeping the faith means remaining faithful to the end. This requires passing the many tests that try to derail our loyalty to the Lord. Life is a test in which our commitment to the Lord may be questioned, even ridiculed. We are tempted to give up and give in. We are tempted to please ourselves instead of God. There are barriers, seductions, and distractions to overcome. Many of our brothers and sisters face tremendous pressure, persecution and execution for their faithfulness.

Keeping the faith through the tests of life

I have often wondered why God chose not to liquidate our lower nature at the moment of conversion.* I have also wondered why He allows so much pain and suffering in the world. I now believe that, at least part of the answer lies in the fact that planet earth is one big testing ground. Life is a test, or a series of them.

During our time of testing here on earth, we not only have to contend with our lower nature, we are also engaged in spiritual warfare.

> The enemy in this spiritual battle is formidable. He is like a lion looking for his kill, and he is dead set on defaming God's glory and destroying God's people. Where the church exists, he works to draw us in through temptation and discourage us in trial. He lures us with possessions and prosperity, and he lulls us to sleep with comforts and complacency. He deceives, deters, and distracts the church from knowing the wonder of Christ and declaring the worth of Christ to the ends of the earth.[9]

(*) Some Bible teachers and theologians believe Christians no longer have lower natures after conversion. I respectfully disagree, yet this is not the place to debate this issue.

Q.: *What do these tests consist of?*
A.: *Difficult but inescapable choices.*
"I, the Lord, explore the mind and test the heart, giving to all according to their ways, according to the fruit of their deeds" (Jeremiah 17:10 - NABRE).

Looking back to the beginning of the human race, we see that when God created man, He immediately presented him with a test, consisting of a negative command and a warning (Genesis 2:16-17). When the man and his wife failed the test, they lost the reward which would have otherwise been accessible to them. "The Lord God said, 'Since man has become like one of Us, knowing good and evil, he must not reach out, take from the tree of life, eat, and live forever'"(Genesis 3:22 - HCSB). The tree of life is yet again offered as a reward "to him who overcomes," to whom God says, "I will grant to eat of the tree of life which is in the Paradise of God" (Revelation 2:7b - NASB)

Today we too are faced with difficult choices on a daily basis. Will we choose what is honest, fair, holy, correct, and righteous? Will we prefer Kingdom Values over being embraced by the world? Will we seek to serve or be served? Will we submit to God's rule or stubbornly stick to our own desires? (1 Kings 18:21).

Q.: *How are we tested?*
A.: *Through difficult circumstances in life.*
These either fall under the category of trials or of temptations. Trials stretch our patience, place us under pressure, bring crisis, suffering and persecution. Temptations try to seduce us with "the easy way out," with pleasure over virtue, comfort over commitment, selfishness over service (James 1:2-4; 13-15). Peter reminded his readers that believers have a great inheritance waiting for them in heaven, saying, "In all this you greatly rejoice, though now for a little while you may have had to suffer grief in all kinds of trials" (1 Peter 1:6 - NIV). While we wait for that great day when pain will be no more, we must endure this time of testing on earth.

Q.: *What are we constantly being tested for?*
A.: *Loyalty and faithfulness.*
Peter continues to speak about the trials and tests, and writes, "These have come so that the proven genuineness of your faith–of greater worth than gold, which perishes even though refined by fire–may result in praise, glory and honor when Jesus Christ is revealed" (1 Peter 1:7 - NIV). Trials and tests will determine if our faith is the real deal.

The main test in life consists of what we will do with Jesus: will we accept or reject Him? Once we do accept Him, will we allow Him to be Lord? Everyday? Every moment of every day? Do we love God more than we love ourselves? Do we love Him more than we love others? Are we truly committed to Him and to His Kingdom? Just how much are we willing to sacrifice for Him? Are we willing to pay the ultimate price? Do we remain strong and committed when faced with insurmountable temptations?**

Consider this verse: "Blessed is the man who perseveres under trial, because when he has stood the test, he will receive the crown of life that God has promised to those who love him" (James 1:12). Here is confirmation that trials are indeed part of a test we are expected to overcome and, in so doing, show we love God. As with the seven churches in Revelation, those who do overcome will be richly rewarded.

The evaluation of the Revelation churches is a reminder that one day each one of us will stand before our Lord and give an account of everything we have done (2 Corinthians 5:10). Will we pass our evaluation as overcomers? Will we hear, "Well done, good and faithful servant"? (Matthew 25:21 - ESV). Will we reap the rewards promised only to those who do overcome? The victory comes from the Lord (1 Corinthians 15:57), but the decision is ours to make.

A word of encouragement. The Apostle Paul acknowledged that life is indeed difficult and full of challenges. "But in all these things," he said, "we overwhelmingly conquer through Him who loved us" (Romans 8:37 - NASB). Now, it is important to understand that the verb "overcome" which appears in the verses above all come from the same term in Greek, *nikaó*, showing this was an important Kingdom Value to the early followers of Christ and to Christ Himself. But here Paul goes beyond *nikaó* and uses the superlative *hupernikaó* to express the condition of those who overcome through Jesus. They are hyper or super overcomers! We might say today they are "overachievers." So let's place our unwavering faith in Jesus, the One Who overcame and can lead us to super victories!

We do face toil and trouble in this life. But "our momentary light affliction is producing for us an absolutely incomparable eternal weight of glory" (2 Corinthians 4:17 - HCSB). And it is refreshing to know that what is coming next includes resting from our earthly toil (Revelation 14:13), because once we get there, the test is over.

(**) Of interest to this Kingdom Value, the dictionary defines *insurmountable* as "too great to be overcome." Humanly speaking there are many such temptations we face; overcoming only happens through deliverance from the Lord, not by our own strength or effort.

Have you been living a victorious life? Are you overcoming the obstacles and challenges that come your way? Have you firmly decided to remain faithful to the Lord for the rest of your life?

Kingdom Value #63: Freedom

When Jesus told His listeners that "you will know the truth, and the truth will set you free" (see *Kingdom Value #60*), some of them took offence. Claiming to be Abraham's descendants, they complained, "We have never been slaves to anyone. What do you mean, 'You will be set free'?" (John 8:32-33 - NLT). Let's see: the people of Israel had been slaves in Egypt for hundreds of years, the northern kingdom had been taken captive by the Assyrians and the southern kingdom by the Babylonians. There had been terrible times under Antiochus IV Epiphanes when the Temple was desecrated, Jerusalem was occupied, and the Jewish population prohibited from going about their religious activities; and now they were under Roman occupation. Perhaps they were not slaves in a more comprehensive sense under the Romans, but were certainly not free to control of their lives or politics.

Even so, Jesus was speaking of another form of slavery. He explained, "I tell you the truth, everyone who sins is a slave of sin." Then He declared, "So if the Son sets you free, you are truly free" (John 8:34, 36 - NLT). His audience still did not wish to concede, so Jesus told them they were under the influence of their real father – not Abraham but the devil, and that was why they opposed and wanted to kill Him. Jesus told them the devil was originally a murderer, a truth-hater, a natural liar and the originator of lying (John 8:44). Those who belong to God gladly listen to His Word (John 8:47 - NLT).

Jesus proved there is a close link between truth and freedom. We could say "know truth, know freedom; no truth, no freedom." Those who refuse the truth open themselves up to the father of lies, live a life of sin, and become devil-driven slaves.

Those who embrace the truth eagerly follow Jesus and find the freedom that only He can offer. Just as the Israelites were set free and redeemed from slavery in Egypt and began their journey towards the Promised Land, so we have been transported from a kingdom which enslaved and oppressed us to the Kingdom of Christ, where we enjoy freedom (Colossians 1:12b-14). Part of this freedom is already realized, and part is reserved for eternity.

But what specifically is the freedom that He offers? What does it consist of?

Arthur W. Pink (1886-1952) wrote about a "Fourfold Salvation:" Salvation from the Pleasure of Sin, Salvation from the Penalty of Sin, Salvation from the Power of Sin, and Salvation from the Presence of Sin.[10] I would like to take this idea and modify it somewhat, as others have done, and define salvation as freedom from the punishment of sin, freedom from the power of sin, and freedom from the presence of sin. These describe the past, present, and future experience of the Christian.

Freedom from the punishment of sin

The Bible speaks of God's wrath, judgment, condemnation, and punishment of sin. God "did not spare the ancient world" but "brought a flood upon the world of the ungodly," and "condemned the cities of Sodom and Gomorrah to destruction," and more: He "did not spare angels when they sinned, but cast them into hell and committed them to pits of darkness" (2 Peter 2:4-6 - NASB).

Those who live only to please themselves and are disobedient to God's Law are "by nature children under wrath" (Ephesians 2:3 - HCSB). It is helpful to remember that "we too were once foolish, disobedient, deceived, enslaved by various passions and pleasures, living in malice and envy, hateful, detesting one another." And it should make us grateful that one day, "when the kindness of God our Savior and His love for mankind appeared, He saved us—not by works of righteousness that we had done, but according to His mercy." He gave us His Holy Spirit, Who washed and renewed us, and we were "justified by His grace" and became "heirs with the hope of eternal life" (Titus 3:3-7 - HCSB).

Being a righteous and just God, He could not simply ignore our sins. The gravity of our rebellion called for punishment, and the penalty was death. Jesus was willing to come, live the perfect life, and die in our place. Those who, by faith, place their trust in Jesus as their substitute sacrifice are justified before God and declared "not guilty." Arthur W. Pink points out that, "Because Christ suffered in my stead, I go free; because He died, I live; because He was forsaken of God, I am reconciled to Him."[11] Pink explains that "justification means that the accused is found to be guiltless, the law has nothing against him, and therefore he is acquitted and exonerated, leaving the court without a stain upon his character" (ibid).

We could say it's like having "NOT GUILTY" stamped across our official record of guilt, shame and sin, signed with the redeeming blood of Jesus Himself.

Freedom from the power of sin

Being free from the punishment of sin, a one time experience which occurs when we inherit the Kingdom, does not mean we are automatically freed from the power of sin. Being set free from the power of sin "is a present and protracted process, and is as yet incomplete."[12] Because this has been an area of great frustration, it will be worth adding a longer quote from Arthur W. Pink on this point:

> Many there are who, having learned that the Lord Jesus is the Saviour of sinners, have jumped to the erroneous conclusion that if they but exercise faith in Him, surrender to His Lordship, commit their souls into His keeping, He will remove their corrupt nature and destroy their evil propensities. But after they have really trusted in Him, they discover that evil is still present with them, that their hearts are still deceitful above all things and desperately wicked, and that no matter how they strive to resist temptation, pray for overcoming grace, and use the means of God's appointing, they seem to grow worse and worse instead of better.[13]

Because God chose to leave the fallen nature in all of us, even after experiencing His salvation, the conflict (potential or real) between who controls our lives – the Holy Spirit or our lower nature (and therefore, the devil), is a daily one. Yes, every day our faithfulness is being tested. The Apostle Paul himself struggled with this conflict and was honest about this fact. He confessed: "For in my inner self I joyfully agree with God's law. But I see a different law in the parts of my body, waging war against the law of my mind and taking me prisoner to the law of sin in the parts of my body" (Romans 7:22, 23 - HCSB; see verses 13-25).

Yet, this same Paul told the Galatians that "you have been called to live in freedom, my brothers and sisters. But don't use your freedom to satisfy your sinful nature. Instead, use your freedom to serve one another in love" (Galatians 5:13 - NLT). And he told the Roman Christians that "sin must not reign over your mortal bodies so that you obey their desires." He expanded, "And do not present the parts of your bodies to sin as weapons for wickedness, but present yourselves to God as raised from the dead to life and the parts of your bodies to God as weapons for righteousness. For sin is not to have any power over you, since you are not under the law but under grace (Romans 6:12-14 - NABRE).

The secret is being "under grace." As long as we try to defeat our sinful desires with our own strength we are sure to fail. But if we cry out to God and allow Him to fight the battle in our stead, then victory will be ours. That is a very important condition, which we tend to have difficulty applying. We must understand that sin is like the giant Goliath and we are like little, puny David. And it is precisely from David that we learn a vital Kingdom Principle in our spiritual warfare. He told Goliath that "it is not by sword or spear that the LORD saves! For the battle is the LORD's, and he will deliver you into our hand" (1 Samuel 17:47 - NET Bible).

Freedom from the presence of sin

No one would dispute that we live in a world where the impact of sin can be felt on a daily basis. Suffering, calamities, oppression, injustice, racial tension, poverty, sickness, corruption, lies, loss, filth, immorality, infidelity, stealing, accidents, wars, torture, persecution, and death. These are featured regularly in the headlines and occur daily in the lives of every human being on earth.

But, "What we are suffering now is nothing compared with our future glory" (Romans 8:18 - NIRV), which is spoken of in terms of "the glorious freedom of God's children" (Romans 8:21 - HCSB; see verses 18-25). "For this light momentary affliction is preparing for us an eternal weight of glory beyond all comparison" (2 Corinthians 4:17 - ESV).

Glory. What all does our glorification involve? "Dear friends, now we are children of God, and what we will be has not yet been made known. But we know that when Christ appears, we shall be like him, for we shall see him as he is" (1 John 3:2 - NIV). God's word only gives us glimpses of our future glory, but being like Jesus will mean being sinless, connected to the Father without interruption, living in perfect peace and harmony with our Lord and His redeemed. Being free from the presence of evil will be for us what every human being desires and aspires to: painless joy, sweet fellowship, loving and being loved, accepting and being accepted, belonging, and being truly free – from conflict, attacks, and oppression. It will include receiving a glorified body, created to withstand eternity without wearing out, growing old or even getting sick.

When God takes us from this life He will also be taking us away from the presence of evil and evil people. And since our salvation will then be complete, there will be no evil in us as well. We will stand before the Father in the righteousness of Jesus, without condemnation, and will forever be the recipients of His tender loving care. We will be home free.

Are you living in the light of God's truth? Are you walking in freedom? When it comes to freedom from the power of sin, how is your process of sanctification coming along?

Kingdom Value #64: Courage

The Bible is full of stories of bravery, people of valor, the demonstration of fear-lessness and boldness. Like Noah, Abraham, Moses, Joshua, David, Daniel, John, and Paul. Gideon and Peter had their moments of fear and weakness but came around and proved to be just as courageous as the other heroes of faith (as exemplified in Hebrews 11).

There is a list of those who will suffer horrible punishment close to the end of Revelation. They are contrasted with the "victors" or "overcomers," so we could say they are the real "losers," because they do not make it into the Kingdom. The first to be listed are the "cowards" (Revelation 21:8 - NLT; "unbelievers" actually comes in second).

Living for God in a fallen world takes a lot of courage. Many would like to believe, but they are afraid of their friends' and family's reaction. They are unwilling to challenge long-standing traditions or new "values" which are trending and being promoted – such as "tolerance" – and break away from what is acceptable to society at large or to their special, smaller group. They are unwilling to face the consequences of going against the current. Yet, little do they know that the current leads to a great waterfall that none can survive. They ignore the fact that, ultimately, the consequences of **not** following God are much greater than those of following Him.

Courage does not mean facing challenges or opposition without fear. It means facing them in spite of fear.

Imagine the courage of our brothers and sisters living in predominantly Muslim, Buddhist, or Hindu countries. The whole culture and state religion are, to varying degrees, opposed to any form of Christianity or Christian expression. According to an e-mail newsletter from Voice of the Martyrs (dated April 28, 2015), Christians are learning a lot through persecution and have much to teach us. In fact, the Church is thriving even under areas controlled by ISIS.[14] "The Gospel thrives in a climate of persecution," says Tom Doyle in his interview on this same site. Author of the book, *Killing Christians*, he says, "These are Hebrews 11 type people living today."[15]

225

In these last days Christians will need to exert more and more courage, as persecution intensifies. It took courage for the first disciples to leave family and work and follow Jesus. It took courage to stay by His side during those three years and to continue following Him after His crucifixion, resurrection, and departure. It took courage to stand up to the officials and authorities who threatened them with jail and execution, and to go about proclaiming the Gospel of the Kingdom and planting churches, as seen in the book of Acts. They followed the example of their Master as He, too, had to demonstrate great courage as He was persecuted, misunderstood, slandered, rejected, separated from the Father, and executed on a cruel cross.

The disciples were not superheroes (although they are heroes of the faith for us today). They were common – even simple – people. One day Jesus crossed the Sea of Galilee with His them after a very busy day of ministry. He went to sleep while a storm began to batter the boat. The disciples came to Jesus, woke Him up and asked Him if He didn't care that they were about to drown. Jesus rebuked the wind and told the waves to be still. Immediately the wind ceased and the waves died down. "He said to his disciples, 'Why are you so afraid? Do you still have no faith?'" (Mark 4:40; the International Standard Version has "why are you such cowards?"). After this they were even more afraid, because they saw that even nature obeyed His command and it dawned on them that they were in the presence of Almighty God (and they had just rebuked Him for being asleep!). This story helps us to see that lack of courage comes from lack of faith, and lack of faith comes from a lack of understanding of Who Jesus really is.

Moses, the great leader and liberator of the Israelites, was dead. Now, the command had fallen to his successor, Joshua. The children of Israel were free from Egyptian dominion, but were still wanderers without a home. God told Joshua that he was to lead his people to "the land I am giving the Israelites" – the land promised to Abraham, part of which had already been their forefathers.

A Kingdom Principle seen in the story of Joshua is that God gives (blessings, land, promises, ministries) but we still must do some conquering. Yet, even the effort of conquering is to be guided and empowered by the Lord. "I will not leave you or forsake you," God promised Joshua. This whole process, this giving and conquering principle, requires a lot of courage on our part. God tells Joshua three times in this passage to "be strong and courageous," placing more emphasis on the charge each time He gives it (Joshua 1:6, 7 and 9). After the third time, which God makes clear is a command, He tells Joshua to "not be afraid or discouraged, for the Lord your God is with you wherever you go" (Joshua 1:9 - HCSB).

In order to fulfill the mission God has given us on earth, we must possess the Kingdom Value of courage, just as the faithful found in Scripture and the history of the church. So many suffered and died for Christ and His cause throughout the history of the Christian Church, beginning with John the Baptist (Matthew 14:10; before the Church was established), and Stephen (Acts 7:59). Polycarp, the Bishop of Smyrna, a disciple of John the Apostle, left us a tremendous example of courage in the face of persecution.

At a festival of Caesar, in Smyrna, Christians were being thrown in the arena to fight the beasts. Soon the crowd demanded Polycarp be brought in. He was finally captured and brought to the stadium. On the way, his captors tried to persuade him, saying, "Now what harm is there in saying 'Lord Caesar,' and in offering incense, and so on, and thus saving thyself?" Polycarp told them he did not intend to comply. As they entered the stadium with him, other Christians who were present heard a voice, saying, "Be strong, Polycarp, and play the man." Again, he was offered a way out of certain martyrdom. "But the Proconsul urged him and said, 'Swear, and I will release thee; curse the Christ.' And Polycarp said, 'Eighty and six years have I served him, and he hath done me no wrong; how then can I blaspheme my king who saved me?'" When threatened with being burned at the stake, he answered, "Thou threatenest the fire that burns for an hour and in a little while is quenched; for thou knowest not the fire of the judgement to come, and the fire of the eternal punishment, reserved for the ungodly." Filled with renewed courage and joy, Polycarp endured the ultimate sacrifice. "And the multitude marvelled at the great difference between the unbelievers and the elect."[16]

How courageous are you when it comes to taking a stand for Christ and the truth? How bold are you when sharing or defending the faith? How willing are you to face your fears and move ahead for the Kingdom, in spite of opposition?

KV64 – **COURAGE**

| Consistently practice | Sometimes practice | Struggle | Mostly fail | Continually fail |

Chapter

10

Overall and Generic Kingdom Values

But let justice roll on like a river,
and righteousness like an ever-flowing stream.
Amos 5:24 - BSB

Kingdom Value #65: Justice

Justice is the social and relational arm of righteousness. Justice describes how we should relate to others in politics, commerce, at work, church, home and in society. Justice seeks to treat others fairly, which includes being truthful and dealing honestly. When someone is just, he or she will always strive for win-win situations. (Mercy will take a step further and, when appropriate, allow for a loose-win situation: being willing to be on the loosing side in order to further bless the other).

For the state it means applying the law equally to all, without favoritism ("the law is blind"). In the workplace it means being fair and giving people an equal opportunity to thrive; rewarding them because of what they have accomplished, not because of their gender, color, age, social status, or who they know.

The prophets' cry for justice
There are important passages in Old Testament books such as the Psalms and Proverbs concerning the just treatment of the poor and needy (Psalm 35:10; 72:13; 113:7; Proverbs 14:31; 22:22; Proverbs 28:3; see also Deuteronomy 15:7,

11). But no one alerted the people of Judah and Israel about social injustice more than the prophets. In fact, a "prophetic ministry" implies a confrontation of sin by the Lord's "mouth piece." More than foretelling, the prophets were primarily "forth-tellers:" proclaimers of the will of God. And much of the sin being confronted was social injustice. And many being confronted were the rulers themselves. God's calling to the prophet was to, "Cry out loudly, don't hold back! Raise your voice like a trumpet. Tell My people their transgression and the house of Jacob their sins" (Isaiah 58:1 - HCSB).

The prophet Isaiah was God's instrument to tell the population of Jerusalem and Judah to purify themselves, to stop committing evil, and to "learn to do what is right! Promote justice! Give the oppressed reason to celebrate! Take up the cause of the orphan! Defend the rights of the widow!" (Isaiah 1:17 - NET Bible).

God told them that even on the days they were fasting, "you do as you please and exploit all your workers." God then told them, "Is not this the kind of fasting I have chosen: to loose the chains of injustice and untie the cords of the yoke, to set the oppressed free and break every yoke?" (Isaiah 58:6 - NIV).

God then explains that true justice means "to share your food with the hungry and to provide the poor wanderer with shelter — when you see the naked, to clothe them, and not to turn away from your own flesh and blood." God promises to reward them if they stop oppressing people and dedicate themselves to caring for the hungry and oppressed. "Then your light will rise in the darkness, and your night will become like the noonday." God also promises to bring healing, lead them in righteousness, answer their prayers, satisfy their needs, strengthen them, allow them to rebuild their ruins, and allow them to find joy in the Lord (Isaiah 58:7-14 - NIV).

In a different context, God declares, "For I Yahweh love justice; I hate robbery and injustice" (Isaiah 61:8 - HCSB). If the King loves justice, so should we!

Another prophet, Jeremiah, was sent by God to confront the king of Judah (probably Jehoiakim) because of his practice of gross injustice. God told him exactly what to say: "Hear the word of the Lord, king of Judah, you who sit on the throne of David—you, your officers, and your people who enter these gates. This is what the Lord says: Administer justice and righteousness. Rescue the victim of robbery from the hand of his oppressor. Don't exploit or brutalize the foreigner, the fatherless, or the widow. Don't shed innocent blood in this place" (Jeremiah 22:1-3 - HCSB).

230

Again, Jeremiah lashes out against King Jehoiakim, declaring, "Woe to him who builds his house without righteousness and his upper rooms without justice, who uses his neighbor's services without pay and does not give him his wages" (Jeremiah 22:13 - NASB).

The Lord told Ezekiel why He was bringing such severe judgment upon the nation. "'The house of Israel and Judah is guilty—and theirs is a stubborn guilt, at that!' he replied to me. 'The land is filled with blood, and the city overflows with injustice, because they keep saying, 'The LORD has abandoned the land,' and 'The LORD isn't watching'" (Ezekiel 9:9 - ISV).

And there was the prophet Amos. The Lord told Israel that what He wanted was not a bunch of noisy worship. "But let justice roll down like waters, and righteousness like an ever-flowing stream" (Amos 5:24 - ESV). "Amos is particularly vehement in denouncing the lack of social concern in his time."[1]

In fact, "The improved economic situation in Israel led to an increase of the wealthy, who not only neglected the poor but used them to increase their own wealth. The social concern inherent in the very structure of the law was forgotten. God's will, as it applied to the nation of Israel, was ignored; and this spurred the eighth-century prophets to action."[2]

We have glanced at a few examples of God's demand for justice through some of His prophets, applicable to rulers and commoners alike. Now we will look at some examples from the New Testament.

Justice in the New Testament

Jesus, the Righteous One, valued justice and consistently demonstrated this in His teachings and ministry. Jesus always showed compassion towards the poor, needy, suffering, and sick among the population (see *Compassion – Kingdom Value #46*).

There was concern in the early Church for the poor within their ranks. "In those days, as the number of the disciples was multiplying, there arose a complaint by the Hellenistic Jews against the Hebraic Jews that their widows were being overlooked in the daily distribution" (Acts 6:1 - HCSB). The apostles decided that while they could not afford to divert their attention and energy from the task of proclaiming the Gospel, they understood the need and had the group elect seven men of good character and full of the Holy Spirit, to serve the widows and needy in their midst (see Acts 6:1-7).

I worked at World Vision at a time the question was being asked by churches whether it was their mission to devote themselves to the proclamation of the Gospel or to *serving* the poor. These were seen by some as mutually exclusive or at least as competing against each other. Much of what came out of the early Lausanne documents helped to clarify the issue and the conclusion was that it is the Church's responsibility to do both.

Paul promoted a fundraising effort to help the church in Jerusalem in its hour of need. "For you see, the believers in Macedonia and Achaia have eagerly taken up an offering for the poor among the believers in Jerusalem" (Romans 15:26 - NLT). Both the emphasis of the early Church and Paul's fundraiser are consistent with the Kingdom Principle Paul shared with the Galatians: "So then, as we have opportunity, let us do good to everyone, and especially to those who are of the household of faith" (Galatians 6:10 - ESV).

But the principle does begin by stating we should "do good to everyone." And this applies to relationships in general – even to masters and their treatment of slaves. "Masters, treat your slaves justly and fairly, because you know that you also have a Master in heaven" (Colossians 4:1 - ISV). We can apply this same principle to leaders and their followers or supervisors and their employees today.

James claims that "pure and undefiled religion before God and the Father is this: to visit orphans and widows in their trouble" (James 1:27a - NKJV). He makes a strong case against personal favoritism and showing partiality towards the wealthy in church to the detriment of the poor (James 2:1-13). He also calls out those who have a "virtual" or theoretical faith which lacks hands and legs to serve others, especially the needy. He asks, "If a brother or sister is naked and destitute of daily food, and one of you says to them, 'Depart in peace, be warmed and filled,' but you do not give them the things which are needed for the body, what does it profit? (James 2:14-26 - NKJV).

James warns the rich to not take pride in their wealth, because it is temporary and will testify against them. James warns that, "Indeed the wages of the laborers who mowed your fields, which you kept back by fraud, cry out; and the cries of the reapers have reached the ears of the Lord of Sabaoth." The rich he struck out against were accumulating wealth, living in pleasure and luxury, and had condemned and murdered the just (James 5:1-6 - NKJV).

The term "justice" does not appear in the passages above, but the practical application of social justice is clearly there.

Though our world has seen the advance of democracy and freedom, there is still a great need for justice in all levels of society. Human trafficking has become an epidemic in our world today. Women are still treated unfairly in the workplace and usually earn less than their male counterparts. Children are being sexually abused and whole countries exploit other, less fortunate nations for economic gain. Politics has become so partisan that there are now two standards for truth and justice: one for "us" and another for "them." It's like this: "whatever *we* do is right and whatever *they* do is wrong" (even if it's essentially the same thing). And, many churches and Christian organizations overwork and underpay their employees while creating an atmosphere of mistrust, competition, and office politics.

What the world needs now is... justice!

Do you treat your family members, colleagues or employees at work, and fellow church members fairly? Are you concerned enough for the less fortunate, the poor or needy to do something about it?

Kingdom Value #66: Authority and Power

"For the kingdom of God is not a matter of talk but of power" (1 Corinthians 4:20 - HCSB). Any reader of the Gospels and of Acts of the Apostles will readily realize authority and power are essentials in the Kingdom of God. We are commanded to "be strong in the Lord and in his mighty power" (Ephesians 6:10 - NLT).

While both authority and power are Kingdom Values, they will here be presented together because they are as inseparable as the two sides of the same coin. Notice that Jesus "called the twelve together and gave them power and authority over all demons and to cure diseases and he sent them out to proclaim the kingdom of God and to heal" (Luke 9:1-2 - ESV; see also Luke 4:36, Ephesians 1:21, Colossians 2:10). There is no authority except that which has been *given* by God (Romans 13:1). Jesus said "all authority in heaven and on earth has been *given* to me." (Matthew 28:18 - ESV). Jesus, the Son of Man, "was *given* authority, honor, and sovereignty over all the nations of the world, so that people of every race and nation and language would obey him" (Daniel 7:14a - NLT).

Only those under authority have authority. "For I myself am a man under author-

233

ity, with soldiers under me" (Matthew 8:9 - NIV). The Roman centurion in this passage understood that he only had authority because there was an army behind him and an emperor above that army. He applied that principle to the spiritual realm, understanding that Jesus too had the power of angels and of God the Father Himself behind Him. Jesus knew the centurion had understood this concept and exclaimed that He had not seen that much faith anywhere in Israel.

Transferred Authority occurs when God's authority, given to a spiritual leader, is no longer needed. The original bearer of authority relinquishes this authority, which is then transferred to a successor. When Moses was close to death, he asked God to anoint a new leader over Israel. God told Moses to "take Joshua son of Nun, a man who has the Spirit in him" and "confer some of your authority on him so that the entire Israelite community will obey [him]" (Numbers 27:15-20).

God informed Shebna that because he had been a disgrace, his death was imminent and that "I will remove you from your office; you will be ousted from your position." God declared that "on that day I will call for my servant, Eliakim son of Hilkiah. I will clothe him with your robe and tie your sash around him. I will put your authority into his hand" and "place the key of the House of David on his shoulder; what he opens, no one can close; what he closes, no one can open" (Isaiah 22:15-25).

Delegated Authority takes place when the person passing on authority retains his or her own authority over others. Moses told the Israelites on their way to the Promised Land to select their own leaders, who were "wise, understanding, and experienced," and he would place them over the people (Deuteronomy 1:15-18).

Concerning the government, Paul implies that it operates on delegated authority when he stated, "Everyone must submit to the governing authorities, for there is no authority except from God, and those that exist are instituted by God" (Romans 13:1 - HCSB). Pilate, who had received authority from the Roman empire, told Jesus he had the power (authority) to release or execute Him. But "Jesus answered, You would not have any power or authority whatsoever against (over) Me if it were not given you from above" (John 19:10-11a - AMP).

When it comes to a confrontation with evil spirits, things change. The Christians' authority is different when related to Satan or demons than when it relates to human beings. "When Jesus had called the Twelve together, he gave them power and authority to drive out all demons and to cure diseases" (Luke 9:1a - NIV). Notice that their authority towards demons was negative – to drive them out, and towards humans positive – to heal. Paul speaks of "our authority, which the Lord gave for building you up and not for destroying you" (2 Corinthians 10:8 - NASB),

234

and that Christian leaders can and should "encourage and rebuke with all authority" (Titus 2:15 - HCSB).

Partnership Authority is shared authority. In a very special way, God the Son shares the Kingdom authority with His Father. And in a similar, yet lesser way, the Son shares His kingdom authority with His own (John, chapters 5 and 14 through 17; see "The Mirroring Principle," in *The King of the Kingdom of God*, volume 4 in this series).

The relationship between the Father and the Son serves as a model for our relationship with the Lord Jesus. Jesus taught that the Father is in the Son and the Son is in the Father, and that He is in the believer and that the believer is in Him. Jesus shares His Kingdom inheritance with those who believe and follow Him.

Seven types of power
Power is the ability to get things done in the way one wishes them to be done. We are often frustrated and disappointed because of our inability to control people, circumstances, and outcomes. As we confront our limitations, we can either despair or we can have faith, trusting God's character and guidance. This means being willing to use the authority and power God *has* given us. Christians have no magical powers but they know the Almighty. In fact, He is their Father. Christians go to the Father, in the name of the Son, to dispense His power in the world. This connectivity is called *prayer*. Through prayer and by the Holy Spirit, people are given power in the areas below.

1) God-given political, financial, and administrative power
"Wealth and honor come from you alone, for you rule over everything. Power and might are in your hand, and at your discretion people are made great and given strength" (1 Chronicles 29:12 - NLT). Such a recipient of God's power was King Nebuchadnezzar, to whom Daniel referred as, "You, your majesty, king of kings— to whom the God of heaven has given the kingdom, the power, the strength, and the glory" (Daniel 2:37 - ISV).

2) Power to perform wonders and miracles
The power to perform signs and wonders was especially evident in the early Church. Even the deacons were endowed with power from on high. "And Stephen, full of grace and power, was doing great wonders and signs among the people" (Acts 6:8 - ESV). Paul was no exception. He told the Church in Rome that his ministry among Gentiles was done "in the power of signs and wonders, in the power of the Spirit" (Romans 15:19a - NASB). Signs and wonders were invariably done in the context of the proclamation of the good news of the Kingdom.

3) Power to cast out demons and heal sickness

"Amazed, the people exclaimed, 'What authority and power this man's words possess! Even evil spirits obey him, and they flee at his command!'" (Luke 4:35-36 - NLT). The Lord Jesus delegated this power to His disciples: power to heal, cleanse, and set free. He gave them these marching orders: "As you go, proclaim this message: 'The kingdom of heaven has come near.' Heal the sick, raise the dead, cleanse those who have leprosy, drive out demons. Freely you have received; freely give'" (Matthew 10:7-8 - NIV; see Luke 9:1 and Acts 10:38). Just as with wonders and miracles, the context is proclamation.

Disciples today have this same authority and power, demonstrated especially in areas where missionaries share the Gospel with unreached peoples. I have heard of some of these experiences and they are truly amazing. And where there is no Christian witness there are frequent reports of those who come to the Lord through dreams in which He appears and calls them to Himself.

4) Power to witness

"And with great power the apostles were giving their testimony to the resurrection of the Lord Jesus, and great grace was upon them all" (Acts 4:33 - ESV). Boldness is the courage to speak out, witness, stand firm and hold fast to your faith, even in the face of persecution and death. Such as with 80-year old Victoria, part of a small group of elderly survivors in a town which had been raided by ISIS. They were told they must convert, and that Islam could offer them paradise.

> Victoria and Gazella responded: "We believe that if we show love and kindness, forgiveness and mercy we can bring about the kingdom of God on earth as well as in heaven. Paradise is about love. If you want to kill us for our faith then we are prepared to die here and now." [ISIS] forces had no answer. The dozen Christians, who included many elderly and infirm, were let go ... and they made it to safety."[3]

Peter and John (Acts 4:13 - ESV), as well as Paul, were involved in "proclaiming the kingdom of God and teaching about the Lord Jesus Christ with all boldness and without hindrance" (Acts 28:31 - ESV). But they were not alone. During a prayer meeting the believers "were all filled with the Holy Spirit and began to speak the word of God with boldness" (Acts 4:31 - NASB).

5) Inner power over sin (sanctification)

"I pray that He may grant you, according to the riches of His glory, to be strengthened with power in the inner man through His Spirit" (Ephesians 3:16 - HCSB). We need God's power in order to succeed in our Kingdom mission as well as for the sanctification of our inner self. Bad characters don't produce good ministries.

"A good tree cannot produce bad fruit, nor can a bad tree produce good fruit" (Matthew 7:18 - NASB). That is another Kingdom Principle.

Only the Father, through His Spirit, "is able to do above and beyond all that we ask or think according to the power that works in us" (Ephesians 3:20 - HCSB). "His divine power has given us everything required for life and godliness through the knowledge of Him who called us by His own glory and goodness" (2 Peter 1:3 - HCSB).

6) Power over the enemy

The Apostle John told his readers that it was "for this purpose the Son of God was revealed: to destroy the works of the devil" (1 John 3:8 - NET Bible). The Church is to continue Jesus' ministry on earth, which is why He told His disciples, "Look! I have given you the authority to trample on snakes and scorpions and to destroy all the enemy's power, and nothing will ever hurt you" (Luke 10:19 - ISV). Don't get caught up in the snake and scorpion trampling (both allusions to demonic powers). Focus instead on this: Jesus gave His followers "the authority... to destroy all the enemy's power."

7) Power to teach and disciple in order to lead to maturity in Christ

"We proclaim Him, admonishing every man and teaching every man with all wisdom, so that we may present every man complete in Christ. For this purpose also I labor, striving according to His power, which mightily works within me" (Colossians 1:28, 29 - NASB). Paul could sense God's power (*dunamis*) leading him on as he accomplished his mission, which involved proclaiming, discipling, and church planting. His end goal was to present them as mature disciples to the Lord.

My spiritual gift is teaching. Many times I will approach my class with my head swirling with noisy thoughts. Sometimes I feel emotionally drained or hesitant. But when I begin to teach, I feel the Lord takes over and I become focused, encouraged, and "inspired." I know it is the Lord Who is making this happen, and using me as He wishes, because in my own power I could never teach that way. Perhaps more than in any other situation, when I teach God's Word I sense God's power working in and through me.

Do you need more spiritual power and authority? Have you been exercising that which you already have in Christ and through the indwelling Holy Spirit?

KV66 – AUTHORITY AND POWER

Consistently practice | Sometimes practice | Struggle | Mostly fail | Continually fail

Kingdom Value #67: Life

This Kingdom Value is about the sanctity of life. Life and consciousness are precious, and distinguish beings from things. God created human life in His image and likeness, gave the directive, "Be fruitful and multiply and fill the earth and subdue it" (Genesis 1:27-28a - ESV), and commanded: "You are not to commit murder" (Exodus 20:13 - NIV). Life is not a random result of evolution but a priceless miracle of incalculable worth. Human life has intrinsic value because it was given by God and reflects His likeness. And, because every human being receives from Him a set of general purposes and specific missions (Psalm 139:13-16). All of this leads us to the conclusion that God is the only One Who has the right to terminate human life (with a few possible exceptions, a couple of which could be justifiable war and self-defense).

Adopted by Congress on July 4, 1776, the Declaration of Independence of the United States of America declares: "We hold these truths to be self-evident, that all men are created equal, that they are endowed by their Creator with certain unalienable rights, that among these are life, liberty and the pursuit of happiness."[4] Notice that the Founding Fathers gave the "Creator" the credit that is due Him: it is He Who endows humans with these rights. These rights are said to be unalienable, meaning inseparable and non-transferable.

Taking the lives of the unborn
Governments, the declaration goes on to explain, are in place "to secure these rights," and yet some become "destructive to these ends."[5] Although not necessarily the intended original purpose, we can take this principle and apply it to any form of degradation of, threat to, violence against, or attack on life and liberty. And yet many governments today have abandoned their protection of life and have not only allowed but promoted the killing of unborn babies. Recent government authorities demonstrate an "undying passion for, support of, and belief in abortion."[6]

When a person's "choice" is valued more than God-given human life – by government and society – then it is a clear sign that God and His standards are being substituted by the cultural views of the day. There is no way to ignore or outlaw God's values and principles and get away with it: everyone who does so will be held accountable by Creator God Himself.

Abortion goes to the core of God's first stated mission for humanity: to multiply and fill the earth. It cuts short the process of reproduction and extinguishes a

238

human life. A beating heart is silenced forever. Abortion is so appalling because it is aimed at those who are the most vulnerable, the weakest, who have no way of defending themselves, at the request of the parent or parents, who should be the baby's first line of defense.

There are extenuating circumstances that can lead someone to have an abortion, such as conception due to being raped or when having to chose between keeping the mother alive or delivering the baby alive. These are complex issues and cannot be addressed here. But an overwhelming majority of abortions are performed as birth control or for one or both of the parents' "convenience." These fall squarely under the principle being discussed here. This said, it is important to be reminded that there is forgiveness even in such cases, if there is true repentance. God is a God of second chances.

Taking lives through violence

God cannot stand violence and murder: "The LORD abhors the man of bloodshed and deceit" (Psalm 5:6b - NASB).

Speaking of a figurative Esau or Edom, God announces, "You will be covered with shame and destroyed forever because of violence done to your brother Jacob" (Obadiah 1:10 - HCSB). Jacob stands for Israel, but for whom does Esau stand? Who are his descendants? More importantly, what have they done or what are they doing that has caused God to declare their final destruction? During a study on Obadiah, Brian Stephens explained:

> God is angry with Esau. God is angry with his violence. That word in Hebrew is *hamas*. What does *hamas* mean? It is a specific type of violence. Let's say I am a thief. I like to steal things. And you have something of value that interests me. So I try to take it but you resist, so I hit you, I stab you or I shoot you, so I can get that and run away. What was my objective? To steal. That's violence and that is wrong; so is stealing.

> But that violence does not fit the definition of *hamas*, because it had a purpose behind it. *Hamas* means violence for the sake of violence. Violence for the sake of seeing someone suffering, feeling pain and hurt.

> That is the same type of spirit that Satan has. He loves to devour, to cause hardship and pain, and to make people suffer. That is his nature. And God says that is the spirit of Esau. That word *hamas* is a Semitic word. This terrorist organization that took on this name enjoys seeing Jewish people in pain. They don't want a peace agreement because they want to see Israel no more. They want to see every Israeli driven into the sea and they want to see, as they have said, the Mediterranean turned to blood – Jewish blood.

As if the terrorist group Hamas were not bad enough, along came ISIS, the likes of which none had seen in modern times. Their disregard for human life is simply astonishing. All who do not agree and conform to their brand of Islam are tortured and executed in the most cruel ways imaginable. Mexican drug cartels have begun to practice some of the same forms of atrocities in order to eliminate their competition and any opposition.

Halloween costumes and Hollywood movies promote zombies, skeletons, demons, and spirit-monsters. Popular lyrics glorify death while fashion includes cartoon skulls and scary skeletons. We live in a culture of death, as exemplified by Dr. Jack Kevorkian ("Doctor Death"), who popularized the concept of physician-assisted suicide, and "Santa Muerte" (Holy Death) in Mexico, a cult which venerates death.

Suicide has reached near epidemic levels. According to the World Health Organization, "Close to 800,000 people die due to suicide every year, which is one person every 40 seconds."[7]

If we do not stand up for life, we run the risk of repeating some of the darker pages of history. Hitler's Nazi Germany engaged in "many radical eugenic measures" which included the euthanasia of what they esteemed to be "life unworthy of life," that is, "individuals who—they believed—because of severe psychiatric, neurological, or physical disabilities represented both a genetic and a financial burden on German society and the state."[8] "The term 'euthanasia' means literally 'good death.'"[9]

Satan is a fallen celestial being who is "filled with violence" (Ezekiel 28:16 - HCSB). He is a thief who wishes to destroy and kill. But Jesus came to offer abundant life (John 10:10). God is pro-life.

We've heard it said: *we're free to choose but we are not free to choose the consequences of our choices.* That was, in essence, what God told the people of Israel before they entered the Promised Land. The Lord told them, "See, today I have set before you life and prosperity, death and adversity" (Deuteronomy 30:15 - HCSB). He explained that if they loved Him and followed His lead they would live, multiply as a people, and be blessed. If, however, they allowed their hearts to turn away and go after false gods, they would not live long and would perish.

God repeats His offer in the strongest of terms. "I call heaven and earth as witnesses against you today that I have set before you life and death, blessing and curse. Choose life so that you and your descendants may live." And, again He stresses the need to "love the Lord your God, obey Him, and remain faithful to Him" because, quite simply, "He is your life" (Deuteronomy 30:19-20 - HCSB). "Starting from scratch, he made the entire human race and made the earth hospitable, with plenty of time and space for living so we could seek after God, and not just grope around in the dark but actually find him. He doesn't play hide-and-seek with us. He's not remote; he's near. We live and move in him, can't get away from him!" (Acts 17:24-29 - MSG).

The Lord is the author of life (Acts 3:15) and the One Who "keeps me alive!" (Psalm 54:4 - NLT). When Jesus came to earth, "In him was life; and the life was the light of men" (John 1:4 - KJV). The One Who joined His Father in creating the universe is, Himself, life (John 14:6).

Have you valued and protected the universal right to life? Are you grateful for the gift of life God has given you? Are you ready to stand for the protection of human life – from the unborn to the elderly?

Kingdom Value #68: Family

God's Kingdom on earth is made up of people, and people don't just appear out of thin air. What a great privilege and tremendous responsibility God gave us when He endowed the human race with the ability to multiply (Genesis 1:28). God meant for this process to take place in the context of marriage and the family (Genesis 2:24).

Under "Our Passion," ***Focus on the Family*** states:

> We believe that marriage is the foundation of family life, and that God's design for marriage is a relationship where both husband and wife are committed to loving and caring for one another for a lifetime.
> We believe children are a gift from God, and thrive best in a home where both mother and father are committed to raising them with love, intention, and care.
> We believe sex is given by God as an expression of love to be shared and enjoyed exclusively between a husband and wife.[10]

241

There is a reason the enemy ruthlessly attacks the family and traditional marriage: God's purpose for humanity could not be accomplished without the family. Destroy the family and you will have all but done away with any hope for God's Global Kingdom on earth.

When God commanded the first man to "rule... all the earth" (Genesis 1:26), He did not mean humans had the right to change the structure of the family, His moral laws, or His Kingdom Values. Humans received delegated authority, to be exercised in a consistent manner with God's final authority. Humans ignore God's orders at their own peril, as the first couple discovered very soon (Genesis 3).

Consistent with ***Focus on the Family***'s statement above, new families should start with marriage, where sex and reproduction follow, and where the father and mother figures nurture, protect, and educate the children in love, leading by example, and encouraging them to seek and serve the Lord. There should be no need to state the obvious, but society has grown so far from this Biblical model it is important to emphasize this truth.

I must say that Hollywood movies have me confused with their standard story line: *Man likes woman, man and woman live together for months with no commitment, man finally decides to propose marriage to woman, woman becomes teary-eyed, then excitedly tells all her friends.* The reaction seems so far-fetched: what blissful joy, what mysterious discovery of each other, what appeal could there be in "getting married" after you have already been living together? Is this what the woman has to settle for? It's anti-climatic and meaningless. It *is* better than staying unmarried together, but it is certainly not to be compared with the rush which comes from waiting, committing, then celebrating.

Problems in the family are nothing new. In fact, in the very first family there was parental failure, filial rebellion, and fatal brotherly rivalry (Genesis 3, 4). From the first to the last book of the Old Testament, there are stories of infidelity and strife in family after family. In the last book of the Old Testament, the prophet declares that "the LORD has been a witness between you and the wife of your youth, against whom you have dealt treacherously, though she is your companion and your wife by covenant" (Malachi 2:14 - NASB). God's plan is that husbands should be faithful because God is seeking "godly offspring" (Malachi 2:15). The Biblical ideal is to grow old together. "Let your fountain be blessed, and take pleasure in the wife of your youth" (Proverbs 5:18 - HCSB).

How the family reflects God

"For this reason I kneel before the Father, from whom every family in heaven and on earth derives its name" (Ephesians 3:14-15 - NIV). There is another reason the

242

family is so fundamental. It has to do with God's revelation of Himself to humanity. When God reveals Himself as Father, Jesus as Son, His people as brothers and sisters, and the Church as the bride of Christ, we can understand these concepts because we have experienced what it means to belong to a family. That is why it is so important that families truly fulfill their mission, because broken homes where a father or a mother is missing (due to abandonment), or families where there are more conflicts and fights than love and cooperation, do not adequately reflect God's character and purpose.

That is not to say that establishing and maintaining a cohesive and harmonious family is easily achieved. In fact, perhaps more than ever, this is one of the biggest challenges many of us face. When my wife and I celebrated our 41st wedding anniversary, someone asked me about the secret to staying married so long. I thought about that question and two things came to mind: forgiveness (requested and granted) and commitment. We have had to learn (and are still learning) how to ask for and offer forgiveness. And we have not given up on each other in the face of conflicts because we see marriage as a covenant made with each other and with God. Ultimately we seek to please God, and that is what keeps us going even when things are a little rocky.

The family is so important to God that it was the first human institution He established in the Global Kingdom. Families are where we find our identity. Where we are first taught values, how to relate, how to respect authority, how to be responsible, and more importantly, how to love. Parents have the mission of providing their children with the **roots** they need, then giving **wings** to fly away and live on their own.

In his insightful book, **Why You Do What You Do,** Bobb Biehl makes quite a strong case for the fact that adults are more the product of their childhoods than their teen years. He developed a chart that correlates childhood experiences, perceptions and feelings with the current emotional strengths and weaknesses in adults. This is just one more example of how critical it is to raise our children and grandchildren in a home where there is love, acceptance and respect. And where God's Kingdom Values are taught and practiced.

I work with *The Mailbox Club,* a ministry that reaches close to three million children in close to 80 countries each year. We are constantly reminded, by Josh MacDowell, George Barna and other Christian leaders, that if someone does not come to the Lord before the age of 14, most likely they never will. And the age is dropping. That's why Christian families, raising Christian kids, are so vital to God's Kingdom.

Families should safeguard traditional values and be safe a haven for all members, especially the little ones. Yet there is so much emotional, verbal, physical and sexual abuse going on between spouses and their children. Many children do not receive the attention, time, and tender loving care they need. And, children learn through social media, movies, from each other and those in school not to respect or obey their parents. Teens are engaging in premarital sex at alarming rates. Husbands and wives have allowed themselves to become increasingly unfaithful to each other.

Although the family is being attacked, there is hope for the ones that turn to the Lord and asks for guidance, protection, and blessings. The Lord is in the business of restoration and recovery. He can turn things around and bring reconciliation, mend broken hearts, and use bad experiences for our ultimate good.

Joseph is the classic example of this principle. Brotherly rivalry landed him in a pit, being sold to random strangers, working as a slave in a foreign country where he was sexually harassed and falsely accused, then thrown in prison. After he had been made second in command over the Egyptian empire, he both confronted and comforted his brothers – firmly but lovingly – by telling them, "As for you, you meant evil against me, but God meant it for good, to bring it about that many people should be kept alive, as they are today" (Genesis 50:20 - ESV).

How is your family life? Do you promote an environment of harmony and understanding? Are you doing your part to serve and bless each family member? Does your family inspire others and reflect God's glory?

Kingdom Value #69: Morality

We have evolved as a race in many areas: technology, knowledge, and scientific discoveries, reaching a level of sophistication which vastly surpasses that of our ancestors. But when it comes to our human nature and basic morality, we are just as crude, rude, and sinful as the first humans who walked this planet.

Our human nature has not evolved. Neither have God's laws and Kingdom Values. Jesus promised, "For truly I say to you, until heaven and earth pass away, not the smallest letter or stroke shall pass from the Law until all is accomplished" (Matthew 5:18 - NASB).

While the Bible does not use the word "moral," it does use "virtue" – a close equivalent. Peter said: "Make every effort to supplement your faith with virtue" (2 Peter 1:5 - ESV). Virtue is translated as "moral character" (ISV), "moral excellence" (NASB), or simply "goodness" (NIV), in different versions of the English Bible.

Instead of "morality," the Bible sometimes uses the term *example* "in illustrating different aspects of Christian conduct."[11] Paul said, "Join together in following my *example*, brothers and sisters, and just as you have us as a model, keep your eyes on those who live as we do" (Philippians 3:17 - NIV). "The proper life style and value systems are thus demonstrated individually and collectively in the lives of Christ (Jn 13:15; I Peter 2:21), the prophets (Jas 5:10), Paul (Phil 3:17; II Thess 3:9), and the churches and their leaders (I Thess 1:7; I Tim 4:12; Tit 2:7; I Peter 5:3)."[12] Essentially, these are examples of morality as it relates to holy and righteous living.

Morality is not only a character trait or an individual virtue. It is a societal mindset, a value system which should permeate the whole culture. It is so fundamental because, as the dictionary defines it, morality has to do with "principles concerning the distinction between right and wrong or good and bad behavior."[13] Since it affects all areas of life, morality is a value that must be addressed and taken seriously.

The Bible uses the Greek term ***porneia*** when addressing sexual immorality, especially when referring to fornication, such as in Galatians 5:19, where it is first on the list of the works of the flesh. Yet, though usually used to refer to sexual conduct, "morality" is much broader than that. Corporate greed, unfair treatment of minorities or aliens, the persecution and execution of others for the beliefs they hold, lying, stealing, cheating, scamming, and slandering are examples of immoral behavior.

Morality influences – and should be the basis for – standards of decency, decorum and modesty. Modesty is dictated, to a degree, by one's culture (the native tribes in the Amazon region would not have the same standards of modesty or same dress code as the inhabitants of New York city). Instead of trying to legislate through legalistic means, principles should be established and guidelines provided by the community of faith.

For instance, years ago there was a pastor of a country church in Brazil who

245

used to stand at the entrance and measure the length of women's dresses as they entered the building. Would it not have been better for the older women to teach the young ladies that they should not dress so as to flaunt their bodies and deliberately provoke the guys? As a leader taking a group of young people on a volunteer mission trip told the girls, who were attracting just a little too much attention among the nationals, "don't advertise what's not for sell." And young and older men should be taught how to control their thought life. Although women are responsible for the way they dress, "lust is in the eye of the beholder." Men are, therefore, ultimately responsible for the way they react and respond.

When standards of morality get inverted

"He's a decent guy." The reference was to a conservative Christian politician who believes in marriage as being between a man and a woman. It came from a liberal politician, who received an immediate backlash from his base. "Nobody who opposes the LBGTQ+ could be 'decent,'" was the argument. The liberal politician just as quickly issued a retraction.

"Moral" and "decent" used to refer to what was correct, pure, fair and definitely not promiscuous. And those standards were mostly defined by people's understanding of the Holy Scriptures. Now, "immoral" and "indecent" have nothing to do with God's standards, but a new set of values aggressively promoted by those who have no interest in Christian principles.

Movie heroes today have a great sense of duty, are honest, distinguish themselves for not allowing themselves to be corrupted, but see no problem in sleeping around. In fact, bed hopping is portrayed as the acceptable norm. So acceptable that it has become a non-issue. Most would identify them as decent, moral people. The concept of "sin" has been lost on this culture.

Promoting worldly standards in place of Kingdom Values is nothing new. The prophet Isaiah declared: "Woe to those who call evil good and good evil, who substitute darkness for light and light for darkness, who substitute bitter for sweet and sweet for bitter" (Isaiah 5:20 - CSB). Sounds very relevant to our situation today!

We are moral beings, created in the image of a moral Supreme Being. He will hold us responsible for the way we have conducted our lives in the 21st century just as He did those who lived in the first. "For this you know with certainty, that no immoral or impure person … has an inheritance in the kingdom of Christ and God. Let no one deceive you with empty words, for because of these things the wrath of God comes upon the sons of disobedience" (Ephesians 5:5-6 - NASB; see Romans

2:8). See Purity (*Kingdom Value #6*), Holiness (#53), Integrity (#55), and Justice (#65) for values related to Morality.

You may have great moral standards, but how does your thought life and personal conduct measure up?

Kingdom Value #70: Exposing evil

I don't like confronting people. For me, that's a very difficult thing to do. But sometimes we just can't sit back and let the darkness try to snuff out the light! There comes a time when we must take a stand.

While we are called to expose evil, we are not called to be "Kingdom police," or tasked with sniffing out and catching evildoers in order to teach them a lesson. "Vengeance is mine, I will repay, says the Lord" (Romans 12:19b - ESV). We are not on a witch hunt. We are not bounty hunters. We are not to be legalistic like the Pharisees, in or out of the church setting. We are not even supposed to judge people, which poses the question: how does one expose evil without judging people? The answer can be tricky, but let's look into this issue.

Newark Mayor Cory Booker was outraged that witnesses who saw a young man stripped and whipped over a $20 debt kept this information to themselves instead of calling 911 or the police. The authorities only became aware of the violence after a cell phone video of the scene went viral on the Internet. "Laughter from those watching the beating is heard throughout the video," the report states. "In the face of evil, those who remain quiet are participants in that evil," the mayor said.[14]

First, we are to expose evil for what it is. That means we *call* it what it is. Euphemisms like "pro-choice," "alternate lifestyle" or the inversion of values relabeled as "tolerance," or repackaged in acceptable – even positive – terms, have been so overused by politicians and society at large we tend to grow used to them. We should not. We don't name-call, but we do call sin what it is. Paul told the believers in Ephesus to "have nothing to do with the unfruitful actions that darkness produces. Instead, expose them for what they are" (Ephesians 5:11 - ISV).

Second, we need to expose the person, people or institutions behind the evil. Although this calls for extreme caution, think of the "Me Too" movement. This movement has dealt a long overdue blow to those who thought they could engage in sexual abuse and get away with it because of their privileged position. This movement has the purpose of exposing evildoers, and that is a good thing. Many, from filmmakers to pastors, were forced to face their shameful behavior and abandon their leadership positions.

Things are less complicated when a crime has been committed and the perpetrators have been caught "on tape," as in the story above. But there are non-criminal situations where things are fuzzy or difficult to prove. One should be very careful not to commit the sin of slander when exposing people who may or may not be harming the church or society. Some are innocent and their reputation must be maintained. Others are guilty but are willing to admit, confess, repent, be held accountable and restored. Some are not. Each case should be handled with care and prayer but the victims, not the predators, are the ones who should be protected.

One of the main complaints against Christians and churches today is that we are judgmental. They claim Jesus did not judge anyone and that we should not either. But when Jesus said, "Do not judge, so that you won't be judged" (Matthew 7:1 - HCSB), He was referring to condemning people's inner motivation and measuring their worth by their outward behavior. Jesus was not saying that if you see someone practicing something that is condemned in Scripture and the person confirms this action, is proud of this behavior, and promotes this activity as though it were acceptable or even noble, we are to remain quiet or even applaud them, lest we judge or offend them. No, remember Jesus also declared, in the same chapter, that "just as you can identify a tree by its fruit, so you can identify people by their actions" (Matthew 7:20 - NLT). While we are not called to judge, we are allowed to be "fruit inspectors."

And, when it comes to "your brother" (a friend, a family member, or a brother or sister in Christ), Jesus taught there are important steps to be followed: first "go and rebuke him in private." If that doesn't work, "take one or two more with you." Then, "if he pays no attention to them, tell the church. But if he doesn't pay attention even to the church, let him be like an unbeliever and a tax collector to you" (Matthew 18:15-17 - HCSB).

There are times and situations when the Lord takes it upon Himself to expose those who practice and harm others with their evil. "I expose the false prophets as liars and make fools of fortune-tellers. I cause the wise to give bad advice, thus proving them to be fools" (Isaiah 44:25 - NLT). A large portion of the Old Testament prophet's role was to strike out against injustice, rebellion, and sin. The prophet's mission involved confronting the nation, in the name of the Lord (see Ezekiel 16:2; 20:4; 23:36, etc.).

The Church is called to be "the salt of the earth" (Matthew 5:13). Without its presence, society would be insipid and in a state of decay. The Church is also called to be "the light of the world" (Matthew 5:14). It only takes a little flicker of light in a dark room to make a big difference. The presence of a Christian person in a workplace otherwise devoid of Christian influence can be felt even when there is no verbal witnessing involved. The mere presence of the Christian will, many times, bring an uncomfortable feeling to the other employees. Sometimes this opens doors for witnessing. Sometimes there will be a negative reaction. The Christian's presence has pierced their conscience and exposed their sinfulness, and they may not appreciate it! What they don't know is that much of this is involuntary and unplanned. The Christian is being used by the Holy Spirit to reach out and touch lives with the light of truth.

Does the glorification of sin trouble your spirit? Does the world's inverted value system make you sick to your stomach? Do you speak up for Kingdom Values when the opportunity presents itself? Do you call sin sin? Do you lovingly confront or expose evil when appropriate?

249

Conclusion

Sanctify them by the truth; Your word is truth.
John 17:17 - HCSB

The challenge ahead

The Christian faith is future-oriented. We live between two extraordinary events: the day we inherited the Kingdom and the day we will enter into the fullness of the Kingdom. While we wait in anticipation, we must still contend with our fallen nature, our fallen world and our fallen enemy. Were we already free from these forces a book like this would be unnecessary.

This in-between experience is a time in which our loyalty will be tested on a daily basis, with the goal of teaching us how to love God above all and those around us – or across the globe – as much as we love ourselves. It is the growth process of sanctification. Even Jesus, Who is fully God and fully Human, went through this process and came through it absolutely victorious. Now, He expects His followers to be overcomers as well.

In order for us to succeed, the Lord sent us the Holy Spirit, founded His Church, and gave us His teachings. The popular acronym B-I-B-L-E, standing for "Basic Instructions Before Leaving Earth," reminds us that while we wait, we follow the teachings from His Word. God's Word shows us the "what" and the "how" – and has life-changing power. That is why so many Scripture verses were quoted in their entirety throughout the pages of this book.

The purpose of categorizing and commenting on Kingdom Values has been to aid you as you seek God's Kingdom and His righteousness as a priority. Hopefully, these pages have helped to remind you of truths you already knew, provided you with new or deeper understanding of Kingdom Values and Principles, and encouraged you to apply them daily in practical ways.

May the Lord accomplish His will in us until we go to be with Him or He comes to be with us.

"Let the unrighteous go on in unrighteousness;
let the filthy go on being made filthy;
let the righteous go on in righteousness;
and let the holy go on being made holy"
(Revelation 22:11 - HCSB).

Notes:

Introduction
1. *Thomas Dreier*; https://www.inspiringquotes.us/quotes/Qnzd_jJie1I2n. Cited January 31, 2019.

Chapter 1 – Righteousness: The Standard of the Kingdom
1. *Apple's electronic dictionary*; Copyright © 2005–2014 Apple Inc.; Version 2.2.1. I am using accepted definitions not only to clarify the meaning of "standards," "values" and "principles" but to make the case that society instinctively knows what these are, being indicative of an internal moral compass provided by our Creator.

2. *Kingdom Living Here and Now, On the Beatitudes*; John MacArthur, Jr.; Moody Press, Chicago; © 1980; p.p. 9, 10; used with permission. (Republished in 1998 as *The Only Way to Happiness: The Beatitudes*).

3. *Apple's electronic dictionary*; Copyright © 2005–2014 Apple Inc.; Version 2.2.1.

4. *BusinessDictionary*; www.businessdictionary.com/definition/principles.htm; cited January 2017.

5. *Wikipedia*; en.wikipedia.org/wiki/Principle#cite_note-0

6. *A Survey of the Old Testament*; Andrew E. Hill & John H. Walton; Zondervan Publishing House, Grand Rapids, Michigan, 1991; p. 268.

7. Ibid, p. 278

8. Ibid, p.291

9. Online *NAS Exhaustive Concordance of the Bible* with Hebrew-Aramaic and Greek Dictionaries; Copyright © 1981, 1998 by The Lockman Foundation, Lockman.org; cited May 17, 2013.

10. Ibid

11. *Holman Illustrated Bible Dictionary*®; General Editor Trent C. Butler, PH.D.; Author of Righteousness article, Marion Soards; Copyright © 2015 by Holman Bible Publishers; p. 1194. Reprinted and used by permission.

12. Ibid, p. 1194-5

13. *Kingdom Living Here and Now, On the Beatitudes*; John MacArthur, Jr.; Moody Press, Chicago; © 1980; p.125; used with permission. (Republished in 1998 as *The Only Way to Happiness: The Beatitudes*).

Chapter 2 – Righteousness: The Foundation for Kingdom Values
1. www.bloomberg.com/news/2010-11-16/pink-diamond-sells-for-record-45-6-million-in-geneva.html; cited August 2013.

2. www.vggallery.com/misc/faq.htm and en.wikipedia.org/wiki/List_of_most_expensive_paintings; cited August 2013; more recently the price has gone up to close to $300 million.

3. http://www.bpnews.net/37310/obama-sin-is-what-doesnt-match-my-values; cited August 2013.

4. *Character Is the Issue: How People with Integrity Can Revolutionize America*; Mike Huckabee

with John Perry; Broadman & Holman Publishers, Nashville, Tennessee, 1997; p. 89

5. http://www.alplm.org/272viewessay.aspx?id=800; cited June 27, 2015

6. http://cyberhymnal.org/htm/g/o/godgrace.htm; cited September 2013

7. http://www.stjoan-center.com/twain/atheists.html; cited September 12, 2015.

Chapter 3 – Kingdom Values – The Beatitudes
1. *The Inspirational Writings of C. S. Lewis*; from *The Business of Heaven – Daily Readings*, by C. S. Lewis; Copyright © 1958, 1956, 1955 by C. S. Lewis. Inspirational Press, LDAP, Inc. 1991; a division of the now defunct Harcourt Brace Jovanovich Inc.; p. 346

2. ibid, p. 347 (extracted from *Mere Christianity*)

3. ibid, p. 347 (extracted from *Mere Christianity*)

4. *Easton's Illustrated Bible Dictionary*; Matthew George Easton; Repentance; Database © 2008 WORDsearch Corp.; www.mywsb.com; public domain.

5. Ibid

6. *HELPS™ Word-Studies*; online version, for "meekness;" http://biblehub.com/greek/4239.htm; cited September 15, 2014

7. www.phrases.org.uk/meanings/absolute-power-corrupts-absolutely.html; cited October 23, 2014

8. A possible exception: the fig tree He cursed in Matthew 21:19; but this was almost certainly a prophetic act meant as a warning against Israel for its unfruitfulness.

9. *Strong's Concordance*, NAS Exhaustive Concordance and HELPS™ Word-Studies in reference to these two Greek terms.
10. Dictionary; Copyright © 2005–2014 Apple Inc.; Version 2.2.1

Chapter 4 – Kingdom Values – The Fruit of the Spirit
1. *On Loving God*; Bernard of Clairvaux; Christian Classics Ethereal Library; www.ccel.org/ccel/bernard/loving_god.html; Public domain.

2. http://edition.cnn.com/SPECIALS/2010/chile.miners; cited March 26, 2015

3. *Apple's electronic dictionary*; Copyright © 2005–2014 Apple Inc.; Version 2.2.1.

4. http://biblehub.com/text/psalms/136-19.htm; and http://biblehub.com/hebrew/2617.htm; cited June 10, 2015.

5. *HELPS™ Word-Studies*; from http://biblehub.com/greek/4741.htm; cited September 15, 2014.

6. Quotes for Charlie Brown (Character) from A Charlie Brown Christmas (1965) (TV); from http://www.imdb.com/character/ch0029401/quotes.

7. *The Expositor's Bible Commentary*; James Montgomery Boice; Galatians; Zondervan Publishing House; ISBN 0-310-2301-8; electronic version from CD; www.zondervan.com

8. *Strong's Concordance* and THAYER'S GREEK LEXICON, Electronic Database; Copyright © 2002, 2003, 2006, 2011 by Biblesoft, Inc.; All rights reserved. Used by permission. BibleSoft.com via http://biblehub.com/greek/1466.htm; cited June 10, 2015.

Chapter 5 – Kingdom Values – The Five Purposes of the Church
1. *The MacArthur Study Bible* by John MacArthur Copyright © 1997 Word Publishing / John MacArthur. Used by permission of Thomas Nelson. www.thomasnelson.com.; p. 1648

Chapter 6 – Kingdom Values – The Mutuality Commands
1. *The Expositor's Bible Commentary*; Zondervan Publishing House; ISBN 0-310-2301-8; electronic version from CD; www.zondervan.com.

2. *Wycliffe Bible Dictionary* by Charles F. Pfeiffer, Howard F. Vos, John Rea, copyright 1999 by Hendrickson Publishers, Peabody, Massachusetts. Used by permission. All rights reserved.; p. 816.

3. Ibid

4. http://www.christianpost.com/news/report-isis-fighter-who-enjoyed-killing-christians-wants-to-follow-jesus-after-dreaming-of-man-in-white-who-told-him-you-are-killing-my-people-139880; cited June 12, 2015.

5. Ibid

6. *The Incredible Power of Kingdom Authority*; Adrian Rogers; Broadman & Holman Publisher, Nashville, Tennessee; 2002; p. 83).

7. Ibid

8. See more on the Mirroring Principle in *The King of the Kingdom of God*, volume 4 of this series, under "Mirroring God's authority in the family."

9. By Georgy; www.turnbacktogod.com/story-long-handled-spoons; cited November 1, 2018; see also https://en.wikipedia.org/wiki/Allegory_of_the_long_spoons.

10. En + courage; http://www.etymonline.com/index.php?term=encourage; cited June 4, 2015.

Chapter 7 – Kingdom Values– In Relation to God
1. *Character Is the Issue: How People with Integrity Can Revolutionize America*; Mike Huckabee with John Perry; Broadman & Holman Publishers, Nashville, Tennessee, 1997; p. 97

2. Ibid, p. 100.

3. *The Secret of the Kingdom of God*, Volume 1; John Hatton; ©2016 by John Hatton; Kingdom Secret; www.kingdomsecret.org

4. *The Inspirational Writings of C. S. Lewis*; from *Reflections on the Psalms*; Inspirational Press, LDAP, Inc.; 1991; p. 180.

5. https://carm.org/what-is-the-shekinah-glory-of-god; cited December 14, 2018.

6. See Chapter 3, "Access to the Kingdom of God," of *The Secret of the Kingdom of God*, the first volume in this series.

7. Chapter 6, "The Millennial Kingdom" in *The Secret of the Kingdom of God*, the first volume in this series.

8. See Chapter 7, "The Eternal Kingdom" in *The Secret of the Kingdom of God*, the first volume in this series.

9. *The Inspirational Writings of C. S. Lewis*; from Reflections on the Psalms, by C. S. Lewis; p. 180.

Copyright © 1958, 1956, 1955 by C. S. Lewis. Inspirational Press, LDAP, Inc. 1991; a division of the now defunct Harcourt Brace Jovanovich Inc.; p. 179.

10. *A Passion for Prayer; Experiencing deeper intimacy with God*; Tom Elliff; Living in the Word Publications; Oklahoma City, OK 73189-1474; 2001; p. 19.

11. *Empowering Kingdom Growth, To the Ends of the Earth; Churches Fulfilling the Great Commission*; Jerry Rankin; Published in 2005 by the International Mission Board, SBC; P.O. Box 6767, Richmond, Virginia 23230-0767; p.p. 58, 59.

Chapter 8 – Life Mission Kingdom Values
1. See "The Son of God and the Mirroring Principle" in *The King of the Kingdom of God*, volume 4 in this series. See *Dynamic Discipleship: The Biblical Force of Christlikeness,* by Dr. William Goff.

2. *The Joshua Project*; https://joshuaproject.net; cited January 4, 2019

3. Ibid

4. *GPS - Go, Plant, Serve, Navigating through Missions*; Ken Sorrel; A Volunteer Debriefing Handbook; p. 13.

5. Apostolos; https://biblehub.com/greek/652.htm under Strong's Concordance; cited November 22, 2018.

Chapter 9 – Character Kingdom Values
1. *The Atlantic*, digital online edition; http://www.theatlantic.com/health/archive/2013/01/theres-more-to-life-than-being-happy/266805; cited March 29, 2015.

2. Ibid

3. *Emotional Intelligence*; Daniel Goleman; Bantam Dell; Bantam 10th anniversary hardcover edition; October 2006; p. 21.

4. *Apple's electronic dictionary*; Copyright © 2005–2014 Apple Inc.; Version 2.2.1.

5. Thayer's Greek Lexicon, online version; https://biblehub.com/greek/5048.htm; cited July 10th, 2017.

6. *Timeless Truths*; Free Online Library; http://library.timelesstruths.org/music/I_Have_Decided_to_Follow_Jesus; cited April 14, 2015).

7. *The Seven Levels of Lying*; Sarah Sumner; http://www.christianitytoday.com/ct/2011/may/7-levelslying.html; Christianity Today, May, 2011.

8. *The Bible Exposition Commentary*, Vol. 1: New Testament ©2003 by Warren Wiersbe. Used by permission of David C Cook. May not be further reproduced. All rights reserved.

9. *Spiritual Warfare and Missions, the battle for God's glory among the nations*; Jerry Rankin and Ed Stetzer; B&H Publishing Group, Nashville, Tennessee; 2010; p. vii.

10. http://www.pbministries.org/books/pink/*Four_Fold_Salvation*/ffsalvation_01.htm; cited April 30, 2015. Public domain.

11. Ibid

12. Ibid

13. Ibid

14. *The Voice of the Martyrs*; www.persecution.com; cited May 2, 2015.

15. Ibid

16. (Documentss of the Chritian Church; Selected and Edited by Henry Bettenson; 2nd edition; © 1963 by Oxford University Press; p.p. 9-12).

Chapter 10 – Kingdom Values – Overall and Generic
1. *The Expositor's Bible Commentary*; Thomas Edward McComiskey; Zondervan Publishing House; ISBN 0-310-2301-8; electronic version from CD; www.zondervan.com.

2. Ibid

3. Article by John Pontifex, for www.catholicherald.co.uk, on 3 October 2014; http://www.catholicherald.co.uk/commentandblogs/2014/10/03/the-iraqi-christian-who-told-isis-if-you-want-to-kill-me-for-my-faith-i-am-prepared-to-die-here-now. Cited October 15, 2014.

4. http://www.earlyamerica.com/declaration-independence; cited May 28, 2015.

5. Ibid

6. http://www.theblaze.com/contributions/scott-walker-was-too-nice-its-incredibly-obvious-that-barack-obama-isnt-a-christian; cited February 23, 2015.

7. https://www.who.int/mental_health/prevention/suicide/suicideprevent/en; cited March 24, 2019.

8. https://encyclopedia.ushmm.org/content/en/article/euthanasia-program; cited March 24, 2019.

9. Ibid

10. http://www.focusonthefamily.com/about_us.aspx; cited on March 25, 2015.

11. *Wycliffe Bible Dictionary* by Charles F. Pfeiffer, Howard F. Vos, John Rea, copyright 1999 by Hendrickson Publishers, Peabody, Massachusetts. Used by permission. All rights reserved.; p. 559.

12. Ibid

13. *Apple's electronic dictionary*; Copyright © 2005–2014 Apple Inc.; Version 2.2.1.

14. http://www.reuters.com/article/2013/02/13/us-usa-newark-crime-idUSBRE91C1KJ20130213; Wed Feb 13, 2013 4:39pm EST; By Edith Honan.

About the Author

John Hatton has been a Bible teacher for over 40 years, teaching in English, Portuguese and Spanish, in the United States, Brazil and Chile. More recently, he taught at the *Instituto Bíblico Teológico* in Orlando, Florida, where he was the Director. He is presently one of the pastors at the *Primera Iglesia Bautista de Orlando*.

His parents, William Alvin and Lydia Catherine (Katie) Hatton, were missionaries to Brazil for 40 years, serving under the *International Mission Board* (*IMB*). They had four children: Lidia Dell, William (Bill), Sarah Janell and John.

John and his wife Monica joined the *IMB* and served for 23 years, living and ministering in El Paso, Texas; Hollywood, Florida; Santiago, Chile; and Rio de Janeiro, Brazil. For the last three years, John and Monica have served with *The Mailbox Club* as Area Coordinators for Brazil, where children are being reached, evangelized and discipled via weekly *Explorers* Bible Clubs.

John began writing **The Secret of the Kingdom of God** series over 20 years ago, first organizing relevant passages about the Kingdom, then commenting on them according to the pattern that emerged. The idea of categorizing the Kingdom under four distinct aspects naturally followed, being original with this author.

As a graphic designer and illustrator, John enjoys creating Bible charts and illustrating Bible characters, scenes and concepts. He has used his spiritual gift of teaching and natural talent of illustrating to better convey Bible truths.

John is the thankful husband of Monica, his wife of 41 years, the grateful father of Monique and Melissa, and the proud grandfather of Heidi Joy, Derek James and Asher Blue.

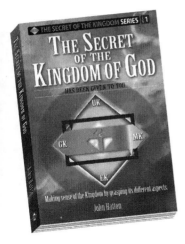

The Secret of the Kingdom of God is volume 1 of this series.

Finally, a book about the Kingdom of God that brings all the different aspects together in one volume! A book that helps the reader fit the pieces together, stand back and see the big picture.

Dr. David Garrison describes this book as "a well-written, beautifully constructed, and clear exposition of God's Kingdom," and says it is "a remarkable gift to the body of Christ."

If you haven't yet, read this book to gain an even better understanding of *The Values of the Kingdom of God*!

COMING SOON!

Look for Volumes 3 and 4 of *The Secret of the Kingdom* Series.

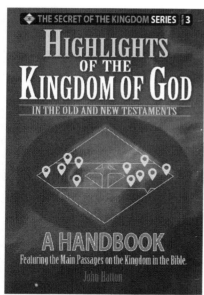

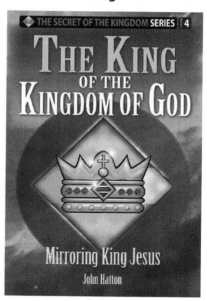

Highlights of the Kingdom of God is volume 3 of this series. It's like a *Kingdom handbook* since all major references to the Kingdom are listed, book by book, in the Old and New Testaments, with a short commentary on each.

The King of the Kingdom, fourth and last volume of the series, focuses on the identity, work and example of the Lord Jesus Christ.

www.kingdomsecret.org

61139388R00150

Made in the USA
Columbia, SC
24 June 2019